Understanding
SOCIAL
SCIENCE RESEARCH

SECOND EDITION

THOMAS R. BLACK

SAGE Publications
London • Thousand Oaks • New Delhi

First published 2002

SAGE Publications Ltd
6 Bonhill Street
London EC2A 4PU

SAGE Publications Inc
2455 Teller Road
Thousand Oaks, California 91320

SAGE Publications India Pvt Ltd
32, M-Block Market
Greater Kailash - I
New Delhi 110 048

British Library Cataloguing in Publication data

A catalogue record for this book is available from the British Library

ISBN 0 7619 7368 0
ISBN 0 7619 7369 9 (pbk)

Library of Congress Control Number 2001132891

Typeset by SIVA Math Setters, Chennai, India
Printed in Great Britain by The Cromwell Press Ltd,
Trowbridge, Wiltshire

Contents

Preface to the Second Edition

The first aim of this book is to provide the knowledge and skills necessary for someone to read and evaluate research reports, journal articles, conference papers, etc., that include some aspect of measurement and quantitative analysis. It could be considered a 'consumer's guide to quantitative research' and it has been written for anyone in the social sciences, education or related areas who reads about research. The second aim is to provide basic guidance on how to design a first piece of research through encouraging critical analysis of existing studies. The decision-making skills encouraged here should prepare new researchers to be aware of many of the pitfalls in designing, carrying out and reporting research, as well as providing a sound background in basic concepts related to research design. This edition does provide more information on a limited set of statistical procedures than the first. It also includes exercises showing how to implement them in Microsoft Excel, thus providing a more comprehensive introduction to elementary quantitative data analysis. Thus it has the potential to be a major resource in a first course in research design and statistics for both consumers and producers of research.

While the book could be read on its own, it was designed to be used as the basis of a course for those whose main concern is reading the literature intelligently and critically. The advantage of using it as part of a course as opposed to reading it in isolation comes from the interaction with others. The aims of the book are at a high cognitive level: to acquire evaluation skills. There are definite benefits in discussing one's analysis with others, with or without the guidance of an 'expert', but there will be little chance of achieving the objectives of this set of materials if it is taken as just another book to be read. These skills require practice to master, which means actually dissecting articles and papers.

A course on evaluating research can be an end in itself (there are more consumers of research than producers), or a precursor to a subsequent course on research design methodology or statistics. All students and researchers should read broadly, including literature that describes tools and approaches that they have no intention of using themselves. Therefore, even if there is no intent to carry out a measurement- and statistically based study, everyone should be able to read about other research that has used instruments (questionnaires etc.) that generate quantitative data for statistical analysis, not only with basic understanding, but with a critical eye. This book aims to prepare one to do just that. Based on the research question and hypotheses provided in a report or journal article, you will be looking at the choice and justification for the use of

- research design
- samples
- measuring instruments
- statistics
- analysis

as well as logical continuity within the study.

For those interested in greater depth, this book could be used as a prereq-uisite to such books as Howell (1997), Black (1999) or Kerlinger and Lee (2000) which are more advanced formal texts on research design and statistics.

Part of the motivation for writing the original text was the author's encounters over the years with postgraduate research students and col-leagues who tended not to read articles that had statistics in them. Some have actually expressed a fear of statistics, having apparently had a bad experience with numbers in their youth. Others have sincere doubts about the use of statistics, some of which the author shares when reading certain articles and papers. No tool is universally applicable to all problems, and there have been some notable occasions when quantitative data has been col-lected in situations that were not appropriate and 'statistically' analysed. But as a scientist the author would prefer any doubt to be rationally based, allowing one to have an open mind when reading a report of a research pro-ject. Having used the first edition for the past eight years, students have identified a number of improvements and provided feedback that hopefully will enhance the achievement of these goals. One significant change has been to expand the two chapters on statistical inference to four to cover better a range of basic techniques.

The book is organized such that the first chapter provides an overview of the research process and an outline of the skills and knowledge to be cov-ered. Subsequent chapters introduce the concepts and criteria for evaluating the various aspects of research. Each chapter contains two types of activities: the first are intended to help clarify new concepts and criteria, while the second (at the end of each chapter) actually involve readers in the critical analysis and evaluation of research reports. This second type of activity should be carried out on one or more articles or parts of reports the reader may find in the literature. These will require the reader to use progressively more columns (sets of criteria) on the Profiling Sheet, a complete copy of which is found at the end of Chapter 11. Some of these could be used for for-mal assessment in a course of study. The idea of using a Profiling Sheet to guide researchers in the critical analysis and evaluation of research reports is not original – the author used a simpler one as a postgraduate student (Gephart and Bartos, 1969) and found it immensely useful. The Profiling Sheet has been expanded in this edition to include a column for evaluating ethics and, at the top, a place to classify the type of research, helping to eval-uate the intent of the paper being considered.

If this book is used with classes or seminars, it is suggested that optimally three sessions (about an hour each) per chapter are needed, one to discuss the concepts and another two for comparison analyses of articles. To what depth the analysis is carried will determine the amount of out-of-class reading necessary in addition to the chapters of this book. There is the potential for about 120–150 h of activity to be generated by reading this book and carrying out all the activities, depending on background and previous experience.

The author wishes to thank his numerous postgraduate students who used the earlier edition and the few who emailed from other countries, with pertinent questions, offering most useful comments and criticism. As is always the case, ultimate responsibility for the content and style still lies with the author.

T.R. Black
University of Surrey

REFERENCES

Black, T.R. (1999) *Doing Qualitative Research the Social Sciences: An Integrated Approach to Research Design, Measurement and Statistics*, London: Sage.

Gephart, W.J. and Bartos, B.B. (1969) 'Occasional Paper 7: Profiling Instructional Package', Phi Delta Kappa.

Howell, D.C. (1997) *Statistical Methods for Psychology* (4th edn), Belmont, CA: Duxbury Press.

Kerlinger, F.N. and Lee, H.B. (2000) *Foundations of Behavioural Research* (4th edn), New York: Harcourt.

1

Evaluating Social Science Research:
An Overview

Social science research involves investigating all aspects of human activity and interactivity. Considering traditional academic disciplines, psychology tends to investigate the behaviour of individuals, while sociology examines groups and their characteristics. Educational research can be viewed as an endeavour to expand understanding of teaching/learning situations, covering the cognitive, affective and psychomotor domains, thus drawing upon the perceptions of both psychology and sociology. Many other disciplines such as nursing and health-related studies, business and economics, political science and law, address analogous issues and employ many of the same research tools. Ideally, the research community should be able to address itself to general, global questions, like what enhances learning in primary school, what contributes to poverty, why individuals engage in crime, which would in turn generate a set of specific research questions. To resolve such issues would require researchers to choose the appropriate research tool or tools for the chosen specific question(s). Individual researchers (or teams) would select an aspect of the problem of interest that was feasible to tackle with the resources available. Their contribution would then be added to the growing body of knowledge accumulating through the combined efforts of the research community. To a certain extent, this does happen, but unfortunately many of the disciplines in the social sciences seem less able to achieve such a coherent approach to research than some other academic areas.

This shortcoming stems at least partially from the fact that carrying out social science research involves considering many more variables, some of which are often difficult if not impossible to control. This is unlike research in the natural sciences which commonly takes place in a laboratory under conditions where control over potentially contributing factors is more easily exercised. Second, there is less widespread agreement about underlying theories and appropriate methods for resolving issues in the social sciences than in many natural science disciplines. Consequently, a wide variety of measuring instruments, research tools and approaches are employed, some of which may seem unnecessarily complicated. These complexities and idiosyncrasies of social science research present a challenge for the person new to the scene.

Adding to the difficulty of extracting the most out of published research are the various 'schools of thought' relating to social science research. On a more public level, note the dissonance between clinical and experimental psychologists. In some academic departments, staff who 'use statistics' have not been spoken to by their colleagues who 'never touch the stuff' for years. On a more intellectual level, there has been considerable discussion about such schisms. Cohen and Manion (2000) present a comprehensive discussion leading to the classification of two research 'paradigms', though not all researchers conveniently admit to belonging to one or the other, or even fit the categories. Historically, these derive from objectivist (realism, positivism, determinism, nomothetic) and subjectivist (nominalism, anti-positivism, voluntarism, ideographic) schools of thought. Briefly, as Cohen and Manion (2000: 22) note:

> The normative paradigm (or model) contains two major orienting ideas: first, that human behaviour is essentially rule-governed; and second, that it should be investigated by the methods of natural science. The interpretive paradigm, in contrast to its normative counterpart, is characterized by a concern for the individual. Whereas normative studies are positivist, all theories constructed within the context of the interpretive paradigm tend to be anti-positivist.

Though the anti-positivists level the criticism that science tends to be dehumanizing, it can be argued that science (or more appropriately, a scientific approach) is a means, not an end; with it we can both better understand the human condition and predict the consequences of action, generalized to some degree. How this understanding is used or what action is taken will be based upon values, the realm of philosophy. Thus it may not be science that de-personalizes, but the values that the people who apply it have; thus if there is any corruption of the human spirit, it lies in beliefs and human nature, not in a scientific approach. To recall an old ditty based upon a murder case in New England in 1892,

> Lizzie Borden took an axe
> And gave her mother forty whacks
> And when she saw what she had done
> She gave her father forty-one.

To say that science is evil is like convicting the axe, instead of the murderer who used it as a tool for the destruction of human life.

Science is no more susceptible to abuse in the form of depersonalization and human degradation than any other competing intellectual endeavour. We have seen, and still see, wars in the name of God, carried out by virtually every major religion in the world, most of which have a major tenet against killing. There has been and will be oppression in the name of political systems that purport to represent and protect the masses, resulting in everything from dictatorships of the proletariat under communism to restrictive voting practices to 'protect' so-called democratic societies. Science or a scientific approach in viewing the world, like religion, political theory or humanistic psychology, is a means to understanding, and is depersonalizing in the study of people *only* if the social scientist wants it to be.

One goal of scientific research is to be self-policing through rigour and consistency of practice. This is necessary if the conclusions drawn at the end of a piece of complex research are going to be valid and replicable. Logical consistency from one stage to another, combined with reliable procedures, are essential. While achievement of this goal through so-called good practice is implicit in any study, scientific research is just as prone to bias and/or poor practice as any approach. The unresolved case of Cyril Burt's studies of identical twins comes to mind, unresolved in the sense that there is not con- clusive evidence that he falsified his data, but there is strong statistical evi- dence that he did. As Blum and Foos (1986) note, scientists are human beings and susceptible to common foibles including stupidity and dishonesty. They summarize their view of the academic world as follows:

> Whereas some scientists espouse the view of self-correcting mechanism whereby scientific inquiry is subject to rigorous policing, others believe that academic research centers foster intense pressure to publish, to obtain research and renewal of grants, or to qualify for promotion. Still others believe that finagling is endemic and that public exposure is to be continually encouraged.

This does not mean that there is widespread fraud and that reading research reports is like trying to buy a used car from a politician. Evaluating research requires a more measured approach: many reports will have faults, most will provide some valuable insights, but judging the validity of these will require knowing what to look for.

There are limitations to both 'paradigms', particularly when applied in isolation from one another. Quantitative research is quite good at telling us *what* is happening, and often qualitative studies are better at determining *why* events occur. When poorly conducted, normative (quantitative) studies can produce findings that are so trivial as to contribute little to the body of research. On the other hand, interpretive (qualitative) studies can be so iso- lated, subjective and idiosyncratic that there is no hope of any generalization or contribution to a greater body of knowledge. When ideologies are taken to less extremes, it can be said that the two paradigms complement each other, rather than compete. It often takes both to answer a good question comprehensively. To choose one as the basis of research prior to planning may be a philosophical decision, but it also could be likened to opening the tool box, choosing a spanner and ignoring the other tools available when faced with a repair task. To reject the findings of researchers who appear to subscribe to a supposed opposing paradigm is to ignore a considerable body of work. Cohen and Manion (2000: 45) summarize the position nicely when closing their discussion on the subject:

> We will restrict its [the term research] usages to those activities and undertakings aimed at developing a science of behaviour, the word *science* itself implying both normative and interpretive perspectives. Accordingly, when we speak of social research, we have in mind the systematic and scholarly application of the princi- ples of a science of behaviour to the problems of people within their social contexts; and when we use the term educational research, we likewise have in mind the application of these self same principles to the problems of teaching and learning

within the formal educational framework and to the clarification of issues having direct or indirect bearing on these concepts.

The particular value of scientific research in the social sciences, as defined above, is that it will enable researchers and consumers of their research to develop the kind of sound knowledge base that characterizes other professions and disciplines. It should be one that will ensure that all the disciplines which are concerned with enhancing understanding of human interaction and behaviour will acquire a maturity and sense of progression which they seem to lack at present. It also does not limit researchers in their choice of research tools, but does demand rigour in their application.

This book will address the issue of evaluating the quality of a major subset of social science research: those involving various forms of observation and measurement (some of which will employ statistics as a decision-making aid) as reported in research journals, conference papers, etc. It is felt that this covers some aspect of the majority of all social science research since most involves collecting data of one form or another, and all data gathering should be well defined and verifiable (Blum and Foos, 1986). While this begs the issue as to which 'paradigm' is being employed, it does mean that the criteria and evaluation approaches described here will apply to some aspects of almost any study that collects data, quantifiable or not, though the emphasis is on quantitative research. Consequently, this book does leave out philosophical studies, assuming they do not refer to observation- or measurement-based research.

There are two practical reasons for emphasizing this aspect of social science research. The first is to assist readers in overcoming the problem of interpreting existing publications containing numerical data and statistical analysis. The second is to assist designers of research, since the cause of much low-quality social science research (and not just statistically based studies) is often rooted in problems of measurement and data collection. Too often, new researchers base their techniques unquestioningly upon the practices of others. They read the research reports and journal articles and assume that if they are published, they must have followed acceptable procedures. This is not a sound assumption in an age when academics suffer from the 'publish or perish' syndrome, and not all journal referees are equally proficient in separating the wheat from the chaff.

Having made what may seem to be a somewhat cynical, if not damning, comment on the editorial capabilities of research publications, one must accept that it is not a trivial task to analyse a research paper critically. There can be errors of omission as well as faulty logic and poor procedure. Many of these must be inferred from reading a written discourse and their relative severity weighed against some vague standard of acceptability. Consequently, it must be realized that it is very unlikely that a consumer of research will become highly proficient at evaluating studies just by reading this book in isolation. Like most complex skills, such proficiency will be acquired through practice and application to a variety of situations, and thus there is a considerable number of activities built into this material.

As with most higher level intellectual skills, the acquisition of these can benefit from discussions and interaction with fellow researchers. Therefore, most of the activities will focus on the discussion and evaluation of research papers; thus it would be desirable to have a forum in which to defend and justify your position, in order to ensure your logic and criteria are sound. This can be done in a class, tutorial or computer-based classroom, but it could also be carried out by your discussing an article with a friend.

In general, the consumer of research reports should learn to be critical without being hypercritical and pedantic, able to ascertain the important aspects, ignore the trivia and, to a certain extent, read between the lines by making appropriate inferences. The ability to identify true omissions and overt commissions of errors is a valuable skill. It is not so much a matter of right and wrong, but one of considering the relative quality. No research carried out and reported by humans is going to be perfect, and at the other extreme, little published material will be totally useless. Therefore, as consumers, we must be able to ascertain the worthwhile and ignore the erroneous without rejecting everything.

RESEARCH DESIGNS

Regardless of which research approach is eventually chosen, all research endeavours have some traits in common. This is based on the assumption that the primary purpose is to expand knowledge and understanding. It is doubtful that an endeavour to justify a stand regardless of the evidence available can be considered research: these are the domains of irrational opinion, beliefs and politics. Figure 1.1 outlines the key components of almost any quantitative research activity, though the actual order of events may vary somewhat from the sequence shown and each step may be visited more than once, the researcher reconsidering a decision having changed his/her mind, or wishing to refine a point.

Beginning at the left, an *overall question* will have arisen in the potential researcher's mind, based on previous experience(s), reading and/or observations. For example, what enhances learning, why do people forget, what social conditions contribute to crime, what influence on attitudes does television have?

For a researcher to begin a project with no question formulated but with a research approach already chosen, like a case study, survey, statistical model, etc., is, as suggested earlier, roughly equivalent to opening one's tool box, grasping the favourite spanner, and dashing about to see what needs fixing. On the other hand, this does *not* mean that the statement of the question should be so restrictive as to hamper the quality of the research by placing an unchangeable constraint, but a question does need to be identified to provide a touchstone for subsequent steps in the process. In any case, one would expect when reading a research paper to find a statement of the overall question being addressed, or the question whose answer to which the researcher intends to have his/her results contribute.

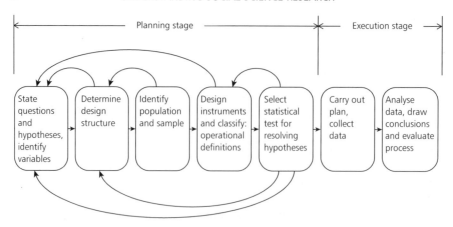

FIGURE 1.1   *Stages of design and carrying out a study, including iterations*
for modifications and improvements during planning (adapted
from Black, 1999)

Starting with a general interest area or problem, a *specific research question* should be explicitly stated. This helps to focus attention on the purpose of the research and assists when making decisions about such matters as appropriate research tools. Obviously, the statement of the question could be refined in the light of experience at a later date, if necessary. An informed change of direction in a project is not unheard of, though extreme changes may indicate inadequate initial planning. But putting pencil to paper at an early stage helps to avoid problems arising from ambiguities at a later time. The research question described in a final report, therefore, may have been revised several times. This is quite reasonable; what can be frustrating to a reader is not to find any statement of a research question, or to find a different question has been answered at the end of the report.

Also as part of this stage, a refined statement of what is expected as the outcome of the research, the *hypotheses*, should be generated. It is difficult to believe that a researcher would engage in a study that he/she did not have some expectation of the outcome. What is essential is that this is an expectation and not a foregone conclusion. All research approaches have procedures to follow when being carried out and stating hypotheses is one that is common to most. Very little, if any, respected research is totally unstructured and unplanned. Research does not just happen, as Nisbet and Watt (1978: 49) in their description of case studies, maintain:

> Both survey and case study involve formulation of hypotheses. Without hypo-
> theses, both become merely a formless and uninformative rag-bag of observations.

Hypotheses help fix the direction of a study and are a more formal way of expressing the research questions. They too can be revised, though which set of tools one eventually chooses may limit how much flexibility there is in changing the specification of hypotheses. These usually include a specific statement of the variables of interest in the study and the nature of any expected relationships. The criteria that will define an adequate hypothesis will be discussed in detail later.

The *design structure* of any study should be logically consistent with the research questions and hypotheses. We will examine a range of designs that will potentially contribute to resolving hypotheses.

Another issue that the reader expects to be addressed early in a study, and described in the report, is *to whom will the results apply*? To what group will the conclusions be relevant? The answer to this may have a strong influence on what research tools are eventually chosen, particularly when the question of the limitations of resources (money, time and effort available) are brought to bear. There are several views about the generalizability of results, deciding to whom they apply, as will be seen later. The group or *population* (no matter how large or how small) to whom the results will extend needs to be clarified and an adequate justification provided. Issues related to this will be discussed in Chapter 3 in detail as one of the major criteria.

Having looked briefly at characteristics common to all research, this book will henceforth focus on the problems associated with measurement-based studies and those using statistics. Such research will include case studies and surveys where no statistical tests are used, but data is collected in numerical form from observations, questionnaires or other instruments. The only research to which this book is not relevant is that which generates no data. A word of warning, though: one should not be misled into thinking that just because numbers and statistics are used that a study is trying (or even should be trying) to establish causality. This is a desirable goal, but one that is notoriously difficult to achieve. Statistical techniques are a tool that might be used as *part* of an argument for establishing causality, or for establishing an explanation of relationships between variables that cannot, from the design or structure of the study, be established as causal. Many variables that we choose to investigate vary together without one causing the other to change.

A brief word on statistics

Regardless of which approach is eventually chosen for resolving a research question and which set of research skills you master, it will be necessary to have some understanding of measurement-based and statistically analysed research. Very few areas of educational and social science research are completely devoid of applications in this area and consequently when engaging in background reading, you will inevitably encounter articles or papers that report the use of a measurement instrument and maybe even employ some statistical analysis. When reading such papers, it is desirable not only to understand the point the author is trying to make and defend, but also to begin to be able to evaluate any claims. This is usually not a simple matter of either accepting or rejecting the study, but assigning a relative value to the claims made, based on the quality of the research. The question of quality of research is confounded by the fact that some shortcomings of published work will simply be attributable to poor writing style or unjustified interpretation of statistical outcomes, as opposed to inappropriate research design or faulty procedure. One must assume in the professional research world that Disraeli's view 'There are three kinds of lies: lies, damned lies, and statistics' (Huff, 1954) is *not* necessarily true, and should probably be changed to 'There are lies, damned lies, and distorted or poorly presented statistics'. Your skill in identifying the last should be enhanced through critical reading and practice in evaluating research papers.

On the other hand, one must not be fooled into thinking that just because there are numbers to support the results that the results are 'the truth'. With statistical studies, the answer is more accurately 'probably the truth'. In the past, there have been overly optimistic expectations of statistically based research, which when the reality became apparent led to a decline in interest in the approach (Campbell and Stanley, 1963). Answers in social science research are no easier to come by (and usually harder, considering what is being studied) than answers in any other discipline, be it science, humanities or art.

How critical one is of any research will often depend on how the results are to be used. If decisions are to be made that are a matter of life and death (say, the use of a new drug), then the reader is very critical of the process of arriving at the results. But if you are interested only from the viewpoint of looking at possible variables to study in your own research, then you are really looking for clues and quite reasonably will be less critical. In any case, it is best to be able to evaluate what you have read and not accept everything blindly or, at the other extreme, ignore it.

A key aspect to evaluating statistics-based research is to realize that to justify adequately his/her results, a researcher must have followed the rules and met the underlying assumptions; failure to be rigorous can cast doubt on any claims or completely invalidate them. To check this requires some understanding of what is involved in carrying out quantitative research. The first objective of this book is to provide you with sufficient insight into the problems a researcher faces to evaluate research. This will also introduce you to major issues that must be addressed if you are going to carry out successfully this type of research, but also requires additional skills that are the subject of other books. This is not intended to discourage, but to warn you that statistically based research requires care and skill if it is to produce acceptable (valid and reliable) results. Too often in the past, potential researchers have shown up at the computer centre, clutching piles of data, asking, 'what do I do with it?' Without careful planning at all stages, the results produced by the computer will follow the old computer saying 'garbage in, garbage out'. The First Law of Social Science Research should be:

> No amount of massaging by a computer-based statistical package will rescue a poorly planned research project.

Having made that point, let us return to the overall question of evaluating research reports, *some* of which will use statistics.

CRITERIA FOR EVALUATING RESEARCH

A two-dimensional model showing the cyclical nature of research is provided in Figure 1.2, one that includes iterations and revisions. Starting with the two boxes in the upper left part of the picture, most research starts its life as a combination of accepted ideas and new insights. The resulting proposal is to test the limits of a theory, its applicability, or even its veracity, resulting in a modified theory. This might be a completely new one, or simply determining whether the existing theory applies to a given situation. This is then stated in terms of a hypothesized outcome. Taking the variables described in the hypothesis, these are now operationally defined as observable events (like using an intelligence test as an indicator of intelligence). The instruments are designed and the data collected. If the process has been carefully carried out, then the data can be used to accept (or refute) the hypothesis and the theory (or its limits) will be redefined. But since there is no perfect theory, the process is open to repetition. A theory is only viable as long as no one can refute it. While this may seem disconcerting, just remember that we are talking about modelling reality, *not* reality itself. We as humans endeavour to make sense of our complex environment through models and theories; these are the tools of communication amongst ourselves. Presenting arguments that can withstand scrutiny and testing is part of the process of refining and more accurately describing events, making valid predictions and basically supporting decisions. The key to the above process is its openness to scrutiny, since the validity of the process is the basis of the strength of the argument. Figure 1.2 does remind us that real life is rarely simple and *the* answer is unlikely to be found in one piece of research!

In order to examine the processes involved in formulating a valid argument from research outcomes, let us expand the process outlined in Figure 1.1. Since we will concentrate on evaluating research reports, a simpler, more linear model will be used following a single cycle of the process. Assuming that the research questions designated by the researcher indicate a need for the measurement of variables and possibly the use of statistical analysis, then a linear version of the process will be something like that shown in Figure 1.3.

In order to help you to evaluate research, a condensed set of criteria have to be identified and set up as a Profiling Sheet (a complete version is provided at the end of this book). These criteria will serve as guides for evaluating studies and summarize the more extensive criteria introduced below and elaborated on in the rest of the book. By the end of this course of study, you should be reasonably proficient in using the Profiling Sheet as an evaluation tool. This sheet will be used in stages in activities in subsequent chapters that will involve you in evaluating a variety of research papers, including those which will be of your own choice. The columns on the Profiling Sheet reflect decisions made at the stages in Figure 1.3, to help you to link the evaluation process with the overall research design process. Also, each column is dealt with in greater detail in a subsequent chapter. The following paragraphs start at the bottom of Figure 1.3 with Action 10 since it is the conclusions that are of prime interest. This way, it will be possible to take the results and

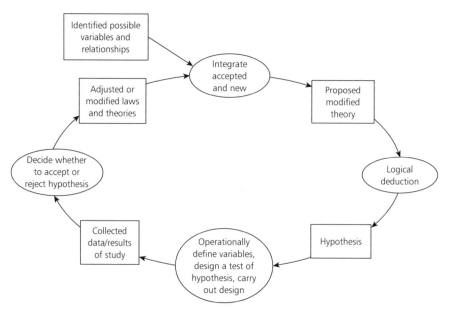

FIGURE 1.2   *The principal information components (rectangles), methodological processes (ovals) and information transformations (arrows) of the cyclic ongoing scientific process*

claims made by a researcher and see how strongly they are justified. How the validity of these depends on the whole design will become more apparent as the analysis proceeds back up through the chart. The brief discussion below is intended to provide an overview of research planning to put the whole practice into some perspective. The Profiling Sheet may be photocopied for future use in evaluating research papers. Each column will be fully covered in later chapters, as indicated by each action summarized below.

Action 10.   Draw conclusions (Chapter 11)

Some conclusions verge upon blatant speculation, while others tend to be overly conservative. While there are some studies that make outrageous claims, the main criticism usually is not on whether the conclusion is right or wrong, but on the strength of the support provided, which includes how well the researcher has justified the processes involved. Very little in human behaviour and activity can be predicted exactly, so most studies are looking for evidence for trends or tendencies, rather than absolute cause and effect events. No matter what the findings may seem to prove, there are always exceptions. Therefore, when reading reports of studies, one looks for not only claims of relative confidence in a conclusion, but also supporting evidence. Much of the latter will be found (or not found, as the case may be) in decisions and processes in the other nine actions that precede the conclusions in

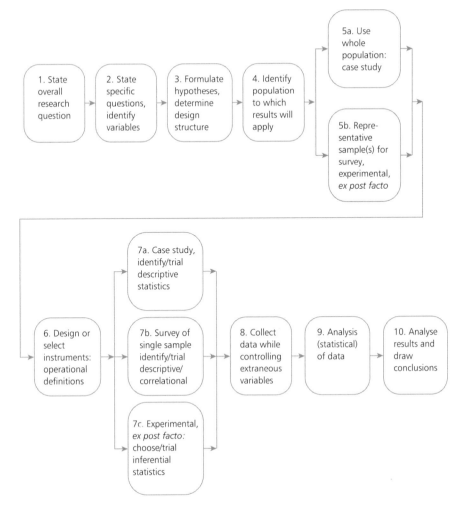

FIGURE 1.3   *Summary of the processes involved when designing and carrying out measurement-based studies: case study, survey, ex post facto and experimental/quasi-experimental*

the report. The strength of the conclusions is no stronger than the relative level of rigour with which the other steps are executed, as will be seen.

What you must check as a reader of research is how well the researcher has accounted for all the other possible causes and how well he/she has justified the identification of the cause of the observed effect, if this is the case. When a report omits a discussion on this, then the reader begins to wonder about the quality of the research. Later discussion in Chapter 11 will point up some subtle and not so subtle potential sources of faulty conclusions. In addition, a conscientious researcher will make recommendations and identify limitations of the study, mainly in terms of implications for practitioners and other researchers who might make decisions on the basis of the study.

Action 9.   Statistical analysis of data (Chapters 7–10)

One type of outcome does merit special consideration. Statements often appear in statistically based reports such as there was a *significant* difference between the scores of two groups. This is often used to justify the existence of a cause and effect relationship between two variables. What is meant by statistically significant? It simply means that *it did not occur by chance alone,* that any differences are greater than what could be accounted for by natural variation. In other words, there is probably some external cause. For example, the IQ (intelligence quotient) scores of two identical groups of children are found to be 'significantly different'. This means the difference is so great that it is probably not a chance occurrence and is not due to the natural variation in IQ scores in the population. It does not *prove* that the variables being investigated caused the difference, it only says that the difference exists and is probably not just a random occurrence. It is up to the researcher to prove that the variables under consideration are the actual cause and eliminate the possibility of any other variable(s) contributing to the results found.

In addition, there are situations where the use of statistical tests is not even appropriate. Just because there is numerical data does not mean that it is necessary or justified to carry out statistical tests on it. The most common situation where statistical tests are inappropriate is when the whole population is used. *Inferential statistics,* which is the formal name for the study of such tests, assume you have a representative sample of a well-defined whole population. Inferences about this population are made on the basis of the sample through the statistical tests. Thus, if the whole population is used, for example in a case study, inferential statistics are inappropriate. Later in Chapters 7–10, we will consider criteria for the appropriate use of inferential statistics, introducing a range of specific statistical tests.

Action 8.   Collecting data (controlling variables)
             (various chapters)

One might be tempted to think that this is a straightforward process, but there can be many problems. In addition to those associated directly with how the data is actually collected, ranging from the wording of covering letters for questionnaires to the interpersonal skills of an interviewer, there are other sources. A prime one may be the measuring instrument itself, like a test, questionnaire or observation schedule, which will be discussed under Action 6. The sampling procedure (Action 5) will also affect how effectively this step is carried out, as will one's choice of statistics (Action 9).

Any report should describe the data collection procedure in sufficient detail so as to allow the reader to judge its appropriateness. Ideally, there would be enough detail to allow another researcher to replicate the study, something that happens all too rarely, in this author's estimation. In most natural science disciplines, before the results of a study (especially a statistically based one) are widely accepted and acted on, the procedure must be replicated. For reasons that are probably associated with the dictum that all research *must* be something 'new', this tends to be unfashionable in the social sciences. If the guiding principle was truly that research should reflect some originality as stated by most institutions of higher education, then replication would constitute a part of the evaluation of a research methodology. Research does not have to be entirely new to demand considerable original thought in the processes of planning and execution.

Action 7a.   Plan case study data collection and
*   trial of descriptive statistics (Chapter 5)*

Going into a situation without a plan, intending only to observe whatever happens with no strategy as to what to look for, has been shown to be a good recipe for disaster. A researcher needs to prepare for the data collection, the exact nature of the preparation depending on the type of study. For example, to conduct an interview, questions must be prepared (Action 6) and tried out, recording systems (paper and pencil as well as electronic) devised, dates arranged with subjects, etc. Observation in classrooms requires an observation schedule, a list of categories of events to look for related to the concepts being investigated. Failure to carry out such preparation is often the source of problems that manifest themselves at other stages. Even a decision made before collecting data on just how it will be presented can point up omissions as well as superfluous data. This includes trying out descriptive statistics on trial data to see if it will provide the appropriate evidence for the arguments to be made. While journal articles often report only the salient parts of data collection, research reports can reveal the problem of poor planning and resultant weak data.

Action 7b.   Plan survey and trial of descriptive
*   statistics/correlations (Chapters 4–8)*

The design of the questionnaire or measuring device is the focus of Action 6, but by trying it out before distribution the researcher can avoid oversights. Deciding on what descriptive statistics will be used (graphs, charts, etc.) and what correlations will be calculated *before* collecting data can help in identifying omissions as well as requests for superfluous data. At first, this may seem unnecessary, but failure to do so has resulted in attempts to measure too many variables and contributed to an overly long questionnaire which in turn have affected whether the recipients were willing to complete the form. This in turn has affected whether a sample was considered very representative of a larger population, or just volunteers and therefore of questionable representativeness. Also, it can help in deciding ahead of time whether the data collected will potentially answer the research question.

Action 7c.   Formulate null hypothesis, select and trial statistical model/tests (Chapters 7–10)

The *null hypothesis* is just a way of stating the expected outcome of the research in terms of the statistical model used. Such a statement basically says that no statistically significant difference is expected to be found, for example, between (among) groups or that a correlation found is not different from zero. Statistical significance, though, is no guarantee of educational, socio-logical or psychological significance. But let us be optimistic and consider a study that has the general hypothesis that one set of learning material is more effective than another. The researcher might state it as a null hypothesis:

> There will be no significant difference in improvement of performance by the two groups using the two different sets of learning materials.

Having selected two representative groups of students to try the materials, the researchers would then look at the difference between pre- and post-test scores (gain scores: one possible measure of learning) and compare the scores of the two groups. If the test showed there was a statistically significant difference in gain scores, then the null hypothesis would be 'rejected'. All that the researchers know is that the difference probably did not occur by chance alone. It would still be up to them to justify that the superior nature of one set of material over the other was the sole cause of the difference observed (not necessarily a trivial task). Such experimental designs were originally developed by researchers in biological disciplines, but have been found to be of value in some situations in social science research.

Stating a null hypothesis tends to compel the researcher to think about what the statistical test is *really* going to tell him/her. Occasionally, null hypotheses are stated in a form to suggest that there is no cause and effect relationship; thus a significant statistical result rejecting this would confirm the causal relationship. This is an improper usage of statistics. Remember, rejecting a null hypothesis only indicates that whatever has happened very probably did not happen by chance alone. Assuming the truth of this, it is still up to the researcher to justify the cause by ensuring nothing else could have possibly caused it.

Ex post facto studies are also looking for differences in group characteristics, traits or preferences, but due to life experiences (e.g. education, gender, social class). These are referred to as such since the researcher is collecting data on the consequences of these life experiences. Owing to the rather complex nature of such variables (life experiences) it is rarely possible to claim unequivocally to have proven causal links. While 7-year-old girls may tend to read better than 7-year-old boys, this does not necessarily mean being of that gender *causes* them to read better. Other variables linked to being either a boy or a girl (e.g. expectations, gender of teacher role models, contemporary cultural influences on boys and girls) may be the real causes, but these influences (variables) are much more difficult to isolate.

The criteria for selecting an appropriate statistical model and test are numerous and complex because of the diversity of tests available. But any report ought to justify the choice of statistical tests for the questions to be answered. Some guidance will be provided in Chapters 9 and 10, but researchers often have to consult experts or refer to more advanced texts on the subject of statistical research design to begin to resolve completely the detailed question of appropriateness.

All the points about measurement, data collection, sampling and interpretation of statistical significance must be considered when evaluating a report. One supposed advantage of selecting research reports from refereed journals is that the selection process has prevented reports of poorly conducted studies from being published, though as one might expect this is not a perfect process.

Action 6.   Measuring instruments as operational definitions (Chapter 4)

Most research studies in the social sciences involve rather abstract concepts devised by the researcher or other members of the discipline, like intelligence, wealth, class, social mobility, knowledge of a language. This means that to investigate a problem based on an abstract idea, a way of quantifying (measuring) that idea is going to be required. This will mean devising or selecting a measuring 'instrument' that will constitute an operational (observable) definition of this abstraction. The best known example is that of intelligence, something that we all talk about but cannot observe directly. Often impressions are formed of someone's relative intelligence based on observations, but a more objective process is needed in many situations. Consequently, over the years, a number of IQ tests have been devised that purport to reflect objectively a person's intelligence. But there are still arguments as to what constitutes intelligence and, therefore, what should be included in such tests. There have been discussions focusing on such undesirable influences on existing tests such as the potential for cultural bias, what constitutes language, and gender bias. These leave the reader in a difficult position as to knowing whether any test used was a valid test of intelligence for the study under consideration.

But this is not the only problem. What if an appropriate test does not already exist? To create a measuring instrument requires another set of skills, the time to develop the test, and persons to try them out before they are used in the research project. The reliability and validity of researcher-designed tests can be suspect, though often an indication and justification of these are provided in the research report for the reader's perusal.

In addition, when evaluating a study, a researcher should look for logical consistency across the original question, the concepts/constructs from the theory applied, and the measuring instruments used as the operational definition. A sound underlying theory and references to previous work lend credibility to any study. It is not necessary to have earth-shaking discoveries or to create new theories in a study to make a meaningful contribution to the realm of research. Most studies are built on the work of others; research tends to progress in small steps, not huge leaps.

Actions 4 and 5.   Identify the population and select
a representative sample (Chapter 3)

In a statistically based study, you can expect to find that the group(s) chosen to participate in a study tend to be one of the following:

- a whole population;
- a randomly selected sample from a population;
- a purposively selected sample from a population;
- volunteers;
- an unspecified group.

The further one goes down the list, the less representative a group is of a larger population. Rarely is it possible to use a whole population of a worthwhile size; consequently samples are taken and inferences made about the whole population based on the sample (recall the term *inferential* statistics). Also, it is possible to find a combination of the above five levels. For example, it is possible to have randomly selected a sample to participate in an activity, but not all those selected agree to do so. While the original sample was randomly selected (very desirable), the resulting study was carried out by volunteers. In such cases, to strengthen his/her case, a researcher would have to ascertain why some chose not to participate, to assure the reader that it was not for reasons pertaining to the research (offended by a questionnaire, afraid to do a test). Any study using volunteers should address itself to the question of why some did and others did not volunteer. Obviously, the further up the list a study is, the stronger the generalizability of the results. In summary, the way a sample is selected affects how strongly a researcher can justify the generalizability of a study.

Action 3.   Formulation of hypotheses and determining
design (Chapters 2 and 3)

As noted at the beginning of this chapter, stating the expected outcome of a study (hypothesizing) tends to focus the researcher's attention on relevant problems and inform the reader of the purpose of the study. If the research does not use inferential statistics, then a general statement is quite acceptable, whereas the use of inferential statistics really requires a null hypothesis. This all leads to the design of the study and how the hypotheses will be resolved. As noted earlier, quantitative research is potentially quite good at confirming the existence of differences in groups, telling us *what* happened. But this does require a plan to ensure comparisons are appropriately made.

Actions 1 and 2.   Statement of general and specific
research questions (Chapter 2)

These do not have to be presented in any formal terms, but should be supported by a rationale for the study that includes references to relevant models, theories and previous studies. A general statement of the area of research should be followed by some indication of what specific research question the report is addressing itself to. Articles that describe the process involved in data collection, the measurement instruments, statistical tests and conclusions without indicating the reason for decisions made may describe research that lacked direction, or may just be poorly reported.

EVALUATING THE REPORT OF A STUDY

To ensure the validity of claims and reliability (replicability) of their work, researchers need to adhere to the kinds of guidelines outlined above. Limitations of resources, the fickleness of subjects, and just plain bad luck, to name a few, can reduce the strength and generalizability of results of a study. The more complex a process such as this, the more places things can go wrong.

Obviously, the results of this type of evaluation are going to depend not only on the quality of the research, but also on the comprehensiveness of the written report. Writing about research is not an easy task, especially when it is done for a journal that may have limitations on length of articles. Such constraints can affect writing style and contribute to the omission of essential information that would facilitate the evaluation of the study. Thus, the process of evaluating a research report will reflect not only the quality of the research, but the quality of the report, since any report should provide the reader with sufficient information to assess the quality of the study, or ideally even replicate it. In some disciplines, this last criterion is most important.

As can be seen from the previous sections and the Profiling Sheet that will serve as a guide to evaluation, a reader expects to find certain types of information about the implementation of a study, as well as the results. The following list summarizes what could be considered as the essential components of a report or journal article, though not necessarily presented in this order:

- Clear statement of research question and hypotheses, supported by literature references.
- An indication of the design or processes to be employed to resolve the hypotheses.
- Description of the subjects, and if a sample, the population to whom the results are to apply.
- Description of the measuring instrument(s), with some indication of validity and reliability.
- An account of (typically) the conditions under which the data was collected.
- Presentation of the results, graphically where appropriate.
- Summary of any statistical analysis, with clear indication of why the specific test(s) were chosen.
- A statement of the conclusions with limitations, and recommendations for further research.

The evaluation of a report will involve determining sins of omission as well as sins of commission, and consequently, there will be occasions when the lack of information is more frustrating than being able to identify poor procedure. While a full report may provide sufficient detail to allow the replication of a study, most journal articles have such length restrictions placed upon them that this is not possible. There is nothing to prevent the reader from contacting the author of a journal article and asking for greater detail.

A problem of rigour

With so many possible pitfalls, how does anyone ever produce decent research? While the task is complex, it is not impossible and is based upon a long tradition of skill development. It can be maintained that it is desirable to take a more scientific approach, which includes an eclectic view towards data collecting approaches, encompassing case studies, experimental and survey research, all complementing each other where appropriate. Carried out with intellectual honesty and with adequate skills, endeavours that depend upon the systematic observation of people are more likely to contribute to the advancement of understanding the human condition than those that depend more heavily upon eloquence of argument. Such an approach basically maintains that to understand where we are going, we must know where we are. One overall criterion for the quality of a study is the relative potential to replicate the process with a different group or sample, and arrive at much the same conclusions, regardless of the paradigm employed.

What skills do such approaches demand? These do not consist of the more easily identifiable ones that are closely associated with the natural sciences, such as measuring weight or assembling apparatus, but there are skills that all scientists possess none the less. In order to investigate exactly what these are, let us first engage in a bit of fun. Please carry out Activity 1.1 *before* reading any further.

ACTIVITY 1.1

This exercise will illustrate some of the problems facing a researcher. Take a candle (large or small, it makes no difference) and make a list of 30 of its characteristics. You can do anything you like to it (e.g. light it, throw it, drop it in water.) Restrict your list to about 30 items, otherwise you can go on for ever. Set the list aside for a while; it will be used in Activity 1.2.

PROCESS SKILLS OF SOCIAL SCIENCE RESEARCH

While one usually associates the content of such subjects as biology, chemistry and physics with the word 'science', it is more realistic to think of this word as describing a set of *intellectual processes*. Many of these we all acquire with maturity as part of life's survival skills, but some need special training and all can be applied to investigations in social science as well as the natural sciences. A useful scheme for isolating these is the set of 13 'process skills' produced by The American Association for the Advancement of Science (AAAS) in the 1960s, which are closely related to the 'objectives' defined by the Science 5–13 project in the UK and other international science curriculum projects (Lockard, 1980). These were defined in an effort to encourage science teachers to consider science as more than a set of facts, and to treat science more appropriately as a verb instead of a noun. The aim of both projects was to develop enquiring minds and a scientific approach to problem solving, one that should extend to social science research as well. Not surprisingly, this implies that any scientific discipline is not going to be static, but dynamic.

Below are a set of suggested *social science process skills*, based on the above two schemes. The order (slightly different from the originals) is hierarchical, each process being a higher level skill than the ones before it. As you progress through this book, you will be given opportunities to evaluate the possession of these skills by researchers who publish their work.

1 *Observation* Events occur round us all the time, some of which we notice and others we do not. Observing is necessarily selective: we see what we try to see, otherwise our senses would be overwhelmed. In social science research, there is some necessity to be trained as an observer, since some of the events that need to be observed and recorded are so common as not to seem significant to the untrained. For example, to study the use of positive reinforcement in a classroom may require a researcher to count up how often it is used within a lesson. This may require knowing what the children perceive of as reinforcement and watching the classroom interaction carefully. Whether the reinforcement is effective may be a separate question.

2 *Event/time relations* This involves investigations that are time dependent, for example where frequency of an event may be important. This may result in considering rates of occurrence, sometimes over relatively short periods (minutes) and for other studies over relatively long periods (months, years). For example, if one were investigating alcoholism, there would be a considerable difference between subjects who consume a half-litre of whisky in an evening and those who take a month to consume the same amount. The rate of consumption would be of more interest than the amount.

3 *Communication* It is often assumed that educated adults can communicate, at least in writing. But there is a considerable difference in writing a letter to a friend, an essay, or a novel, and writing a research report. Many studies fail to communicate essential aspects of the process, leaving the reader wondering if the conclusions were really justified.

4 *Prediction* An intelligent guess, extrapolation or interpolation ultimately may be the source of a question that will be the basis of a research project. A 'What if ...?' question can stimulate speculation that only becomes accepted fact if followed by an investigation to answer it. Being able to make predictions and confirm their veracity are important skills.

5   *Classification* We all classify objects and events as a way of bringing order to observations. Some schemes have relatively wide acceptance, like physical characteristics, professions, cognitive level of questions on a test, while others generate considerable discussion, such as social class. Devising a classification scheme can be a very complex task that may involve creating new concepts, isolating characteristics into which persons or events can be categorized, and/or operationally defining (see 9 below) abstract concepts. In any case, the defining of mutually exclusive categories that can be used effectively by researchers is not a trivial task.

6   *Inference* Distinguishing between observation and inference is not always easy. An inference is a subjective explanation of an observation. One may observe the wick sticking out each end of a candle and infer that it is a single string going through the candle, but this is not the only possible inference. Further investigations would be necessary to resolve any doubt. Observing a teacher praise a child for an answer in class and the child subsequently smiling, you may infer that the child is encouraged. Alternatively, the child could be smiling for other reasons (a giggle in the class, a sign of relief, an embarrassed smile, a smile of self-satisfaction for getting it correct). Resolving conflicting inferences in human situations is much more difficult than deciding which is most accurate in material ones like the candle. This makes the choice of what to observe even more difficult, since to decide which of several conflicting inferences is best may require multiple observations.

7   *Number relations* Quantified data can be more meaningfully presented and analysed in tabular and graphical form. Some statistical tests will help to resolve issues after the data has been collected, in a way which would not otherwise be possible. For example, a correlation coefficient may not mean as much to some people as the scatter diagram from which it is derived. Selecting the most appropriate mathematical tools will often help in conveying one's results to chosen audiences.

8   *Measurement* In a physical sense, measurement means using instruments like rulers and balances. Here we shall take it to mean designing and using measuring instruments like tests, questionnaires and interview schedules. There is a considerable technology associated with the design of these, covered extensively in other texts, but some of the main characteristics of which will be considered in Chapter 4.

9   *Making operational definitions* As noted with respect to Action 6 in Figure 1.3, most concepts that tend to be investigated in the social sciences are abstract. This means that there is a necessity to select or devise an observable activity that is indicative of the concept. For example, a score on an IQ test is an operational definition of intelligence. There is no direct, physiological way of measuring intelligence; thus, if this concept is to be used as part of an investigation, then an indirect means must be found. Income and educational background may be factors that are used to determine social class. The relative validity of an operational definition may well be dependent upon the possession of measurement skills (see 8 above) and/or the ability to make sound inferences (see 6 above).

10 *Formulating hypotheses* A hypothesis is an educated guess, an expectation. It may suggest a causal relationship, but not necessarily. Whatever the hypothesis, the aim is to test it in some way to see if it is supported or not. Formulating a hypothesis is not an easy skill and one too often neglected by researchers who leap into a study without the adequately defined reason that every investigation needs. A formal statement often compels a researcher to resolve issues that a more woolly statement or question can hide. The whole design of a research study will be affected by a hypothesis; thus it is better to establish one early before too much intellectual effort is invested in a dead end. This process will highlight the need for clear operational definitions and sound concepts, as well as the need to clarify how variables will be identified and controlled (see 12 below).

11 *Interpreting data* Data appears in many forms, some of it numerical, some of it as transcripts of interviews. Raw data has little meaning and must be turned into understandable information. Numbers and statistical results by themselves are of little interest and difficult to make any sense of. What does it mean to have a correlation of 0.45? It is not easy for a reader to understand the significance of a graph on its own. For example, does the shape of a histogram of scores make any difference in a study? Something can be statistically significant without, for example, being educationally significant. What does a statistical significance level of 0.05 tell us in a specific case? A researcher's ability to interpret the data collected in a logically consistent manner without making unwarranted claims or under-rating the strength of the findings is an essential skill.

12 *Identifying and controlling variables* This is a difficult enough task in the physical and biological sciences, where the experimenter has a reasonable amount of control of the environment and any subjects. In the social sciences, it is even more difficult. Just being able to identify variables in a social interaction requires considerable perception, and is related to other earlier skills. For example, what causes a 'discipline problem' in a classroom? The pupil's behaviour? Provocation by the teacher? Domestic (home) problems on either side leaving one party short-tempered?

  To control variables can be even more difficult. For example, an investigation into the effectiveness of a set of learning materials has little or no control over what the children do outside class or what they see on television at home. If some effect is observed, it is up to the researcher to justify that this was the result of a specific variable, which is usually achieved through the careful design of the investigation (see 13 below).

13 *Designing an investigation* This is the integration of all the above skills in the design of an investigation that will collect data and ultimately provide meaningful information. The design will take into account problems of determining the question and hypothesis, of defining, controlling and measuring/observing variables, and of interpreting results and communicating. A well-planned study is done with considerable foresight so that in the final report, few excuses are made for flaws and the results are justifiable *and* educationally or socially significant. We will return to this problem of integrating a complex set of skills in Chapter 12.

Having considered this list of process skills, let us return to the data you collected on the candle in Activity 1.2.

ACTIVITY 1.2

Take your list from Activity 1.1 and classify each item as one of the 13 process skills and consider the following questions:

1   How many of them were something other than observations?
2   For those that were inferences, do you think your fellow researchers would agree with you? Would they have others? Compare notes.
3   Compare those you classify as 'observations' with those of fellow researchers. Does everyone have the same ones? How could you assure that another group observed the important characteristics? What would constitute being 'important'?
4   You have carried out a detailed study of one candle, a 'case study'. Outline briefly how you would extend this into a survey of a variety of candles to see if they possess the same characteristics.
5   If you take a candle, light it and then turn an empty tumbler upside down over it, the candle will burn for a while and extinguish. Briefly describe a plan for an experimental study to determine if there is a difference in post-covering burning time for candles of different colours.

Contending with candles is much easier than investigating people and their traits. As has been suggested, these same skills are relevant to social science investigations. The difficulty in all the skills applied to social science research lies in the variability and complexity of people and their activities, interactions and environments. As noted earlier, objective measurement depends upon the operational definition stemming from an abstract concept described in the hypothesis. You could begin a list of characteristics of social science research that makes it more difficult and challenging than natural science research, and add to it as you progress through the text and its exercises. Now carry out Activity 1.3.

ACTIVITY 1.3

Select and read carefully an article describing a research project in an area of interest to you. In the margins of the copy, note occurrences of employment of as many of the process skills as you can.

SUMMARY

In this chapter, a rough outline of the major actions in designing research has been presented as a skeleton for building a set of identifiable procedures that can be used to evaluate research reports. Each of these actions has been briefly described and the following chapters will elaborate on the criteria for judging the quality of execution of each. These criteria are summarized on the Profiling Sheet, a full copy of which is provided at the end of Chapter 11. The overall aim is to provide you with the opportunity to apply these criteria to articles and reports, providing practice in evaluating research.

Also, this first chapter has introduced a set of intellectual process skills for social science, which researchers tend to employ when carrying out all the actions. The level of acquisition of these will be much more difficult to infer from reports and journal articles, but they should help in identifying the sources of both good and poor practices in research.

It is recognized that the models and skills presented here are not definitive and necessarily widely accepted: there are alternatives. What is of primary importance here is to provide the reader with a basic set of criteria to begin to evaluate research reports. You are encouraged to develop your own model, refining skill sets to suit your area(s) of research, as experience dictates. The only real sin is *not* to have any criteria by which to judge the quality of research reports.

2

Questions and Hypotheses

'Good morning,' said Deep Thought.

'Er...Good morning, O Deep Thought,' said Loonquawl nervously, 'do you have...er, that is...'

'An answer for you?' interrupted Deep Thought majestically. 'Yes. I have.'

The two men shivered with expectancy. Their waiting had not been in vain.

'There really is one?' breathed Phouchg.

'There really is one,' confirmed Deep Thought.

'To Everything? To the great Question of Life, the Universe and Everything?'

'Yes.'

Both of the men had been trained for this moment, their lives had been a preparation for it, they had been selected at birth as those who would witness the answer, but even so they found themselves gasping and squirming like excited children.

'And you're ready to give it to us?' urged Loonquawl.

'I am.'

'Now?'

'Now,' said Deep Thought.

They both licked their dry lips.

'Though I don't think,' added Deep Thought, 'that you're going to like it.'

'Doesn't matter!' said Phouchg. 'We must know it! Now!'

'Now?' inquired Deep Thought.

'Yes! Now...'

'Alright,' said the computer and settled into silence again. The two men fidgeted. The tension was unbearable.

'You're not going to like it,' observed Deep Thought.

'Tell us!'

'Alright,' said Deep Thought. 'The Answer to the Great Question...'

'Yes...'

'Is...' said Deep Thought, and paused.

'Yes...!'

'Is...'

'Yes ... !!! ... ?'

'Forty-two,' said Deep Thought, with infinite majesty and calm.

(Adams, 1979)

Typically, researchers would like to tackle significant problems and find meaningful answers. The most difficult part of starting a research project is often that of identifying the best question to ask, one that is meaningful, whose answer contributes to the discipline, and whose resulting research can be carried out with the resources available. But even with unlimited resources, one has to be careful about the original guiding question, as Adams (1979) so aptly indicates above, because even after 7½ million years of thinking, Deep Thought's answer was difficult to fathom.

Before considering what constitutes a sound research question and good hypotheses, it is worthwhile examining their role in the research process. First, there is the difficulty of the vocabulary, and words like hypotheses and theory are no exception. Terminology often gets in the way of understanding, particularly when technical terms assume common everyday meaning and usage. It is not the intent to delve into a discussion of a philosophy of science applied to social science, but some clarification should prove useful and further reading can be pursued in such texts as Blum and Foos (1986). A simplified definition based upon their work will suffice: *scientific theories* should be considered as explanations of how something functions or why events occur. These are based upon discoveries and data collection resulting in tested *hypotheses*, which can be considered to be proposed relations and expectations. Theories are presented to explain facts (accurately or inaccurately) but are not facts themselves. They are not absolute answers and are continually subject to new, often conflicting, hypotheses. While sometimes research results in refuting an existing theory, more often the consequence is a refinement of the explanation which enhances the power of prediction when applying them. In any case, we are talking about models of reality, not reality itself; therefore it is not a matter of being 'right' or 'wrong', but degrees of quality in establishing the *best* explanation (model) for what we see.

Blum and Foos (1986) are quite adamant that explanations are not in their own right theories. There are explanations that are the result of *rationalism*, based upon reason alone (some of it faulty) and not backed by systematic observation. This can result in almost trite responses to complex problems, such as why are there so many out of work? Saying that it is because of unemployment only provides a label, not an explanation. There are rationalisms that do provide correct explanations and those that do not, but the best description is that of 'dataless reasoning'. It is often heard as the explanation provided for some event by journalists during television news broadcasts: 'Why has the value of the pound dropped today?' The quick answer may be something like 'There has been panic buying of other currencies due to a drop in interest rates.' Has the reporter actually asked even a sample of currency speculators why they have traded today? Not usually. Rationalisms may be a starting point for formulating a research question or hypothesis, but are unlikely to stand up to scrutiny for long.

Having established what these terms mean, let us consider how research questions and hypotheses are formulated and stated.

QUESTIONS

The problem with research questions that tend to be too vague is they do not provide sufficient direction for the research effort. This happens all too often with committees set up to investigate such grandiose topics as Mathematics Teaching or The English Language as Learned in Schools, or The Cause of Poverty. Rarely is everyone satisfied with the answers, since these tend to have multiple interrelated causes, not just one. While a researcher may wish to contribute to the answer of a more global question, the actual project needs to be guided by a more specific question or set of specific questions that are limited to a subset of variables, one that is feasible to answer with the resources available.

Most published research in journals tends to result from reasonable limited statements of research intent. Yet even these can tend to be vague, poorly stated or, on occasion, not even presented at all. The poorly stated ones are often followed by research without direction, producing results that are inconclusive, or projects that generate vast amounts of data followed by attempts to make some sense of it (the consequences of data snooping, fishing and hunting will be discussed later in the chapter). In addition to answering questions directly with definitive conclusions, one of the functions of research is to eliminate alternative explanations or false theories (Popper, 1978). If the original question or hypothesis is weakly stated, then it is much easier to ignore evidence that contradicts the research team's desired outcomes, and there is the danger that they will find what they want to find.

While Popper (1978) feels that the source of a research question is the personal business of the researcher, most statements of research questions build on and are supported by literature citations of previously conducted studies. In particular, Greer (1978) suggests three general categories that constitute sources of research problems in the social sciences:

1 Policy problems that stem from society's values related to poverty, mental health, race relations and crime. These tend to result from a perceived discrepancy between what is considered to be the ideal and the actual situation. This often results in abstract constructs of complex social functions, with a focus on how to achieve some effect or social change.
2 Social philosophy, intellectual problems stemming from the conflict between established ideologies and contemporary events. For example, the study of Marxism leads to the serious consideration of class in society. The aim is to integrate new ideas into established schemas.
3 Previously accumulated propositions, which become the starting points for establishing more comprehensive theories or models. Positive reinforcement may be of prime interest to the classroom teacher, but the educational psychologist will be more concerned with its role in a general learning theory. The problems tend to be of broader interest to the discipline, though to the casual observer this may not always be apparent. Sometimes it is more difficult to see the relevance of a specific study to a specific model or theory. This can be due to a combination of the perceived

need for building on existing theories, collected evidence and structures of the discipline, exacerbated by the rigour required to resolve an individual problem.

All three areas could generate studies that require the collection of data to resolve issues. In each, a clear statement of the questions as well as its links with established thinking (though not necessarily agreement) is essential in the reporting of a study.

Some research questions might be considered to originate from more than one source or a conflict between two. Educational decisions made by politicians can raise public issues that can transcend the categories, such as the desirability of bussing children to schools to maintain a racial balance, and the need for emphasis on basic skills such as spelling and multiplication tables in school in the era of calculators and spell-check facilities on computers. Before going further, please consider Activity 2.1.

ACTIVITY 2.1

Below are three statements of research questions. Suggest and justify what you think the origin of each is from one or more of: policy problems, social philosophy and/or previously accumulated propositions:

(a) How much of intelligence is determined by heredity or environment?

(b) What is the relationship between crime rate and levels of employment?

(c) Why do many people prefer to go on highly structured holidays (pre-booked hotels, guided tours, planned events) rather than more self-organized ones?

How can the reader of research reports begin to evaluate the quality of a research question? Kerlinger and Lee (2000) maintain that there are three criteria for good problem statements in the form of questions. The statement should:

1 express a relationship between variables;
2 be stated in unambiguous terms in question form; and
3 should imply the possibility of empirical testing.

The last criterion recognizes that there are valid philosophical and theological questions to be answered, but these are not in the realm of research covered in this text. This still leaves a problem for the reader when reading a report or article as to deciding the adequacy of a research question. A question could meet all of the above criteria and still be unacceptable. Before considering other issues related to the statement of a research question, carry out Activity 2.2.

ACTIVITY 2.2

Below are three statements of research questions (the first two are adapted from Kerlinger and Lee, 2000). Read each in turn, considering its merits, and then pass judgement on its quality *before* reading the model answers at the end of this chapter. Since these statements are taken out of context, you may disagree with the evaluation supplied, which is quite reasonable assuming you can defend yours.

(a) Does democratic education improve the learning of children?
(b) Do encouraging teacher comments enhance improvement in student performance?
(c) Is it best to provide financial assistance to the unemployed?

You may have found the task in Activity 2.2 an awkward one, since the questions were presented in isolation. Most reports will provide a reasonable rationale supported by other research, presented in the form of references to published reports and journal articles. Occasionally, a reader will find a question that lacks such intellectual support, leaving the feeling that the statement has inadequate justification. In some cases, the question is based solely upon belief, unsupported by previous research. While this is not unheard of, nor totally unreasonable, it is unlikely that a research report will have its basic question unsupported by other research. Even those proposing a radical stance will cite the literature to which it is opposing.

A second reason for expecting a justification for the research question is that the writer ought to be educating his/her readers and promoting further enquiry. Social science research rarely generates questions that involve totally isolated variables, and for the sake of the readership, the author ought to be drawing on the experience of others and encouraging the expansion of interest and effort in that area. Relevant articles have been skipped over by readers because the author has not stated the question unambiguously or presented a sound case for investigating it early in the discussion.

HYPOTHESES

As noted earlier, hypotheses as presented in a report or study are a more formal means of stating expected research outcomes, more firmly fixing the direction of a study. These will have a direct influence on the eventual choice of operational definition(s) of concepts and constructs, which will be the measuring instrument(s) used to collect the data, as will be seen in Chapter 4. This need to consider stages of research planning out of the order described earlier simply points up the somewhat artificial nature of the linear model of research design chosen in Chapter 1, since a researcher most likely will consider these together. It does not negate the need for a statement of a hypothesis early in a report, nor the desirability of a researcher establishing a hypothesis that is acceptable early in the study. Kerlinger and Lee (2000) note:

> After intellectualizing the problem, referring to experience for possible solutions, observing relevant phenomena, the scientist may formulate a hypothesis. A hypothesis is a conjectural statement, a tentative proposition about the relationship between two or more phenomena or variables.

'Observing relevant phenomena' may include surveying the literature and referring to the experiences of others, as well as first-hand observation.

Popper (1978) maintains the need for hypotheses as part of social science research on the basis that such endeavours tend to be deductive, with a statement of hypothesis followed by systematically determining the fallacy of competing answers. He maintains that while we use knowledge of ourselves to make statements about others or people in general, these are hypotheses that must be tested. Too often, one hears statements such as 'A friend of mine buys all his marijuana from this accountant. You know all these accountants deal in drugs on the side. How else could they be so rich?' For 'accountants', substitute all men with beards, a specific ethnic group, profession or social class and such comments are assumed too often to be fact.

While it is human nature to generalize from personal experience, it can result in rejecting research findings because of having seen a counter-example. The result is raising what ought to be hypothesis to the level of fact. How often has something like the following been said: 'My Uncle Charlie smoked three packs of cigarettes a day and died at 96 riding his bicycle. All this research about cigarettes causing heart disease and lung cancer cannot be true.' Part of the fault for the all too common occurrence of such thinking may be rooted in how researchers present their results to the public as direct cause and effect. Or is it a human trait to believe 'it couldn't happen to me'? Here are some interesting hypotheses for someone looking for a research project.

Many seemingly divergent areas of research employ hypotheses as a point for initiating a study. For example, Cohen and Manion (2000) note the formulation of a hypothesis or set of questions and testing them is one approach used in historical research. The main difference is in the use of historical data rather than contemporarily collected data, over which the researcher has more control. Studies related to the past still depend upon the rigorous testing of ideas and sometimes suffer from too much data rather than too little. In such situations, the statement of a hypothesis can assist in focusing a study in a sea of data, helping to take it beyond an exercise in simply collecting facts.

Much later in their book, Cohen and Manion (2000) also note the role of generating hypotheses as one 'method' that can be applied in qualitative studies which involve recording and analysing accounts of events and social episodes. Their statement can clarify and document the expectations of researchers as they enter a situation, providing a baseline for later conclusions. The use of hypotheses should not be considered as only for quantitative studies as they have useful roles in many approaches. What will differ is the nature of the evidence used to resolve the hypotheses.

Stating a hypothesis

Kerlinger and Lee (2000) suggest two criteria for acceptable hypotheses, analogous to those for questions:

a   hypotheses should be statements of possible relationships between variables, and
b   these statements should imply how they are to be tested.

The variables must be potentially measurable, and considering the thinking that goes on during the planning of a research project, the variables are likely to have been operationally defined as part of devising a statement of the hypothesis.

   In social science research, hypotheses can be placed into one of three rough categories:

1   Those that can be confirmed or refuted by direct observation, assuming the skill to make the appropriate observations exists. For example, we are being watched by extraterrestrials, video games are harmful to some children (note the 'some').
2   Those that are confirmed or refuted by considering all possible negative alternatives. For example, all Britons are Christians, people enjoy laughing, politicians only lie when their lips move.
3   Those describing central tendency involving traits of groups. For example, the children in Blogg's School are of average intelligence, workers performing under condition A perform more efficiently than those under condition B. This later group will require a statement of a null hypothesis (to be discussed below) and inferential statistics to resolve it.

   In order to define a hypothesis clearly, it will be necessary at this stage to define operationally the variables involved. This does not mean that the actual measuring instruments need to be described in detail, but some indication needs to be provided as to how data for the variables will be collected. For example, if the research question consists of a statement relating learner intelligence with some learning outcome, then the hypothesis should be in terms that indicate how intelligence, as well as how the learning outcome, is to be measured. The question of validity and reliability of the ultimate instruments used in measurement will be considered in Chapter 4 on data quality.

   Whether stated as a question or more formally as an hypothesis, the research problem statement should conform at this level to five important criteria (Open University, 1973). It should be:

1   *Stated clearly*, with definitions of any technical terms and providing the operational definitions of any abstract variables. Ambiguities and vagueness should be avoided.
2   *Testable or resolvable*, since it is a predictor of outcomes of a study or a statement of a question to be answered.
3   *Stated in terms of relationships between variables*, though not necessarily causal relationships. Relationships should be stated clearly, indicating whether it is anticipated that there will be a positive or negative relation.

4 *Limited in scope*, in other words, realistic. The more global the statement of a relationship is, the less likely it will be possible to confirm or refute it. The desire usually exists among researchers that their study will contribute to a broader field of research, but it is unlikely that any single endeavour will solve all the problems.
5 *Not inconsistent with most known facts*, which is best achieved by references to existing literature. Most journal articles are limited by length, so any review of the literature will not necessarily be extensive, though it should provide adequate justification.

One of the problems that a reader will encounter is to decide whether the lack of a stated hypothesis is a matter of technical writing ability or a sin of omission. Sometimes it is possible to infer the hypothesis, while in other cases it will become apparent that there simply was not one.

Cause and effect, or association?

One aspect of scientific investigation is a common desire to identify what are the causes of certain events or human conditions, for example crime, intelligence, divorce, paranoia, rapid learning. Those variables that are suspected of causing such events or conditions, like heredity, vitamins (or the lack of), good books, are considered *independent variables*. The resulting affected events are the *dependent variables* since they are influenced by (depend on) the other variables and not the other way round. For example, it might be possible that genetics affects intelligence, or even a propensity to crime, but becoming more intelligent or committing crimes will not change one's genetic make-up. Vitamins, or even baked beans, might help children to learn faster in the classroom, but learning faster in the classroom is unlikely to have an affect on the quality of the vitamins or baked beans. While variables are not always overtly labelled as independent or dependent in reports, the relationship will often be implicit.

Are all relationships necessarily causal? No, though sometimes it is difficult to tell from the wording just what the author of a report is trying to prove. Relationships can be ones of *association*, where the two variables change together, though there is not a direct cause and effect relationship. For example, it might be hypothesized that tooth decay is affected by increase sunspot activity. In the first place, not everyone would have increased (decreased) tooth decay, so the proposal would be looking for an increase/decrease in the frequency of tooth decay. Second, we are not observing an experiment where one group is exposed to the possible effects on earth of sunspots and another group is totally shielded. With one group, there is no control over other possible influences that might occur parallel to the sunspots. It might be possible that the increased radiation resulting from sunspots could directly affect teeth, but then there might be an intermediate stage, such as the radiation affecting calcium uptake in cereal grains that children eat. At this stage, the mechanism is not even suggested and the intent is to determine only whether the relative frequency in the population of tooth decay is at all related to the frequency of sunspots. It would take a different type of research to discover the actual causal mechanism, if the association between the two events were even to exist.

It is not difficult to distinguish a potential independent variable from a dependent one: sunspots might have some direct or indirect effect on tooth decay, but there is no way that the frequency of tooth decay in children could affect the sun. This association, when quantifiable, is often expressed as a *correlation*, a numerical value between + 1.00 indicating an exact match between the two events, zero indicating no relationship, and − 1.00 indicating that as one increases, the other decreases, the size of the number indicating the strength of the association. Therefore, a correlation of 0.82 between two variables would indicate a strong positive association whereas − 0.12 would indicate a weak negative one. The value of high correlations is the ability to predict relationships more accurately, but even being able to predict does not prove causality. We can predict with reasonable accuracy children's weight based upon their height, but one does not *cause* the other. Chapter 8 covers this in detail and correlations are mentioned here mainly to emphasize the fact that many relationships are not causal. Thus, the statement of a hypothesis may be in terms of independent and dependent variables, but it may not mean that a potential cause and effect relationship is being investigated.

Another research design that will be covered in greater detail later employs life events as variables, decreasing the likelihood that causality can be established. Some of the most interesting variables in the social sciences are not under the control of the researcher, like social class, education, income, etc. Studies using these as variables appear to have similar structures to experimental designs, but lack the control over the variables: we cannot randomly assign people to social classes and then see how the different groups respond, make them have certain education and find out what different groups do with it, or give them a specific salary to see how the different groups spend it. Such studies, called ex post facto (after the fact), can often at best also establish associations. For example, people in the upper classes *tend* to read more books than those in the lower classes, better educated people *tend* to have jobs with greater responsibility than those with less education, and those with higher incomes *tend* to be more avid consumers than those with lower incomes. While you may think there is a causal relationship, there is little proof available from such studies and the relationships are best described as associational. Activity 2.3 will have you consider some other possible relationships provided in Table 2.1.

ACTIVITY 2.3

Table 2.1 provides some exemplar studies with the data technique, independent and dependent variables provided. Which ones describe potential cause and effect relationships and which are possible associations, but not causal? The issue of operationally defining and measuring these variables will be addressed in Chapter 4, so that does not have to be a concern now.

TABLE 2.1 *Possible relationships between variables*

Research hypothesis	Proposed variables	
	Independent	Dependent
Intelligence is determined primarily by heredity as opposed to environment	Heredity and environment	Intelligence
There is a strong relationship between crime rate and the level of unemployment	Level of unemployment	Crime rate
The preference to go on structured holidays (pre-booked hotels, guided tours, planned events) rather than more self-organized ones is related to social class	Social class	Preferences
Encouraging teacher comments enhance improvement in student performance	Teacher comments	Student performance

The null hypothesis

There will be situations where the researcher wants to make inferences about a larger population based upon a study carried out on a representative sample of that population. To make such inferences requires the use of statistical tests that compare data about groups of subjects and not individuals. For example, if a researcher wanted to consider mathematical achievement under specific learning conditions, one approach would be to investigate the performance of each class or group as a whole without focusing on individuals in the classes. This requires the use of some indicator of group performance, such as the average (arithmetic mean) of the class performance on an examination: individual scores are not of concern, only the class average.

Consider a hypothesis that suggests a comparison of possible effects (variables) on mathematical achievement. One way to determine whether some variables had a greater effect than others would be to subject two (or more) representative groups to these variables (say different textbooks), and see if there was any difference in achievement of the groups as a whole, as measured through the mathematics examination. The problem for the researcher is that the statistical tests will only tell whether the difference in group examination scores is significant; in other words, whether the difference was large enough not to have occurred just by chance. If the significance test says that it is unlikely the difference could be attributed only to natural variability in scores of two groups having the same characteristics (a significant difference), then it is still up to the researcher to prove that the only possible cause was the distinct learning experiences, here the different textbooks (the variables).

As Campbell and Stanley (1963) note, hypotheses are really never 'confirmed' as the truth, otherwise they would not be hypotheses. Thus a statistical test is really a way of rejecting alternative hypotheses and if the test rejects an undesirable hypothesis (shows no difference), then there is some support for the alternatives, even though these are not absolutely confirmed. In a sense, a hypothesis gains strength by having as many alternative hypotheses as possible proven false, or rejected.

This results in a statement of anticipation of outcome in negative terms: there will be no significant difference, a *null hypothesis*. Thus to reject the null hypothesis means that there is evidence to support the conjecture that there was a difference. Why such a convoluted way of thinking? Statistical tests only give *probabilities* of something occurring, so the statistical test will only resolve whether or not two or more groups probably belong to the same group after different experiences. Thus by saying it is highly probable that they belong to the same group means that there was no significant difference. To reject this null hypothesis means there probably was a difference and they probably no longer belong to the same group (for this trait). This would lend support to the hypothesis of interest, but not confirm that it is absolutely true.

Campbell and Stanley (1963) recognize that not being able to confirm a hypothesis directly goes against a scientist's experience and attitudes. In such complex situations as found in social science research where there are so many possible alternative hypotheses because there are so many possible variables, there must be degrees of confirmation. 'Well-established' theories simply have few, if any, plausible alternatives left after extensive investigations. Positive reinforcement does encourage human behaviour, but the widespread acceptance of this statement is based upon an extensive body of research, some contending with such problems as what constitutes 'positive' reinforcement for certain groups may not be true for others. For example, one child deprived of attention at home may consider a rap on the knuckles with a ruler as positive reinforcement for his/her actions: the child received attention rather than being ignored by the teacher. On the other hand, another child may be devastated by such violence. Again, careful definition of the variables is necessary. The control of variables in a study is an exercise by the researcher to make alternative hypotheses implausible. The discussion of the null hypothesis will continue in later chapters, as it is recognized that it can be a difficult concept to grasp.

One other source of confusion arises from the use of the word 'significant'. Just because a study reports a statistical significance does not necessarily mean that it has found anything of sociological, psychological or educational significance. For example, using large samples, it is possible to have statistically significant correlations that are very small. As a case in point, it has been found in the United Kingdom that the correlation between A-level examination results (taken at age 18+ as part of selection for university entrance in the United Kingdom) and subsequent level of success in university, as indicated by degree classification, was of the order of 0.20 (Bourner and Hamad, 1987). This was statistically significant, even though numerically small, primarily because of the very large sample. While the null hypothesis would be rejected (this correlation occurred by chance alone), a correlation of this size means very little in practical terms, except to other researchers looking for ideas for more research. The actual educational significance lies in that there is such a *small* relationship between A-level results and subsequent university degree classification achieved. It is not a good predictor.

Finally, finding a statistically significant difference between two groups using different textbooks still leaves the researcher with the question as to *why* one was better than the other. In other words, there would still need to be other research in parallel, like interviews and observations of children learning, to determine why children learned better from one than the other. This is why quantitative and qualitative research are best conducted in collaboration with each other, to answer both questions: *what* is happening and *why*?

There is no necessity for all hypotheses to be stated as null hypotheses, but if the intent is to make inferences to a larger population through a study that collects data to be processed statistically, then a null hypothesis is in order. While a general hypothesis may propose a cause and effect relationship, a null hypothesis should not, since all the resulting statistical tests will be able to determine whether or not the relationship occurred by chance. The strength of the proof for the causal hypothesis will depend more on how well the researcher controlled or eliminated all the other possible causes.

In *ex post facto* studies, where statistical tests are used to determine whether differences exist between existing groups (like boys and girls), the life experiences associated with gender are the variables, limiting one's ability to talk about causality. The lack of control over these global variables allows one to describe the outcomes as associations rather than causal. For example, if a study shows that 7-year-old boys have a lower reading age than 7-year-old girls, it would be unreasonable to say being a 7-year-old boy *causes* lower reading ability. Many variables (social, developmental, cultural) go into being a 7 year old in addition to the physiological trait of gender. A more reasonable conclusion would be that 7-year-old boys tend to read at a lower age than 7-year-old girls, a subtle difference from saying there is a causal relationship. The null hypothesis still has a role in stating an anticipated no difference in the groups, but not in no causal relationship. Now try your hand at Activity 2.4.

ACTIVITY 2.4

Below are three statements of research hypotheses. Read each in turn, considering its merits, and then pass judgement on its quality *before* reading the model answers at the end of the chapter. Since these statements are taken out of context, you may disagree with the evaluation supplied, which is quite reasonable assuming you can defend yours.

(a) Group study contributes to a higher level of achievement in a class than independent study.

(b) The amount of practice required to master a skill will have no effect on motivation to learn.

(c) Middle-class children more often than lower-class children will avoid finger painting tasks.

What is fact and what is hypothesis?

Unless one is well informed and reads or listens critically, it is often difficult to determine what is fact and what is conjecture or hypothesis, particularly in public statements that tend to be unsubstantiated and taken out of context. For example, in the popular press, Beauchamp (1988) presented an interesting example to consider:

> A report on the effects of the new Housing Bill on homeless people by the West London Homeless Group says: '... It adds weight to the view that ministers do not recognise homelessness as being a problem and that the problem is a product of feckless councils and feckless individuals.'

Such statements require careful dissection. The use of English makes this sound as if there is a contradiction in that the 'problem' is not recognized, but its cause is. In reality, it appears that when the word 'problem' is used in two ways, the first time it refers to homelessness as a condition that might or might not be treated directly, and the second time it refers to a possible cause of homelessness. Let us consider the statement as it was probably intended. If ministers (politicians, not the clergy) do think that the 'problem' is feck-lessness as described, do *they* take it to be fact or hypothesis? But even before this, the question can be asked, is it a fact that ministers do not see that homelessness is a directly treatable problem, or is this really a statement of hypothesis? With no supporting evidence either way, it seems that the best one can do is to treat both these statements – the assumption that ministers have a lack of recognition of homelessness as a directly treatable condition *and* what they identify as a treatable problem (the cause of homelessness) is fecklessness – as possible conflicting hypotheses.

While the general public accepts or ignores such statements (the author's hypothesis supported by the fact that such statements continually appear), possibly because there is a general feeling that political statements are not expected to be substantiated (another hypothesis), research papers generally do not put forward unsubstantiated statements as fact. More appropriately, hypotheses are presented as starting points for research. Having said this, the reader of research can practise the skill in distinguishing fact from hypothesis by simply reading the popular press as suggested in Activity 2.5.

ACTIVITY 2.5

Select a current newspaper article describing someone's stand on an issue, that of a politician or one expressed in an editorial. Read it analytically, particularly considering supposed statements of fact, noting which of these are truly factual statements and which are really untested conjecture or hypotheses.

EVALUATING RESEARCH QUESTIONS
AND HYPOTHESES: CRITERIA

Below are the criteria selected to delineate levels of quality of the statement of research questions and/or hypotheses that will be used when evaluating research articles.

Valid question or hypothesis based on accepted theory with well-justified and referenced support

The validity of the statement will have to be judged based upon your knowledge of the field and the literature, but this is still the strongest basis for a hypothesis. This also assumes that the statement conforms to the five criteria outlined earlier, that hypotheses and questions are stated clearly, testable or resolvable, stated in terms of relationships between variables, limited in scope, and not inconsistent with most known facts.

Valid question or hypothesis based on own theory, well justified

The validity will have to be based primarily upon your knowledge of the discipline and your judgement as to the soundness of the rationale or justification. A new theory may be extrapolating into new areas or contradicting established ones; thus there should be a strong argument for it.

Credible question/hypothesis but alternatives possible, or too extensive/global, or support missing

This level covers three 'sins': (a) there are more valid alternative hypotheses that you can identify; (b) the statement is so global for it to be unlikely that a single study could resolve the issue; or (c) there is an hypothesis or research question stated that on the surface seems reasonable, but there is no justification.

Weak question/hypothesis or poorly stated or justified with inappropriate references

(a) The question or hypothesis is questionable from the view of it being inconsistent with previous research, or unreasonable in terms of your knowledge of the discipline; or (b) it is poorly stated in abstract terms, with variables not clearly or not operationally defined; or (c) the researcher has references that do not really provide credible support.

No question or hypothesis stated, or inconsistent with known facts

Occasionally, one will find a report that has no research question or hypothesis stated. As noted above, the writer either has failed to state the intent of the study, or was just 'data dredging'. In other words, data was collected with no hypothesis or research question in mind and the author is trying to find some relationship. Even so, there should be a statement or question to this effect. The last section of this chapter elaborates on this omission.

More rarely (at least in refereed journals) one will find a paper purporting to investigate relationships that contradict established research. There is the chance that something new has been found, but rarely do we ever encounter 'earth shattering discoveries' in the social sciences. These can occur when someone's beliefs are very strong, such as in articles that purportedly conclusively prove the general inferiority of certain ethnic or racial groups. Sources publishing articles of this quality may not be refereed or may have a strong bias.

DREDGING FOR VARIABLES

Rigorous experimentalists will state that all studies need hypotheses. Other researchers will maintain that there are times when less well-defined statements are necessary to allow one to look for possible relationships and hypotheses. Studies of the second type still have demands made of them in terms of rules to follow. Slevin and Stuart (1978) describe three types of studies that involve data dredging, where questions or hypotheses may be missing,

1 *Snooping* – testing all the (perhaps infinite) predesignated hypotheses possible in a set of data. There are specific rigorous statistical tests for this, so there is at least no reason for not identifying the hypotheses.
2 *Fishing* – an approach of the survey analyst, employed to choose which of a number of potential variables to use in an explanation. This is a common approach employed by economists using standard questionnaires and/or demographic data. Computer programs, for example for correlation and regression, make such a task easier. Two objections arise:

   (a) By selecting to report just some of the variables, the research may produce misleading results, suggesting probabilities that are much higher than justified by the test (this will be considered in greater detail in Chapter 8).
   (b) Collecting data without planned questions can result in the researcher later claiming unjustifiably data to be operational definitions of variables.

   On the positive side, the process can be a starting point for future, more experimentally based or more tightly structured *ex post facto* research by identifying potential variables. Let it suffice to say that if this is the intent, then the researcher still has questions to ask and should admit to fishing.
3 *Hunting* – this approach has no predesignated set of variables to investigate, and subsequently, there are no *appropriate* statistical tests. It can involve searching data, for example demographic data not collected by the researcher, for some relationship(s) worth testing, or testing one hypothesis in several sets of data until something is found. This is one argument for replicating studies, as it is not always possible to tell when someone has been hunting, carrying out a series of studies and discarding data that produces no significance. While this process may also be of use to the survey analyst in helping to identify potential variables, it is the reluctance to admit it and make unwarranted claims for one's results that is the sin. A question can still be stated and the process of hunting admitted.

SUMMARY

This chapter has introduced the criteria for judging the adequacy and quality of research questions and hypotheses, as described in articles and reports. One of your problems as a reader and evaluator when encountering the lack of either or both of these, is whether there were any to begin with, or whether there was an omission in writing the report. Without a clear statement of the research question(s) and hypotheses, it will be difficult to evaluate the logical consistency of operational definitions and the quality of the data subsequently collected. Clear questions and hypotheses provide a sound baseline for you when reading a report, but sometimes these must be isolated from the text by the reader: sometimes the questions are implied and not marked with a nice clear '?'. In Activity 2.6, you will have an opportunity to apply these criteria to a report or article.

ACTIVITY 2.6

Choose up to three articles from your own literature search and rate them according to the quality of statement of research question or hypothesis, using the first column of the Profiling Sheet (at the end of this chapter). Mark your choice of level by circling it. You should justify your rating in each case and include comments where appropriate. Compare your ratings and rationales with fellow researchers or a colleague.

MODEL ANSWERS

Activity 2.2

(a) This is a poor question since it is not going to be possible to test this empirically. First, 'democratic education' will be difficult to define in operational (observable) terms and, second, where is one going to find a non-democratic education against which to compare?

(b) This one is reasonable since it states a possible relationship, the variables are unambiguous, and it is testable.

(c) The term 'best' is ambiguous and would be improved even by referring to 'better than' something else, assuming the something else was definable and the resulting relationship could be empirically tested.

continued

Activity 2.4

(a) The variables 'how they learn' and 'how much they learn' are unambiguous and potentially definable, and the hypothesis is testable. Whether it becomes a case study (two convenient groups in the researcher's own school) or broader enquiry using a number of representative groups is irrelevant at this point, as will be seen in the next chapter.

(b) This is a statement in the null hypothesis form, implying that the two variables, amount of practice required and motivation, are not related. Assuming that a test of motivation to learn can be devised, then this is a reasonable and testable hypothesis.

(c) Kerlinger (1986) suggests that this hypothesis is one level away from the actual hypothesis, which he says is 'finger painting behavior is in part a function of social class'. Thus the above is a prediction based upon a broader hypothesis.

Profiling Sheet: *Understanding Social Science Research*, © Thomas R. Black, 2001

Article: _____

Type of Study: _____ ☐ Descriptive, ☐ Survey/correlational, ☐ *Ex post facto*, ☐ Experimental, ☐ Experimental/quasi-experimental.

**Questions/
hypotheses**

Valid question or
hypothesis based
on accepted theory with
well-justified
referenced
support

Valid question or
hypothesis based
on own theory,
well justified

Credible
question/
hypothesis but
alternative
possible, or too
extensive/global,
or support
missing

Weak question/
hypothesis, or
poorly stated, or
justified with
inappropriate
references

No question or
hypothesis stated,
or inconsistent
with known facts

Comments and rationale for classification:

3

Research Designs and Representativeness

After determining what the purpose of the research is, the reader of a report must answer another question: to whom are the results intended to apply? That is, to what group will the conclusions be justifiably relevant? The answer to this may be partially determined by the initial research questions asked: were there a few variables to be investigated or many? Often the limitations of resources (money, time and effort available) determine who the subjects are and subsequently how far the results can be generalized. Looking ahead, the ultimate level of generalization decided upon will have had an influence on what research tools and types of analysis were chosen by the researcher. This chapter will consider both the implications of how the subjects for a study were chosen and the criteria for rating articles and reports on this aspect. Later chapters will consider the consequence of the choices made at this stage.

One of the factors a researcher will consider when deciding on the sample is which of a number of approaches that use quantitative data to resolve hypotheses will be employed. What becomes apparent is that some designs are more suited to answering some types of questions or testing certain kinds of hypotheses, so the choice is necessarily based upon the nature of the research question and hypotheses. Maintaining a logical thread throughout a study is not as simple as it might seem and more than one researcher has apparently lost the plot during a study, at least from what one can see from the report. Before looking at populations and samples, let us clarify what the choices of designs are.

RESEARCH DESIGNS FOR QUANTITATIVE RESEARCH

In Chapter 2 on questions and hypotheses, it was noted that ideally statements of hypotheses would describe possible relationships between variables. A few will aim to establish causality, a very difficult relationship to establish in social science research, and many will endeavour to identify relationships that are only associational. Some will not aim to resolve hypotheses and will only provide information about a group. Therefore, the following classification scheme is based upon the *intent* of the design and what type of hypotheses, if any, they are capable of resolving:

- *Descriptive* studies intending to provide only descriptive data on either larger or small (even case studies) groups. They will tell us something about the group and may identify the existence of variables and characteristics of the group.
- *Surveys* usually involve a random sample of a single group. The intent is to determine whether relationships exist among specific variables measured by the survey instrument. These often result in measures of correlation or association between variables, allowing predictions, but do not determine causality. They are sometimes referred to as *correlational* studies because of the frequent use of correlations to show relationships among variables.
- *Ex post facto* studies endeavour to determine whether differences exist between groups with different characteristics, traits or preferences. The groups are defined on the basis of life experiences (e.g. education, gender, social class). Here it is usually not possible to establish causality since the classification variables tend to encompass many components and life experiences.
- *Experimental* studies are those where the researchers have a representative sample of a population and randomly assign them to two or more groups. They have control over one or more of the variables and are able to compare the outcomes of treatment groups with each other or with a control group that receives no treatment. This model is used with evaluations of interventions in local environments as well as to test more global hypotheses (e.g. the effects of classroom innovations, counselling techniques, or nurse interventions).
- *Quasi-experimental* studies endeavour to achieve many of the same goals, but have to use less representative, locally available groups.

Such a classification scheme helps in checking on the continuity of design of a study and can assist in determining the intent when it is not clearly stated in a report or article. Each of these is described in greater detail in the following sections.

Not all studies you will encounter that use quantitative data will meet the criterion of resolving a hypothesis that describes relationships. They may question or hypothesize the existence of characteristics or a range of characteristics of the target group. We will start with this basic approach. Most quantitative research depends on the fact that not everyone is the same even for a trait commonly possessed by all. Within that supposedly homogeneous group of people there will be *natural variability* for any given trait. This is easier to see for physical characteristics, such as height and weight. We do not all weigh the same nor are we all the same height. Even for specified populations, such as all children born on 23 February 1994, there will be a range of values for these traits.

More abstract traits are often of interest to social scientists, such as attitudes. If the attitude is defined carefully in the statement of the research question, then not everyone in a population will necessarily feel equally strongly about it. Of course it is possible to group people according to attitudes and views by their membership of an organization, for example. Yet not all members of the Labour Party agree on every issue. Human beings are extremely individualistic, yet there will be some commonality shared among them within limits.

Descriptive studies

Exploratory descriptive studies may occasionally aim to see what the nature of the variability is within a group for a given trait. For example, rather than asking whether all abandoned unmarried mothers hate men, it would be more profitable to find out the range of attitudes towards men on several key issues. How callous, uncaring or irresponsible are men seen to be? What level of trust or dependability can be found in them?

Such studies are likely to gather quantitative data, but to describe the outcomes descriptively, without making statements about relationships. They will report their observations and comment on the range of traits found in the sample. This may apply to case studies where a number of subjects participate in, say, interviews, or they are observed in social groups. It still might be of interest to describe the group as a whole according to other less contentious traits, such as age, years of experience, qualifications, number of children, etc.

For example, it might be desirable to identify the characteristics of adults participating part-time in higher education, in order to determine their needs. A questionnaire sent to a sample of participants would be appropriate, but the difficulty may be in acquiring a list from which to choose the sample if the population is to be more than the students in a single institution.

Surveys

The survey of a single group, even randomly selected, precludes one from establishing causality. It is possible to go one step beyond just describing the characteristics of the subjects and to look for relationships between pairs of traits. For example, in the study on part-time adult learners in higher education above, is there any relation between age and number of courses or modules taken, grades achieved, or time taken to meet the requirements for a degree? If there were a desire to determine attitudes towards higher education provision, is there any relationship between attitudes and age, previous education, type of employment or social class? Even if significant correlations were found, this would not establish causal links, but would allow some predictions to be made in the form of tendencies, for example for attitudes to change with age: the older the students, the greater the desire for more structured teaching. Such a result would not mean that all older students want structured learning, but that there is a tendency within the group. This can be schematically represented as

$$RS \rightarrow O_a, O_b, O_c, \ldots$$

where *RS* indicates a randomly selected group and the *Os* are different observations/measures made on each member of the group corresponding to the traits and/or attitudes of interest.

Ex post facto *studies*

Such studies tend to look for *differences* in group characteristics, traits or preferences based upon life experiences (e.g. education, gender, social class). The statistical tests employed in such studies often are the same ones used in experimental and quasi-experimental studies, which can seem misleading. What one must remember is that statistical tests tell us nothing more than whether a *difference between groups exists*. In *ex post facto* studies, life experiences determine group characteristics and since these tend to be quite complex, it is often difficult if not impossible to determine causality.

Consider a hypothetical study that shows that 8-year-old girls read better than 8-year-old boys, gender being the life experience. It would be unwise to claim that having a certain sexuality will always *cause* 8 year olds to read at a different level. Why? Being a girl or a boy may lead to a set of experiences that are culturally dependent. In some societies, boys are encouraged to succeed in school more than girls; therefore a study replicated there might present just the opposite results. Examining *why* girls perform better than boys in the study described might reveal other causes. For example, since most primary teachers are women, they may form better role models for little girls than little boys; thus girls try harder, spend more time practising, etc.

Such studies are quite good at determining whether a difference exists, but not so good on their own at determining why. It might be possible to complement such data with classroom observations and interviews to resolve why, but in this case determining causality on the basis of just reading ability and gender would not be justifiable. The researchers do not have sufficient control over all the variables to establish a strong causal link. In fact, much of social science research falls in this category, since it is 'in the field' or deals with 'real' issues. Not being able to establish causality may be frustrating, but the results of such studies do lead to a better understanding (and further research) about contemporary problems. When based upon sufficiently representative samples, they can provide a greater understanding of events in society and institutions, what variables are interrelated, and the strength of these relationships. And when complemented by qualitative research (e.g. interviews and observations), the causes may be better understood.

Ex post facto designs can be schematically described as

$$LE_A \rightarrow RS_A \rightarrow O_A$$

$$LE_B \rightarrow RS_B \rightarrow O_B$$

where LE_A and LE_B are the life experience (e.g. gender, occupation, social class) populations from which the representative samples, RS_A and RS_B, are selected, and the *Os* are the observations or measures on each group that are to be compared.

Experimental studies

These are structured in such a way as to allow the researchers to have control over one or more of the variables. Here the aim is to try to establish whether or not there is a causal relationship between an independent variable (usually some sort of treatment, activity or structured experience) and a dependent variable (the outcome). The study provides one or more groups with different experiences, methods of learning, counselling techniques, etc., and looks at the intended outcomes to see if there is any difference compared with a group that did not have the experience, or had a different one. This approach is commonly used in educational settings to establish which of several approaches or media may be better than another, for specified groups of learners. The difficulty is ensuring that the planned treatment is the only possible event that could have an impact on the outcome (amount and quality of learning). It becomes even more difficult when the aim is to change attitudes, since these are much more fluid than achievement of skills or acquisition of information or concepts. As we will see later, a number of other events could make it difficult for researchers to guarantee that what they provided as experiences were the only possible influence.

Such studies require careful consideration of the continuity across the research question, hypotheses, null hypotheses, sample and design. It is possible to control for many *extraneous* variables (those other than the ones of interest that might influence the outcomes) by an appropriate choice of design. Random selection of subjects followed by random assignment to treatment groups protects against some groups having an advantage from previous learning or higher overall IQ. All groups would have roughly the same distribution (amount of variability around the same average) of previous experience and IQ, as well as equivalent distribution of gender, attitudes, etc., factors that might influence learning. In other words, all the groups would be influenced equally by the extraneous variables.

This approach can be schematically described in two ways:

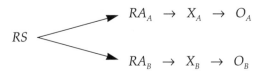

$$RA_A \rightarrow X_A \rightarrow O_A$$
$$RS$$
$$RA_B \rightarrow X_B \rightarrow O_B$$

In words, this says that members of a group that is a representative sample of a population are randomly assigned to two groups (it could be more), one of which receives treatment *A*, X_A, and the other treatment *B*, X_B; then members of each group are measured or observed for the trait to be compared.

Alternatively, it may be desirable to compare changes in scores, or gain scores as they are sometimes called. This would involve each group being measured twice, once before the treatment and once after. This can be described as

$$RS \begin{cases} RA_A \to O_{1A} \to X_A \to O_{2A} \\ RA_B \to O_{1B} \to X_B \to O_{2B} \end{cases}$$

The difference in scores, gain scores, being used to compare the groups.

Quasi-experimental studies

These studies endeavour to provide an experimental structure, but lack control over all the factors. Most commonly in educational and social science research, the sample tends not to be random, but convenience, for example in the form of available classrooms, wards in a hospital, offices in a business, or counselling groups. It is up to the researcher to justify that the classes are sufficiently 'typical' to be representative of a larger set of classes. For example, they have a specified range of IQ scores, come from an identified group of socio-economic backgrounds, are balanced for gender, have specific prerequisites, etc. Without such supporting information about such groups, it is difficult to generalize to a larger group, which limits the value of the study. Readers need to know about the samples even to be able to determine whether or not the study applies to their learners or a specified group on which they would wish to conduct a study, which takes us on to the problem of selecting them.

POPULATIONS AND SAMPLES

As human beings, we tend to go through life drawing conclusions from our experiences. We try a tandoori chicken dish, we meet a couple of Germans, we drive a Rover car, but it is not possible to taste every tandoori chicken, meet every German, nor drive every Rover car. So generalizations tend to be made on the basis of these limited samples and it is decided that tandoori is delightful, Germans do not speak much English, and Rover cars steer differently from other cars. The only problem is, were our samples truly typical? Are our conclusions warranted, and extended fairly and appropriately to all tandooris, all Germans, and all Rover cars? What happens when we eat at a different tandoori restaurant, meet yet another German, and drive a Rover made in a different year? When our samples are taken in such a haphazard way, it is unlikely that our conclusions or inferences based upon a single or limited number of encounters are necessarily going to be valid for all tandoori chickens, for Germans in general, or for all Rover cars. In order to find a solution to this dilemma, let us first consider some common words that have specific technical meanings in research, terminology that should help the reader understand the problems associated with drawing valid conclusions.

The larger groups to which generalizations are extended are called *populations*, and for research purposes, they must be defined by the author of any report or article. Common everyday use of the term population tends to mean that people are grouped or classified by national, racial or ethnic origins. But a research population could consist of all 13-year-old children in Scotland, all males between 21 and 31 in the United States, all 1997 Rover cars. It is up to the researcher to identify and adequately describe the population to which the results are intended to apply, and like all other aspects of research, any such claim must be justified. Second, the term *sample* tends to imply a group selected from a larger population in some way so as to ensure that, for the characteristic(s) being investigated, the group is typical. This turns out not to be a trivial task.

Characteristics of populations and samples

Without deviating too far, a brief mention of a parallel consideration should be made. It is not too difficult to define the characteristics of a population so that it could be decided whether an individual actually belongs or not. It is possible to define rigorously what constitutes a tandoori chicken dish (by its ingredients), a German (by his/her passport), and a Rover car (by the badge on the front). We can argue about special cases, but ultimately the decision is binary: the individual belongs or does not belong.

The real problem arises when one begins to look at characteristics of these groups: saying a tandoori is 'good' or 'bad', a German can or cannot speak English, or a Rover car steers or does not steer (assuming it is roadworthy) does not mean much. It is more difficult to classify them in such a binary way because the categories are too difficult to define. This is where some sort of measurement of variables emerges. For example, it is more realistic to find an average rating (say on a scale of 1 to 10) of tandoori chicken dishes in a restaurant, an average English language proficiency examination score, and an average rating of quality of steering on Rover cars. The 'average' is a measure of central tendency; in other words, it is an indication of what the group does as a whole. No two meals, no two Germans and no two Rover cars are exactly the same (though the differences in some cases may be hard to detect). So if we want to talk about the group as a whole, then the average is often used: the group 'tends' to have a certain characteristic. There are several different 'averages' or measures of central tendency that we can use, but this is a topic for a later chapter.

When such numerical characteristics are assigned to populations, for example the average IQ for the whole population, then they are called *parameters*. On the other hand, if the characteristics apply to a sample, continuing the example, the average of a selected representative group, then they are referred to as *statistics* (Open University, 1973; Chase, 1985). Since most data is collected on samples from populations, and inferences are sometimes made about the population from these samples, we hear the term statistics used quite frequently when referring to data presented in articles and reports.

SELECTING SAMPLES

The method employed by a researcher to choose a sample from a population will determine just how *representative* of that population members of the sample group are. In other words, the average (measure of central tendency) found for the sample should be very close to the population average, if the sample is truly representative. Thus, if a representative sample (say 50) of all Germans was acquired, it would be expected that their average score on an English language proficiency examination would be very close to what we would find for the whole population (all Germans) if such data could be collected. Often population parameters with which to compare are not available and the researcher must depend upon the rigour of the sampling process to justify the representativeness of the sample. Therefore, from data collected on a highly representative sample of Danes, a researcher should be able to calculate a good estimate of the average annual income in Denmark. There are a few exceptions, such as IQ tests which tend to be designed to provide a population average of 100.

High sample representativeness can be achieved through one of a number of processes of selection that are designed to ensure this characteristic, most of which are based upon some aspect of random selection. Kerlinger and Lee's (2000) definition provides a starting point: '*Random sampling* is that method of drawing a portion (or sample) of a population … so that each member of the population … has an equal chance of being selected.'

This is incredibly difficult if not impossible to achieve for most human populations that we would wish to define for an investigation. For example, if a study were to consists of collecting data on a specific group of easily available 13 year olds, like Mary Blogg's secondary school physics class in Birmingham, then the results would pertain to the entire population: that specific group of available 13 year olds in her physics class in Birmingham. The group cannot be considered to be a sample that is very representative of any larger population. To extend research conclusions from a study on a sample and make inferences about a larger population requires that the sample is shown to be representative of that population; in other words, typical in all relevant characteristics, variables or aspects. This presents researchers with practical problems. Using the example of 13-year-old secondary school students, where would we even get a complete list of all 13 year olds from which to select? It does not exist, anymore than many such lists, or it changes from day to day (Blum and Foos, 1986). Consequently, the above definition is not very functional.

Kerlinger (1986) does provide a more realistic definition:

> *Random sampling* is that method of drawing a portion (sample) of a population so that all possible samples of fixed size n have the same probability of being selected.

As we will see, this more general definition allows some flexibility in the actual methods to be considered below. For our study of 13 year olds, it means that randomly selecting *groups* (classes) of 13 year olds from all possible groups (classes) would provide what can be considered to be a reasonably representative sample.

Unfortunately, this stipulation of equal probability raises a problem, which at first tends to make one uneasy about the whole business of sampling. Basically, even when taking a random sample, there is a finite probability that a single resulting group will *not* be representative. This is one of the arguments for replicating a study: the more random samples taken, the less likely it will be to get non-representative samples and the stronger the justification for the results. As Kerlinger and Lee (2000) note, while there is no guarantee that the random sample is representative, there is a much higher likelihood that random selection will provide a representative sample than one that is purposely selected. Thus, a researcher is in a much stronger position when using a process of selection that consists of some form of randomization to consider the sample representative, than one who does not. As the various types of selection commonly employed by researchers are considered below, the advantages, pitfalls and implications for the relative representativeness of each will be considered.

Randomization

Having frequently used the term 'random' and extolled the virtues of having randomness, it is now time to describe some processes for actually acquiring a representative sample. Part of the problem lies in what is meant by 'randomness'. Kerlinger and Lee (2000) provide the following definition:

> *randomness* means that there is no known law, capable of being expressed in language, that correctly describes or explains events and their outcomes.

Since randomness is a concept that forms the basis of much of inferential statistics, this is one definition you may want to refer to again. When selecting a sample, randomness is often achieved through schemes based on tables of random numbers, lists of non-repeating numbers which are often created by computer programs that are mathematically based. The simplest approach would be to use a table of random numbers, such as Table 3.1. First of all, while the table looks like 100 three-digit numbers, it can also be viewed as a list of 300 single numerals or digits (these are better words than 'numbers'). As random numbers, it does not make any difference that such a long list of 300 numerals is grouped in sets of three, and one must not worry about how many digits constitute a number. It is then possible to think of them as grouped in sets of three to make 100 three-digit numbers, sets of two to make 150 two-digit numbers (either going across rows or down columns), or even sets of four to make 75 four-digit numbers. The numerals are random, do not know where they came from (to be anthropomorphic), and they have no real value of their own, so we can combine them however we like.

TABLE 3.1 *A short table of 300 random digits grouped in sets of three*

777	841	707	655	297	947	945	743	697	633
297	522	872	029	710	687	614	660	555	489
672	573	065	306	207	112	703	768	377	178
465	436	070	187	267	566	640	669	291	071
914	487	548	262	860	675	846	300	171	191
820	042	451	108	905	340	437	347	999	997
731	819	473	811	795	591	393	769	678	858
937	434	506	749	268	237	997	343	587	922
248	627	730	055	348	711	204	425	046	655
762	805	801	329	005	671	799	372	427	699

There are two basic ways of using a table of random numbers:

1 Assign all subjects a number; then any number drawn from the table would correspond to a subject's number.
2 The subjects are not necessarily numbered, but a number chosen from the table would tell you how many to count down the list to find a subject, repeating this until enough are selected.

Consider the first approach as a way of randomly selecting a list of 20 random numbers in order to choose a representative sample of 20 students from a class of 100. The researcher could close his/her eyes, poke a pencil at Table 3.1 (thus randomly choosing where to start) and then take the next 20 two-digit numbers. While the list itself is a list of numbers as chosen at random, if you started at the beginning each time you used it, you would end up with the same sequence of numbers each time. A researcher doing this would be open to criticism since the lists would be predictable, and would not be considered random. So a little more randomness must be inserted into the process by randomly selecting where to start.

The second approach could be used to determine how far down the list of 100 to jump to select the first person. For example, if the last number of the second column were picked, 805, starting at the top of the list of 100, number 80 would join the sample. Using the 5 from 805 and the 7 from the first digit of the next number on the list, 707, jump 57 down the list to number 137. But there are only 100 in the list, so just continue counting from the beginning again as if it were one continuous circular list and number 37 is chosen. Then jump another 07 to number 44, and so on until 20 students have been selected.

The proof of randomness is that if you start somewhere else in the table, you will get a different group of 20 students. The fact that one group may overlap with another, and some students could appear in two randomly selected groups, does not diminish the randomness – it is the fact that the *groups* are different. How the numbers in a table of random numbers are used to select groups is only limited by the imagination: one can go across the table instead of down, or even go up. The test of the validity of any random number generation scheme is whether or not you end up with two identical groups by starting at two different places in the table: you should not! Other schemes are described in standard texts on statistics and research design. After Activity 3.1, the discussion will move on to different sampling methods that employ randomness.

ACTIVITY 3.1

This will give you an opportunity to prove to yourself that 'randomization' can produce a unique sequence of numbers that could be used to select subjects for a study:

(a) Use Table 3.1 to produce three lists of 10 random two-digit numbers. Are the lists different? Is there any overlap?
(b) If you have a pocket calculator that will produce random numbers, produce three similar lists, and answer the same questions.

Random samples: Several types

There are a variety of ways to apply randomization (which is sometimes referred to as probability sampling) that can be employed to achieve a sample that can be considered representative (Blum and Foos, 1986; Cohen and Manion, 2000; Kerlinger and Lee, 2000). Some of these will deviate from selecting directly from a given population, avoiding the problems of beginning with enormously large lists that may not even exist:

1 *Simple random sampling* does involve taking a random sample directly from the population, achieving Kerlinger's first definition stated earlier of each member of a population having an equal chance of being selected. This approach is limited by the availability of a complete list of the population, one that could be very large and not feasible or even possible to obtain.
2 *Stratified random sampling* consists of taking random samples from various strata in society, such as men and women, employed and unemployed, etc. This depends on what the researcher is interested in: Does the colour of a Rover affect its steering? Does the age, social and educational background, or hair colour of Germans potentially relate to their ability to speak English? Some strata are obviously more relevant than others and thus possible relations are worth investigating. This is actually the result of defining different subpopulations within a larger population.
3 *Cluster sampling* takes into account the difficulty of sampling from a large population (say, all secondary pupils) by randomly selecting clusters of subjects. For example, it would be possible to select randomly 20 schools nationwide and then include all the pupils in these schools for a study.
4 *Stage sampling* is an extension of cluster sampling and is often used in selecting subjects for a survey. This involves successive random selections; for example, a researcher might randomly select 10 local education authorities or school districts, randomly select 3 schools in each, and randomly select 10 teachers in each school, giving a total of 300 teachers.

Combinations of the last three processes might even be applied: for example, 10 local education authorities or school districts could be randomly selected, and then in each of them, 3 boys, girls and mixed schools would be randomly selected (assuming that there were equal numbers of each in the areas chosen), and finally 5 teachers in each school randomly chosen, giving 450 teachers, 150 from each type of school. Now try Activity 3.2.

ACTIVITY 3.2

Identify the population and classify each of the following descriptions of samples as one or a combination of:

(a) random sampling from whole population
(b) stratified random sampling
(c) cluster sampling
(d) stage sampling.

1 A random selection of 120 male and female social workers selected from the union roles.
2 The young people in 16 randomly selected youth groups.
3 A random selection of 100 teachers in a local education authority.
4 Random samples of 20 unemployed men and women between the ages of 18 and 26.
5 Six groups of 30 14-year-old pupils, each group's members randomly selected from one of six randomly selected schools from a list of all boys, girls and mixed schools in England.

Sample size

Having unambiguously defined a population, a research report should describe the size of the sample. Are there any criteria for determining just how large a sample should be? When an average or other statistic is calculated for a sample, the researcher is estimating the value (parameter) for the whole population. Thus, there will be some error, which will be dependent upon the size of the sample, as shown in Figure 3.1. The smaller the sample, the greater the error and vice versa. For example, if you wanted an estimate of average height of all 13 year olds in a school, you would expect a much more accurate estimation from a random sample of 30 than from a random sample of 5. Thus the larger the sample, the more precise the statistic will be; in other words, closer to the population parameter. In Chapters 7 to 10, it will be demonstrated just how the sample size affects statistical tests, but in general it is to the researchers' benefit to have as large a sample as their resources will allow. It is possible to predict optimal sample sizes based upon trial data for specific statistical tests and research designs, but the mathematics is beyond this text (see e.g. Black (1999) for a way to do this on a spreadsheet, and a parallel process by calculator in Kerlinger and Lee, 2000).

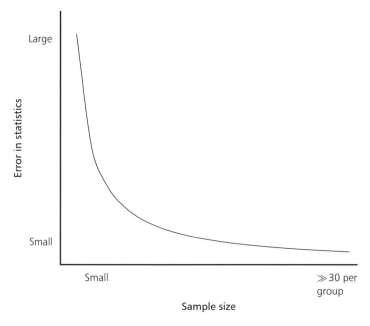

FIGURE 3.1   *Rough relationship between sample size and error, where*
error is considered to be the deviation of sample values
(statistics) from population values (parameters)
(after Kerlinger, 1986)

Non-random samples

There are a number of techniques which provide less justifiably representative samples, though some of these are better than others. Sometimes these
are used because the cost of taking a random sample is too great, or it is very
difficult to obtain a complete list of the members of the whole population.
The ones described below are typical of techniques that have been applied in
research articles and reports (Cohen and Manion, 2000; Kerlinger and Lee,
2000), some providing more representative samples than others.

Purposive sampling   involves the researcher in hand-picking subjects on the
basis of traits to give what is felt or believed to be a representative sample.
To achieve this would require all the relevant variables or traits to be identified so the sample would include a cross-section of persons possessing these.
For example, a sample of teachers in a local education authority could be
acquired by individually selecting from a database a set of 30 teachers in
local schools with the intent to include a variety of ages, subjects taught and
years of experience. The advantage is that one can possibly better ensure a
cross-section of the population in a small sample, which might otherwise
miss certain categories of persons. The main limitations of this approach are
that a researcher may not have identified all contributing variables and characteristics, or individual bias may prevail when carrying out the selection.

Quota sampling   involves the researcher in non-randomly selecting subjects from identified strata until desired numbers are reached. For example, a survey might include interviewing the first 20 people who, in each situation, answer their door in: a housing estate, a set of high-rise apartments, a set of semi-detached (duplex) houses, etc. An extension of this would involve taking into account more than one variable, like 10 men and 10 women as well as type of house, which is referred to as *dimensional sampling*. Such an approach ensures that each group is of the same size, which can be important for some inferential statistical tests. The disadvantage is that the numbers may not reflect the true proportions of subpopulations in the whole population.

Convenience, accidental or volunteer sampling   involves taking a group or individuals that are available, like the local PTA, three classes in a local school, or any students willing to come in after class (a seemingly common practice amongst psychologists who use their own university student volunteers). Radio and television programmes have used the technique of inviting the audience to telephone one of several available numbers as a means of registering a view, while newspapers have invited readers to respond to questions. Moore (1991) describes one such programme presented by Ann Landers, the advice columnist in the United States, who invited readers to respond to the question 'If you had to do it over again, would you have children?' With 10,000 respondents and 70% saying 'No!', parenthood seemed in danger. Yet a random sample of 1373 parents by *Newsday* magazine found that 91% would have children again. The question arises, is the volume response more representative than the randomly selected one? It is often difficult to convince the public that vociferous minorities are not representative. Basically, the 'researchers', if they could be called that, are not dealing with a sample, but a small population, and do not really have the grounds on which to make inferences to a larger population. It is very difficult, if not impossible, to justify that such a group is truly representative of a larger population, no matter what its size. As the advertisement says, 'Can one million people be wrong?' Maybe not, but then there is no guarantee that they are representative of the whole country either.

Snowball sampling   involves the researcher in identifying a small number of subjects with the required characteristics, who in turn identify others, etc. This is of value when a researcher has little idea of the size or extent of a population, or there simply may be no records of population size, for example such groups as illegal drug users, illegal immigrants or homosexual teachers. The disadvantage of depending upon such a sample is that the researcher will have difficulty in defending the representativeness of the sample.

For practice, identify the methods for acquiring the samples described in Activity 3.3.

ACTIVITY 3.3

Identify the intended population and classify each of the numbered descriptions of samples as *one or more* of the following:

(a) random sampling, possibly from whole population
(b) stratified random sampling
(c) cluster sampling
(d) stage sampling
(e) purposive sampling
 (f) quota sampling
(g) convenience, accidental or volunteer sampling
(h) snowball sampling.

1   A study on stress among social workers started with the random selection of 120 male and female social workers selected from the county's employee register. Ultimately, 95% of the men and 85% of the women responded to the questionnaire.
2   The young people in 16 randomly selected youth groups. Actual interviews were conducted by setting up a network of young persons, starting with a few who subsequently talked their friends into participating.
3   A random selection of 50 high streets in villages across the United Kingdom (or main streets in small towns across the United States) was chosen and researchers sent to each to interview 50 shoppers all on the same Saturday morning, obtaining responses to 20 questions from a preplanned questionnaire sheet.
4   Sets of 30 pupils randomly selected from 2 each of chosen boys, girls and mixed schools, recommended as typical of county schools by the Inspectorate.

The sample: Is it representative?

Many public surveying organizations use the telephone as a tool for contacting their sample, be it for predicting election results or market research for a new product. Two sources of numbers exist: (a) a random selection from the telephone directory, which will not have all the numbers since some people have unlisted ones; and (b) computer-generated dialling using a random number, but not everyone has a telephone. In both situations, it is worthwhile remembering the earlier definition of random sampling, and then asking what are the populations for each of these samples? For (a), those with telephone numbers listed in a directory, for (b) those who have telephones. Moore (1991) points out a number of sources of error using the second technique. First, in the United States, 7% of households do not have telephones.

Second, when no one answers, the system moves on to a new number, thus reaching those who are easiest to reach. The result of this in one political survey was that 37% of those who answered were men, when the population is roughly half and half. Women tended to answer the household telephone much more frequently than men. These sort of errors are referred to by Moore as *sampling errors*, since they are the result of actually taking the sample, resulting in a non-random sample.

Alternatively, potentially misleading data can be collected, the cause of the errors being unrelated to the method of sampling. The sample may be random and representative, but the resulting data may not be complete or accurate. Moore (1991) calls these *non-sampling errors* and provides four categories of sources:

1 *Missing data* may be due to the inability to contact a selected subject or not all the selected subjects choosing to participate, resulting in volunteers.
2 *Response errors* will arise from subjects providing inaccurate information, for example about their age or income. Alternatively, the questions may be misunderstood, a problem addressed in the next chapter on data quality.
3 *Processing errors* can arise from coding data or entering it into computer files. This can be prevalent in large projects that employ a team of researchers but do not recheck the entry of data.
4 *Method of data collection*, includes such problems as timing of a survey, wording of questions, and what medium will be used (postal survey, telephone or personal interview). These are all related to data quality and will be discussed in the next chapter.

After having had eight types of sampling described, and some of the pitfalls identified, what does one expect to find when reading research papers and journal articles? Often, a specific sampling strategy is planned, but when all the data has been collected, the actual sample may tend to be something of a combination of the above. For example, a study was planned to investigate the effects of a new curriculum project on learning among 13 year olds. Cluster sampling was used to choose randomly 12 classes of children in the county. Random assignment was employed so that half the classes would use the new curriculum materials and half would use existing materials. The children's achievement of stated objectives was tested both before and after using the materials. When all the results were collected, it was found that 80% of the children had used assigned materials and taken both tests. What type of sample did this study really have? It started as representative and ended with volunteers, though the relative representativeness could still be maintained if the researcher were to determine and report on why the 20% did not participate. If the reason were totally unrelated to the study, like a flu epidemic, then the results could legitimately be extended to the whole population. But if it were found that the 20% were mostly in one-half of the study and the children did not participate because of lack of teacher cooperation, then the researcher needs to answer the question 'why?' If the reason for non-cooperation relates to some aspect of teachers' attitudes towards the project, for example they did not like the materials or the tests were felt to interfere with class work, then it becomes more difficult to defend the representativeness of the remaining part of the sample.

Random assignment: one means of controlling variables

Randomization has another role in research, one that actually follows selecting the sample(s). For truly experimental designs, there will be situations where it is necessary to divide a sample into equivalent subgroups so that one or more can receive a 'treatment', to use a medical term, and the remaining subgroups constitute the control, not receiving any treatment, or a placebo, or in many cases, an alternative treatment. The random assignment of subjects to subgroups prevents any bias and maintains the representativeness of each of the subsequent subgroups. The resulting tests after the treatment will determine whether all the groups *still* belong to the same population (presumably the treatments had no effect) or that they no longer belong to the same population. In the latter case, the researcher must prove that the treatment(s) were the only possible cause of this difference.

Random assignment is one technique for endeavouring to prevent *confounding*, allowing uncontrolled factors to influence the outcomes or validity of the conclusions of a study. Confounding can be caused by *extraneous variables*, which are unanticipated independent variables(s) of no interest to the study that influence the results. Table 3.2 provides some examples of studies and potential confounding factors. The reader of a report should always be aware of the possibility of extraneous variables. When suspected, it is often difficult to tell whether the researchers failed to identify them early enough to control them, or that it was not possible, for one reason or another, to control them even though they were identified. Kerlinger and Lee (2000) suggest four ways of controlling extraneous variables:

a) choose subjects that are as homogeneous as possible for the independent variable(s);
b) randomly assign subjects to groups or conditions, or randomly assign conditions to groups, for experimental designs;
c) if an extraneous variable is identifiable and of sufficient interest, include it in the design as an independent variable, for example, gender: do boys and girls learn more or less using one or the other of two learning approaches?
d) match subjects for potential extraneous variables when assigning them to groups, so all groups have an equal influence, for example equal percentages of high, medium and low IQ subjects.

Confounding and extraneous variables will be addressed in more detail in Chapter 11 on drawing conclusions. At this point, as a reader, it is simply worthwhile noting that randomization can be applied not only at the original selection of the sample, but also to the creation of representative subgroups to prevent confounding by extraneous variables. Now carry out Activity 3.4.

TABLE 3.2   *Examples of studies with potential independent, dependent and confounding variables identified (extended from Table 2.1)*

Research hypothesis	Proposed variables		Possible confounding factors
	Independent	Dependent	
Intelligence is determined primarily by heredity as opposed to environment	Heredity and environment	Intelligence	Inability to manipulate the environment of any group
There is a strong relationship between crime rate and the level of unemployment	Level of unemployment	Crime rate	Unpredicted events: racial unrest and riots
The preference to go on structured holidays (pre-booked hotels, guided tours, planned events) rather than more self-organized ones is related to social class	Social class	Preferences	Non-respondents to the survey through the holiday booking firms
Encouraging teacher comments enhance improvement in student performance	Teacher comments	Student performance	Not all teachers taught the same age group

---

ACTIVITY 3.4

Consider the potential confounding factors in Table 3.2. Which of them are extraneous variables potentially subject to control: sampling or non-sampling errors, or a combination? It is possible to acquire extraneous variables because of sampling or non-sampling errors.

The consequences of sampling: a link with hypotheses

As noted earlier, the aim of sampling is to ensure that the acquired statistics will be as close as possible to the population parameters. While it is possible that a given sample will provide statistics that are *exactly* the same as the population parameters, it is not likely. At the same time, the statistics should be very close to parameter values. In fact, as will be seen in Chapter 7, it is possible to quantify how close. If one knows what the population parameters are (e.g. IQ tests are designed to have a population average score of 100) there are tests that will tell you whether or not a sample is probably representative of the population. Note the term probably. The unnerving aspect of statistics is that nothing is exact and it is necessary to think continually in terms of 'probably'.

Using the example of IQ scores, if a sample of 20 15-year-old students was selected and a researcher wanted to know whether or not the group (not individuals) was typical with respect to the IQ of all students aged 15, the question would be answered in terms of probability. The null hypothesis could be stated as something like: 'There is no significant difference between the average IQ score for this sample and that for any other sample from the population.' The statistical test will tell what the probability is that the group is typical of samples from the population. If the probability turns out to be 5% or less, then the difference is considered significant, the group is probably *not* typical of the population for this trait, and therefore not a representative group. As noted earlier, this test is often not possible to carry out simply because population parameters are usually not available, but it is a useful one when a researcher does have them. Some reports may actually use such a test to justify the representativeness of a sample. The actual test, a mathematically simple one, will be covered in Chapter 7.

WHY GENERALIZE?

The value of being able to generalize results has been questioned, in particular with reference to evaluation studies that tend to be fraught with local variables (Guba, 1978). On the other hand, the situation can exist where there is such tight control on all the variables to ensure generalizability that any parallel group would be rare. Also, Guba (1978) maintains that in extreme situations, things change so radically that not only is generalizability difficult, but also replication is impossible. But whether this is true is really up to the consumer of the report to determine.

   Not everyone would agree with the suggestion that generalizability is of declining value to researchers. Some of the purposes of research include building models, identifying variables and their interrelations, and generally trying to enhance understanding of human behaviour. The more generalizable the results, the greater the possibility that one can begin to resolve conflicting hypotheses. Without generalizability of results, social science research in general will tend to limp along, not benefiting from the efforts of others, collecting results on a piecemeal basis. It is not easy to design a study so that the results will apply to larger groups, and this chapter has introduced only some of the approaches to enhancing the representativeness of samples. But research is a community effort, to be shared whenever possible; studies of too limited a nature are of little benefit to the advancement of knowledge.

   On the other hand, case studies in convenience groups can provide valuable insights and understanding of a scale not possible to find in large, more representative samples. Convenient groups for case studies overcome the problem of the very large resources needed to collect the same amount of data from a larger representative sample. The limitations of such studies are that it is more difficult to justify extending the results and conclusions to larger populations, though some individual readers may be able to generalize to their local situation. This is a continual dilemma for researchers, whether their results will be of sufficient depth (the question of social science significance) and not trivial, and at the same time have some level of generalizability. If care is taken, studies employing the two extremes, small samples studied in depth and large samples where only a few variables are investigated, can complement each other. This is where it is the responsibility of the researcher to ensure through a literature search that his/her study builds upon that of others. This is true at both extremes: the in-depth study of a small sample can have its generalizability enhanced if some of the relevant variables have been investigated on a larger, more representative scale; the large representative study covering a few variables can have its relative academic significance enhanced through building upon other research, in particular localized studies that have found results whose generalizability is in question. Often, on their own and carried out in isolation, the two types of studies can produce sterile results. Since few researchers have the resources to study an issue as thoroughly as they would like, it becomes the collective responsibility of the research community to ensure that the links are there through literature searches.

REPRESENTATIVENESS: CRITERIA

Defined below are the criteria for judging the relative representativeness of a sample, an expansion of the second column in the Profiling Sheet labelled Representativeness.

Whole population   All findings will obviously apply to the whole population, with any error being attributable only to the measuring instruments. The disadvantage is that it may well be that the population is very small, for example a conveniently available group. As long as the researchers acknowledge this, and recognize that the population is small, then whatever conclusions are drawn will be very sound, since they will be describing and interpreting the parameters of that group directly, and not trying to describe population characteristics based upon statistics from a sample. (Any claims of generalizability to any other larger group would mean unjustifiably extending an inference to that group; thus rating would be the bottom one in this column – see also the later column labelled Conclusions.)

Random selection from a specified population   The researcher has appropriately applied one or more of the techniques described earlier (direct random, random assignment, stratified random, random cluster or staged sampling). While there is no guarantee that the sample is perfectly representative, it is the soundest approach giving the highest probability that a sample is representative.

Purposive sampling from a specified population   Some attempt has been made to select a representative sample through specific criteria or characteristics related to variables that are to be controlled. This is not the best way of choosing a sample, but better than the next.

Volunteers   This level will include quota, accidental, convenience and snowball sampling, as described above. While there is some endeavour to obtain a sample that could be considered representative, such a sample is not very convincing. There is also the situation where the researcher starts with a random sample, but ends up with volunteers from the group selected (thus you may want to circle *both*). The key to justifying a high level of representativeness in this situation is for the researcher to have found out why those who dropped out did not choose to participate. Ideally, the researcher should show that neither the way the study was conducted nor the variables investigated had anything to do with non-participation.

Unidentified group   The description of the sample or the sampling technique is not sufficiently clear either to indicate the population or to justify any generalizability to a population. Alternatively, the claim of generalizability is simply unjustifiable!

CONFIDENTIALITY, ANONYMITY AND ETHICS

Two main issues arise that are best considered here. One is that of *ethics*, the aim of which is to protect all persons concerned with or involved in a piece of research.

The second is *confidentiality*, which simply put means that no one or no institution should be identifiable from a research report (unless, of course, there is good reason to reveal institutional origins *and* permission is secured). The aim is to protect subjects from any adverse consequences (e.g. political or economic) of participating in a study. One way of achieving this is through *anonymity*, by allowing responses to be submitted anonymously – no identification on the questionnaire or achievement test. A way of maintaining anonymity is by not having any coded numbers or names on questionnaires. This is hardly possible in the case of an interview, owing to the personal interaction, unless done through some electronic medium such as the telephone.

The difficulty with this approach is that the researcher does not know who has not replied, and thus cannot either chase them up or find out why they did not reply. Determining why subjects do not respond is important, if for no other reason than to ensure it is not because of something in the instrument or the study is considered invasive or inappropriate. In such cases, non-responses might be thought of as equivalent to negative responses. So while confidentiality is highly desirable and often necessary, anonymity may not be the best way to achieve it.

Carry out Activity 3.5 now.

ACTIVITY 3.5

Obtain a copy of the ethical guidelines for your professional organization or consider a generic set, such as that provided by Reynolds (1979) (also available in Frankfort-Nachmias and Nachmias, 1992) and see how they relate to studies you read.

CRITERIA FOR ETHICAL ISSUES

The criteria for evaluating ethical issues that follow are stated rather vaguely, since they require you to refer to the ethical standards of your profession.

Ethical standards met and data sufficiently confidential that
no individuals or institutions can be identified
Long lists of ethical standards may seem tedious to consult, but they do tend to have underlying themes and standards.

Some weakness in maintaining confidentiality Some authors inadvertently reveal too much when describing their subjects or the institution from which they come. For example, 'a hospital on the east side of Birmingham' might leave a local person in no doubt which one it was.

Ethical issues not addressed or confidentiality not discussed or
maintained when it should have been
While not every piece of research has the potential for serious violations of ethical codes, one would expect some indication that issues have been addressed (e.g. permission from appropriate persons acquired, no information released that would allow individuals or institutions to be identified).

Ethical issues not addressed and/or significant loss of confidentiality
Revealing sources is not acceptable, even if it would appear to strengthen arguments for generalizability of the results.

Ethical standards violated and/or subjects endangered
owing to no confidentiality
There are situations where information is revealed in a study that would potentially damage an individual's career, reputation or even life. Institutions can suffer as well, when you consider that many depend upon their reputation to attract students, clients or customers.

Now carry out Activity 3.6 and consider some research reports.

ACTIVITY 3.6

Select several articles and evaluate them using the criteria at the end of this chapter. This includes those for the Questions/hypotheses columns, as well as the new ones in the columns labelled Representativeness and Ethics and confidentiality. Note that it is worthwhile choosing at least one new article each time to allow you to apply the preceding criteria to a new paper.

MODEL ANSWERS

Activity 3.2

1 All persons on the union roll: (a)
2 Young people who belong to youth groups: (c)
3 All teachers in that authority: (a)

continued

4   Unemployed persons by age, though where the original list came from is not clear: (b)

5   All 14-year-old secondary school pupils in England: (d)

Activity 3.3

1   All those who appear on the county register: it began with (a) but ended with (g), and though this is a very high rate, one would want to know why there was such a difference in the dropout rates.

2   Potentially the 16 youth groups: (h), not very representative.

3   The aim is shoppers in villages: (f), which can be very poor.

4   All pupils in the county: (e) for the schools, though (a) for the pupils in the schools selected.

Activity 3.4

Intelligence: environment is not totally controlled for any group thus making it virtually impossible to differentiate between hereditary and environmental contributions to intelligence.

Crime rate: extraneous variables, events outside the study.

Holidays: uncertainty as to why lack of response; could be unknown extraneous variables that would have affected survey results, like personal questions about incomes on questionnaire that respondents did not want to answer thus missing data (non-sampling error).

Teacher comments: no control of age group which could respond differently to teacher comments, extraneous variable introduced by poor sampling.

Profiling Sheet: *Understanding Social Science Research,* © Thomas R. Black, 2001

Article: _____   **Type of Study:** ☐ Descriptive, ☐ Survey/correlational, ☐ *Ex post facto,* ☐ Experimental/quasi-experimental.

Questions/ hypotheses	Representativeness	Ethics and Confidentiality
Valid question or hypothesis based on accepted theory with well-justified referenced support	Whole population	Ethical standards met and data sufficiently confidential that no individuals or institutions can be identified
Valid question or hypothesis based on own theory, well justified	Random selection from a well-specified population	Some weakness in maintaining confidentiality
Credible question/ hypothesis but alternative possible, or too extensive/global, or support missing	Purposive sample from a well-specified population, with justification for representativeness	Ethical issues not addressed or confidentiality not discussed or maintained when it should have been
Weak question/ hypothesis, or poorly stated, or justified with inappropriate references	Volunteers or convenience, with no justification of representativeness	Ethical issues not addressed and/or significant loss of confidentiality
No question or hypothesis stated, or inconsistent with known facts	Unidentified group	Ethical standards violated and/or subjects endangered owing to no confidentiality

Comments and rationale for classification:

4

Data Quality

Now that the reader has understood the questions/hypotheses (or infers them from the report), recognized the design that will be used to resolve them, and identified the population to which the study refers, it is appropriate to consider in greater detail what the specific variables will be and how they will be measured or quantified. Usually the statement of the questions/hypotheses includes some indication of the concepts to be considered, and it is not unusual for the actual means of defining these operationally to be included in these statements. Therefore, some of the following decisions about data quality may be made at the same time as considering the statement of the research question. In other situations, the reader may find it necessary to read more deeply into a report to determine how the concepts described in the research question are going to be defined operationally, and any justification of the quality of measuring instruments used. Regardless of where one finds the descriptions, criteria are needed to judge the quality of data.

The discussion on data quality will be broken into two components: the first will consider how one judges the range and relevance of variables for which data is collected, and the second will assist in examining the quality of the actual measuring instruments used to collect the data. The issues to be raised in the first part will relate strongly to the subject matter and will depend to a great extent on you, the reader, and your knowledge of the field. It will encourage you to begin to enquire about the academic relevance and the logical consistency between the variables and the rest of the report. As a guide, the chapter will provide you with some general questions you should be asking about the variables investigated in any research.

The second part will be concerned with technical issues related to the operational definition of the variables, including how well and how consistently the instrument measures the chosen concepts. The methodology of designing instruments to measure abstract concepts is an established one, and guidance will be provided to help you identify whether appropriate steps have been taken to ensure the quality of instruments used in a study.

DATA QUALITY, PART I: WHICH VARIABLES?

In the statements of the research question and hypothesis, one expects to find some indication of the concepts to be investigated. The first question the reader tends to ask is, are these relevant to my interests? If so, then the next question to ask is, are they academically significant? The second question is the one that requires some reflection. How do you determine the level of educational, sociological, psychological, economic, health or business significance? The answer is found primarily through knowledge of the field or discipline and often ascertained through familiarity with the literature (journals, conference papers, books, etc.).

The variables that a study considers should be generated by the research questions and hypotheses. If the questions are insufficiently specific, then it is likely that the variables will be vague or ill-defined. Too often, this results in a plethora of measurable variables to cover the one overly consuming factor alluded to in the question. For example, a study wishing to resolve the question 'to determine the factors influencing the quality of learning mathematics' is simply too ambitious. First, there are simply too many possible variables that might influence mathematics learning. Second, deciding on what constitutes 'quality of learning mathematics' would result in a large number of components, encompassing the numerous topic areas and the divergent skills that make up the subject. While the motivation for conducting research may start from such a vague question, realistic studies will identify a limited subset of problems that are manageable and involve a set of variables some of which the researcher can hope to have control over. The difficulty comes when trying to ensure that these are significant to the academic area of interest and are not chosen just because they are easy to measure. A study needs to consider a reasonable and manageable number of variables without resorting to trivial, easily measured characteristics alone.

For example, how would you react to a study that investigated the relationship between the colour of a person's hair and the size of his/her briefcase? This might be very interesting if you are involved in helping briefcase salespeople to anticipate attaché case size as customers come into a store, but other than that, as it stands it does not seem to contribute much to social and psychological understanding in the world of business. It would be necessary to look at the justification and references in the literature to make a final judgement, but just because a study produces nice, tidy data does not make it academically significant.

What of a study that reports on 'the use of the telephone as a research instrument'? First of all, what is the question? How about, is the telephone a valuable instrument for social science research? The hypothesis could be that the telephone is a valuable instrument for research. Is this even a worthwhile endeavour from the viewpoint of contributing to research? It seems a bit like asking, is a screwdriver useful? Considering the operational definition for the concept(s) or variable(s) chosen to be investigated may help resolve the issue. For the study on the value of the telephone as a research tool, how is 'valuable' going to be defined operationally? Let us say that the researcher has devised a questionnaire and sent it round to a random selection of researchers to solicit their collective opinion. Does this help in evaluating its significance? And is there a difference between 'valuable' and 'perceived value'? Which would be measured by a questionnaire of this sort?

Considering the discussion in the previous chapter on the problems of obtaining a representative sample, a study that endeavours to identify variables that influence the effectiveness of the telephone as a research tool might be more profitable. There are no simple answers to the question of appropriate variables; one has to depend upon knowledge of the field.

Resolving the question of significance should not be concluded hastily and the reader should allow the author of the report to put forward a case. What at first may seem laughable may provide some significant and relevant outcomes. Ideally, the study should offer to make a contribution to contemporary models or theories, supporting or conflicting with them. This goes back to some extent to the earlier issue relating to the statement of questions and hypotheses. Obviously, it is possible to start with a new theory, but even then the intent of the study will often be to provide a justification for displacing an old one, produce modifications, or suggest new evidence to refute an existing one. The reader again looks to the citation of other studies for support.

Related to the issue of significance is the question of the number of variables or concepts covered by a study. This includes studies that have no hypotheses and purport to 'just look for variables', which can result in considering so many possibilities that the results are overwhelming and contribute little to further understanding. As noted earlier, no researcher is going to answer all the outstanding questions in his/her field of research, much less the big one of 'Life, the Universe and Everything'. Often studies that tackle too many variables have started off with poorly defined questions and probably no hypothesis. Looking for variables is more complex than just casting a net to see what gets trapped. The following sections emphasize many of the potential pitfalls related to choice of variables as reported in research studies, grouping them in the four broad categories introduced earlier: descriptive (case studies/histories), surveys, *ex post facto* and experimental/quasi-experimental designs. Obviously some of the issues raised here will relate back to the original formulation of the research question or hypothesis. One problem the reader may have is deciding which came first: the variables or the question/hypothesis?

Descriptive (case histories and case studies)

Often researchers want to investigate an individual, an individual situation or small group in great depth, rather than many subjects in less depth, as a means of answering their research question. Blum and Foos (1986) describe the approach as a case history (or case study) which is a biographical or autobiographical study and report of an individual, group or phenomenon.

Case histories of individuals are used extensively in areas such as clinical psychology and psychotherapy, but they have been particularly useful in research in general. Piaget's work in developmental psychology involved case histories over time, identifying milestones in the intellectual development of children. Subsequent work by other researchers has involved other approaches to investigate the generalizability of such findings. Educational research tends to define case studies more broadly (Cohen and Manion, 2000), since groups and their activities as well as individuals are often the focus of interest. Regardless of the terminology used, the approach is usually an observational one, with the researcher(s) recording events as they unfold and provide an opportunity to record complex events and the interaction of numerous variables.

Blum and Foos (1986) note that while case histories tend to be valued as a means of recording unanticipated events, they are criticized for being poorly planned. Combined with an inability to generalize to larger groups, this approach tends to be inadequate for testing hypotheses, but of greater value as a source of new hypotheses. Owing to the non-representative nature of individuals or local groups, any evidence to support a hypothesis describing a cause and effect relationship could be discounted since the results could not be generalized to a larger population. The advantages of such an approach do provide an opportunity to identify and suggest possible relationships, and provide evidence to support further study. The richness of information collected by skilled researchers can be of immense value, whether it be the behaviour of an individual child at home or in the classroom, the sequence of events in an unexpected situation like conflict in a riot or cooperation during a disaster, or the detailed interaction of a peer group or classroom of pupils. The limitation lies with the researchers and their ability to record what is happening in an objective and accurate manner. The quality of evidence and information can be enhanced by employing observation schedules and guidelines to focus observers' attention on important events in what is often a time-restricted, intense period of data collection. The design of schedules has an established methodology and means for testing the quality of the data gathered, as will be seen in the next section. Trained observers with schedules are much more effective data gatherers than the untrained sitting waiting for something (anything) to happen. The latter group can be overwhelmed with data or miss those events that would contribute to the research. The reader of research reports of this nature should expect some description and justification of the observation schedule or plan as part of the study. The lack of organized observation can result in missed opportunities or confused reporting, resulting in poorly defined or even omitted records of data.

A second role for in-depth studies *follows* quantitative studies that tell us what is happening or has happened through identifying differences in groups. Interviews with observations within selected groups may be the best way of determining why these differences exist. Such studies provide the opportunity to explore more variables in greater depth with a few subjects, to find out how they are related. The generalizability of any causal relationships identified could then be checked through a subsequent quantitative study using a representative sample. Thus one begins to see the complementary nature of the two approaches.

Surveys

Data from large surveys can come from at least two different sources: surveys conducted by the researchers themselves and surveys conducted by others, for example census data. These usually consist of written or oral questionnaires administered to as large and as representative a sample as possible. A census or demographic survey usually tries to get everyone to respond to a basic set of questions and then members of a representative sample are asked additional detailed questions.

In addition to factual information, surveys can include questions about opinions, attitudes, intentions and beliefs, but all of these are recording data about the subjects' *perceptions* of the issues presented. This presents a problem for some researchers in how they report the results. For example, a study which asks whether a particular political candidate is 'honest' and finds that 95% respond 'yes' might report that he/she is honest, but this is not necessarily true. It is doubtful that the public would have sufficient evidence on the candidate's activities to be able to make such a judgement, and therefore the best the researcher could report would be that 95% of the public *perceives* the candidate to be honest. The reader of a report must keep in mind that there can be radical differences between truth and perception. Consequently, a check can be made between what is stated as a question or hypothesis, and what is actually measured, making sure that there is no loss of logical consistency, subtle or obvious. This issue of consistency across a study will arise again in the next section on technical aspects of questionnaire design as one aspect of validity, and in the last chapter when considering conclusions drawn in a report.

The major issue to consider here with respect to surveys is the one of the potentially large numbers of variables investigated. Census data is a good example of survey data that provides fairly objective factual details of age, income, house size, family size, etc. The problem with a census is that it is primarily a data collection exercise and was not designed to test specific hypotheses. Researchers scouring census data for ammunition to prove or disprove their own hypotheses may have a wealth of numbers to contend with, but it may prove difficult to make any sense of this gold mine. As if one needs to be reminded, the ubiquitous computer and its powerful software are capable of handling large amounts of data, though not necessarily intelligently. Data snooping in the form of correlating every variable with every other variable just to see if anything comes out is quite possible to carry out relatively painlessly on a computer. The pain comes in trying to understand what it all means. Take for example the following seven unambiguous 'census' variables: age, income, number of children, number of rooms in home, number of toilets, number of books in personal library and number of cars owned. There are 21 possible correlations, not all of which mean anything. So what if there is a significant correlation between the number of books in the personal library and the number of toilets in the house? One would hope that no inferences would be drawn about reading habits from such results.

The World Bank has a set of questions widely used in its Living Standards Measurement Surveys (LSMS) carried out in a wide variety of countries (Grosh and Glewwe, 1995). While considerable data has been collected, the limitation of such an approach is the lack of a driving research question behind the instrument. Often, the data is scanned for relationships on a *post hoc* basis, but with questions in the instrument not being the result of a research question with specific variables in mind, the resulting analysis can be of questionable quality (e.g. Black, 2000). Regression analysis has been the popular tool of the economists conducting such studies, trying to combine numerous variables to make predictions. These are then used as the basis for formulating international policy on lending and borrowing requirements of developing countries, as well as imposing structural adjustments that delimit domestic spending on services.

Even if the concepts are meaningful, there is always the probability that a statistically significant result will appear by chance alone. As Blum and Foos (1986) note about such data snooping, when the level of significance is set at 0.01, this still has the consequence that with 100 relationships tested, it is expected that one will be significant by chance alone. Extending this argument, if the significance level were set at 0.05, then 1 in 20 correlations would be expected to be significant by chance. Thus one would anticipate that for the seven census variables above, at least one of the 21 correlations would be statistically significant just by chance alone.

Surveys initiated and conducted by the researchers themselves tend to be more economical in the number of variables tested, simply because of the cost and effort required for collecting and processing the data. There are situations, though, where this is not apparently true. While one can be *reasonably* sure (see the last section in this chapter) that factual data represents the intended concepts (age, income, etc.), the less definite concepts, including perceptions, are more difficult to measure. Occasionally a researcher will try to use the responses to a single question as an operational definition of a concept. For example, to measure perception of the quality of television programmes, a researcher might use the responses from the following question as the data:

	Excellent		Mediocre		Awful
Rank the overall quality of television on the five-point scale.	1	2	3	4	5

Why single questions make poor data will be amplified in the next section, but at this point, the reader ought simply to ask, does this *really* measure attitudes in a way that could be replicated? Would a large number of variables measured this way provide sound data? When reading research reports, one should not assume that because there is a large quantity of variables that this guarantees the research will be of high quality.

Finally, there is the tendency for some researchers using census data or economic surveys to stretch the meaning of some variables to fit their own definitions. Letting someone else do all the hard work of data collecting may seem cost effective, but the results may not be exactly what is needed. This practice of assigning variables to data after the fact is one that can produce questionable studies. For example, to conclude that people below a certain income are almost illiterate because they have only a few books in the house and do not subscribe to newspapers or magazines is equating possession of printed material with literacy. How do we know they do not use the public library? To resolve in a valid way the hypothesis that low-income people do not read would require asking more questions than were in the original survey.

Ex post facto *designs*

These studies are based on grouping subjects who tend already to have had something happen to them as part of life (educational background, social class, age group, sex) and the researcher attempts to ascertain the effect of these potential independent variables on some chosen dependent variable, such as learning ability, attitudes, political preference, etc. *Ex post facto* studies tend to involve real-life variables but lack the control of experimental designs, and thus, as noted earlier, rarely result in proving causal relationships. In addition, there may be designs that combine *ex post facto* and experimental variables, for example gender and two learning styles, to see if there is any interaction between gender and a specific learning approach.

Experimental/quasi-experimental designs

The researchers tend to have control over the independent variables in studies employing experimental designs. Thus, the subjects may be assigned to various 'treatments' as potential independent variables (receiving different amounts of vitamins, using different learning materials, assigned to mixed- or single-sex groups) and the consequences for some dependent variable are measured (IQ, achievement, self-confidence). Such designs tend to be difficult to arrange and are often considered artificial and divorced from reality. Therefore, similar designs are applied using existing groups of people (convenience or purposive samples) and are called quasi-experimental designs.

In either *ex post facto* or experimental designs, there is not much scope for a large number of variables, since to test hypotheses, each variable would need two or more levels or categories of treatment. As we will see in Chapter 11, to have three variables with three levels each would require something in the order of 300 subjects. To acquire 300 persons to participate in an experimental design would be difficult enough, but to find 30 + persons to fit each of the combinations of variables for a study that looks for interactions between variables can be equally difficult. And that is a simple design. Even though multidimensional designs are of great interest since they allow the investigation of interactions between variables, most studies employing such approaches tend to investigate a few, very carefully chosen ones. The impact on, say, bereavement, by a combination of variables, like gender and counselling approach, is potentially more interesting than either of these separately. For such studies, the reader will be concerned not so much with the number of variables, but their relevance and value to research. One criticism frequently levelled at experimental and *ex post facto* designs has been the trivial nature of the variables. The choice of concepts and hypothesized relationships requires substantial background reading and consideration of previous research if such studies are going to investigate potentially meaningful relationships.

Criteria for deciding variable significance

Defined below are the criteria for the column in the Profiling Sheet for Data Quality I, with a brief explanation of each level.

Educationally, sociologically, psychologically, economically, etc., significant and manageable number of concepts

Your knowledge of the discipline or field will determine the relative significance. The number of variables may depend on the sample size and how the data is going to be processed, and should derive from the research question. The variables chosen will probably be unambiguous, well defined and/or supported by a sound theory and literature citations.

Limited academic significance, very narrow perspective   It is possible to be too narrow in one's outlook and to focus on too few concepts or variables in such restricted situations as to make the results not applicable to real life.

Large number of concepts, potentially confusing   At the other extreme, too many concepts, and consequently too many variables measured, can result in a large number of facts, but no new understanding of interrelationships among the variables. This often occurs when researchers have no clear question or hypothesis to guide the data collection process. For the same effort, fewer variables could have been studied with greater understanding of relationships.

Too many concepts and variables investigated to result in any meaning

Surveys using questionnaires that collect vast amounts of information and sent to large numbers of people can produce overwhelming amounts of data. If the questionnaires are not well designed (as will be seen below), then the study will generate many facts, but little new understanding of relationships among variables. Recycling census or demographic data may produce equally dubious results.

Trivial concepts, not academically significant   One of the criticisms levelled at statistically based studies employing experimental or *ex post facto* designs is that they trivialize situations in order to collect quantifiable data. The study is done in such isolation so as to provide relatively little new information. This can happen with survey and case study data as well.

Now consider Activity 4.1.

ACTIVITY 4.1

Choose one or more articles and evaluate the relative significance of the (potential) variables studied, using the criteria outlined above. Use the Data Quality I column in the Profiling Sheet at the end of this chapter.

DATA QUALITY, PART II: MEASURING INSTRUMENTS

When reading a report, one looks for consistency between the hypotheses/ questions and the variables chosen. Questions and hypotheses for educational and social science research tend to be expressed in terms of generally abstract concepts, like reinforcement, achievement, success, leadership, etc. The general question to be answered here is, are the measured variables sound operational definitions of these rather vague and abstract concepts? An *operational definition* is the evidence a researcher uses as justification for the relative existence (sometimes quantified) of the abstract concept. Since much of what is studied is not tangible, this provides a considerable challenge, particularly when there is not a widely accepted operational definition for a concept. For example, take the concept 'leadership'. Not only might a study want to determine whether it even existed in certain circumstances, but it may be desirable to quantify it in terms of quality (rating it against criteria defining good to poor) and quantity (too much to too little).

In addition, it is worthwhile recognizing two separate events that will influence the determination of relative quality of the operational definitions: the actual design of the measuring instruments and the process of collecting the data. Each will have a bearing on the three main concepts that underlie the criteria for judging the data quality: reliability, validity and objectivity.

Translating a description of variables into something that can be seen or measured is not a trivial task, considering the abstract nature of many variables of interest in the social sciences and education. It is one thing to talk about 'efficiency' or 'effectiveness', but how does one observe and quantify it? Asking the recipients of a service will only tell you what their *perception* of that service is, and not necessarily how efficient or effective it is. Questionnaires and interviews are often employed as tools in research, but sometimes they measure something other than what the researcher intended. This is the issue of *validity* of an instrument. It is also necessary to ensure that the resulting instrument measures the concept consistently. This means that the answers or total scores are not influenced by when it is completed or the language used in the questions, the issue of *reliability* of an instrument.

There are numerous textbooks that provide extensive guidance on the design of measuring instruments for use in education, psychology and sociology, such as Thorndike and Hagen (1977), Mehrens and Lehmann (1984), Anastasi (1990), Cronbach (1990), Murphy and Davidshofer (1991), and Oppenheim (1992). It is not intended that this chapter should cover comprehensively such a vast topic, but it will provide some general criteria for judging the quality of measuring instruments employed in research. Reports should provide sufficient background information to judge the level of care taken when designing and using the measuring instruments developed, borrowed or purchased. If you intend to dissect specific instruments or create your own, you should enquire more deeply into the literature.

VALIDITY

Basically, to ensure *validity*, any instrument must measure what was intended. This means that the instrument, as the operational definition, must be logically consistent and cover comprehensively all aspects of the abstract concept to be studied. Ideally, it should be possible to confirm this through alternative, independent observation. The measurement literature traditionally has defined a number of different types of validity, some of which overlap. The discussion of validity in the literature is littered with controversy, but for simplicity, two commonly defined types will be used as the basis for establishing a working definition of validity for measuring instruments used in research: construct validity and content validity.

Construct validity

This is considered to be the most important for research design, since it is concerned with the measurement of abstract concepts and traits, such as intelligence, anxiety, logical reasoning, attitude towards dogs, social class or perceived efficiency. To a certain degree, the validity of each of these is dependent upon a definition or description of the terminology. How is 'anxiety' defined? What constitutes different levels of 'perceived efficiency'? In the latter case, it may be that the operational definition is a score on a questionnaire.

Starting with a definition, one then proceeds to elaborate on all the component characteristics that provide evidence of the trait or construct. The observable, recordable or otherwise measurable aspects will eventually make up the instrument. In particular, this means that it is highly unlikely that a *single* question on a questionnaire or asked in an interview would ever constitute a valid operational definition of anything but a trivial concept. An adequate operational definition would have to consist of a number of questions in a questionnaire (or points in an observation schedule, or criteria for classification, etc.) to incorporate sufficient characteristics to cover all relevant aspects of the concept or construct under study.

For example, consider a variable in a study such as 'the perception of the quality of television', and recall the single question suggested above to measure this. First of all, a valid measure would require that the researcher elaborate on what is meant by the term 'quality'. Is there an interest in the reaction of subjects to the quality of what is presented to the public? Or is there an interest in the reaction to its influence on the public and contemporary culture? If it were the former, then there would be a need to obtain the subject's perception of the quality of variety of types of programmes (game shows, drama, news, chat shows, etc.). Just asking a single question as above to rate television on a scale 1 to 5 would be too vague for the subjects, much less for the researcher, and leaves it up to the subject to define what aspects of television should be considered. How attitudes are defined will determine the wording of questions. With respect to the quality of television, is the intent to determine how much subjects *feel* about television (emotional), or to determine values in terms of information, entertainment or enlightenment (rational judgement), or is the intent to look for negative aspects such as the propensity for the medium to be perceived as time wasting, addictive or providing an unreal view of life?

Even more widely discussed concepts can present researchers with some difficulty when it comes to justifying the validity of the instruments they wish to use. For example, a well-aired, though not fully resolved, controversy exists over what constitutes a valid measure of intelligence. The first recognized tests were developed in 1905 by Binet and Simon, consisting of 30 problems or tests arranged in order of increasing difficulty (Anastasi, 1990). Since then, a wide variety of tests has been developed, some necessarily administered by trained examiners to individual subjects, and others that are paper based and administered to large groups. Even though IQ tests are numerous and diverse in nature, there is a tendency to assume that they are all one in the same, and that they somehow directly, validly and reliably measure intelligence on some absolute scale. IQ scores tend to reflect a set of abilities at a given time as compared with available age norm groups, usually culturally homogeneous. Contemporary research has identified numerous environmental factors that can contribute to rises and falls in IQ, thus potentially complicating any research conducted over time. Anastasi's (1990) book provides an extensive survey of the issues involved, which go beyond the scope of this book. Let it suffice to say that any researchers purporting to use IQ as a variable in their research should describe *which* IQ instrument they are using, its rationale for validity, and its published reliability. The reader will then have sufficient information on which to carry out further investigation of the appropriateness and identify any potential confounding variables if necessary.

Similar comments can be made about most *standardized* tests, those that provide norms for a representative sample of a larger population. Among other applications, these statistics allow researchers to use the tests to group subjects according to traits that would otherwise be difficult to determine. They can be used to justify the representativeness of a sample for proficiency or achievement of some skill, say speaking French, since the group of interest has a mean score not significantly different from that of the published statistics for the test. They can also be used as pre- and post-tests for research to evaluate the relative effectiveness of different teaching strategies, though there would be a need to ensure that the tests and the teaching were covering the same topics at the same cognitive level.

Anastasi (1990) defines another category of standardized instruments, *personality tests*, as 'instruments for the measurement of emotional, motivational, interpersonal, and attitudinal characteristics, as distinguished from abilities', and points out that hundreds are available. The appropriateness of any single test for research will need to be justified by the researchers in some detail, and not just on the basis of a title or brief description. Most are used primarily for clinical practice and counselling, and tend not to be used in isolation.

When reading a report on a study that has developed its own measuring instrument, what does one expect for the justification for construct validity of that instrument? This could be achieved by having the instrument reviewed and evaluated for validity by other experts in the field. Alternatively, the traits to be observed might be sufficiently obvious or unambiguous that justification could be accomplished through reference to the literature.

Finally, Anastasi (1990) and Cronbach (1990) maintain that the other types of validity that follow only expand upon the meaning of construct validity and help to focus our attention on contributing characteristics that may depend upon the nature of the concepts to be defined.

First, *criterion-related validity* can be checked by comparing the data against an alternative set of data. There are two ways of establishing criterion-related validity, depending primarily on the function of the test (Anastasi, 1990), which is best clarified through examples. Consider the situation where it is necessary to check the validity of an instrument constructed to predict mathematical success: a set of results could be compared with the subjects' success in subsequent national mathematics examinations. Alternatively, results on a post-test of a training course could be validated by comparing them with on-the-job performance of the tested skills. Both of these would be also checks of *predictive validity*, how well they predict future performance. So why even have the test if you are going to check up on the subjects later? Standardized aptitude tests are often used as predictors of future success or in identifying potential to learn. In research, this approach is used only on a representative sample of subjects in the population to confirm the criterion-related validity of an instrument to be used on another, possibly larger, sample.

The second form is best illustrated by considering the relationship between the results of a test of arithmetic ability and the independent assessment of a supervisor, like a report that Bloggs continually makes errors in addition. The potential function of this test is to diagnose, not predict, and thus the check is on its *concurrent validity*. The validity of the test is based upon knowing the present condition of a sample of examinees or subjects.

The expectations of the reader evaluating research are straightforward: a report claiming that an instrument has criterion-related validity should have carried out a process of confirmation, or used an instrument for which the criterion-related validity has already been established. For example, a number of studies have been carried out in the United Kingdom investigating the relationship between students' A-level examination results (taken by 18+ year olds and approximately equivalent in content coverage and depth to first-year American university subjects) and the classification of subsequently acquired degrees (roughly equivalent to classifying degrees on the basis of grade-point averages in some higher education systems). It has been shown that for all subjects there were statistically significant correlations between A-level grades and subsequent degree classification; they probably did not occur by chance alone, *but* the correlations (which are sometimes referred to as coefficients of predictive validity) were always low, never more than 0.40 and often of the order of 0.20 (Bourner and Hamad, 1987). Since these correlations indicate the degree of accuracy in predicting degree results from A-level examination results and could range from 0.00 (never an accurate prediction) to 1.00 (perfect prediction every time), this is not very high. In other words, many of those who received low passes (D and E) at A-level did very well (IIi and First) in degree courses, while many of those receiving high passes at A-level did less well subsequently (IIii and Third). This means that the validity of using A-level grades to predict high achievers in higher education is very low. This type of study does not, unfortunately, seem to dissuade many university selectors in the United Kingdom from admitting to their courses only students with high A-level grades.

Content validity

This applies to validating the content of an achievement test or qualifying examination. This might be carried out by comparing the topic coverage and cognitive emphasis of an examination with the original specifications in a syllabus. Examination boards and organizations that produce standardized tests tend to be very meticulous about such processes, while classroom teachers lack the resources and usually collect questions for tests less systematically. If scores on a test or examination constituted an operational definition of 'competency in a subject', the reader would expect some indication of independent verification that the test content was consistent with a syllabus or some other form of agreed content specification. Obviously the problem is that any test will contain only a representative sample of the possible questions that could be asked about a subject. Therefore, to ensure content validity, there needs to be questions that are representative of the cognitive emphasis required by the subject (ranging from remembering facts to solving new and unique problems) as well as the variety of content topics. As an alternative to that of using an accepted syllabus or content list, researchers have been known to define the content of an achievement test and then have this confirmed by other experts in that field. Thus if a project intended to determine if there were different levels of achievement in (say) a university genetics course for different sets of learning resources, then the content validity of the achievement test used would need to be verified and even changed, possibly on the recommendations of a panel of teachers of genetics.

In summary, establishing criterion-related validity is the most relevant form of validity to establish for aptitude tests or selection instruments (predictive), or diagnostic instruments (concurrent). One problem that does occur is that some tests will possibly have a high content validity, for example the A-level examinations, but a low predictive validity. Thus the use of the results must be considered when considering which form(s) of validity are relevant to a study. In other words, it may be very valid to use A-level mathematics results as an indicator of possession of certain mathematical skills (high content validity), but not valid to use them to select for another learning programme (low predictive validity). Reality is such that it is too expensive to make up new and valid selection examinations, so employers and higher education institutions just use existing certification examination results with high content validity to predict success in new endeavours. Construct validity particularly applies to abstract concepts and constructs as used in research, for example when trying to quantify characteristics such as attitudes, personality traits, intelligence, creativity, and the like. Thus A-level physics grades may have high content validity, but without supporting evidence there is no reason to assume that they are valid indicators of intelligence (construct validity). If it were shown that there was a high correlation between IQ scores and A-level physics grades, then assuming the IQ test had high construct validity, there would be *some* validity in saying that someone with a high A-level score was intelligent, but no comment could be made about someone who did not do physics. One must always remember that *the relative validity of an instrument is going to be determined by the intended use of the results in the research*.

Before turning to the second criterion for judging data quality – reliability – please consider Activities 4.2 and 4.3.

ACTIVITY 4.2

Validity is an issue not only in formal research, but in everyday life. Two interesting sources of examples of operational definitions are newspaper editorials and politicians' speeches, particularly when they include statistics as part of their arguments. What constitutes being 'unemployed'? How is the rate of inflation calculated? How are ratings of television programmes determined? What makes a person 'lower' or 'upper' class? Who are the 'workers'?

Read an editorial, the account of a speech, or listen to a speech and identify operational definitions used for specific constructs or concepts. Are they valid? Can you even tell if they are valid and, if not, how might you find out? What type of validity is important in that specific case?

ACTIVITY 4.3

Listed below are three constructs, each having three possible operational definitions. Rank order each set as to validity and note why you have chosen this order *before* consulting the comments in the box at the end of the chapter. None of the choices are perfect and you should try to identify even better ones.

1 *Successful person*

    (a)   personal annual income;
    (b)   attitude towards job and career;
    (c)   investment portfolio (stocks, bank accounts, house value, etc.).

2 *Effective teacher*

    (a)   success rate of teacher's class(es) on national examinations (e.g. General Certificate of Secondary Education (GCSE) in the United Kingdom, Scholastic Aptitude Tests (SAT) in the United States);
    (b)   score on a self-evaluation form covering aspects of self-perception of success;
    (c)   average score on teacher evaluation forms completed by students.

3 *Quality of long-term memory*

    (a)   number of nonsense syllables remembered after two weeks;
    (b)   how often one wins at the game Trivial Pursuit;
    (c)   score on standardized IQ test.

(Consider attitude measures and forms to have been designed, validated and tested by external researchers.)

RELIABILITY

In simple terms, high reliability means that if you measure something today with your instrument, you should get very much the same results some other time (10 minutes from now, tomorrow, next week), assuming that what or who you are measuring has not changed. An instrument with low reliability is like an elastic ruler used to measure a room for a carpet: you are unlikely to get what you want for a fit! Measuring human characteristics with an instrument that is valid but not reliable will produce potentially different results on different occasions. It is interesting to note that while it is possible to have an instrument that is valid but not reliable, an instrument that is not valid will never be reliable. To put this in terms pertinent to the design of measuring instruments in the social sciences, the following succinct definition provided by Mehrens and Lehmann (1984) is most appropriate:

'*Reliability* can be defined as the degree of consistency between two measures of the same thing.'

The 'two measures' can mean a variety of combinations, for example two different tests or measuring instruments, two halves of the same test, the same test or instrument applied on two occasions, two scorers using the same observation schedule, a set of essay scripts marked on two separate days. Reliability coefficients for measuring instruments will give a relative indication of an instrument's reliability, usually on a scale of 0.00 (perfectly unreliable) to 1.00 (perfectly reliable). Since nothing is perfect, most reliability values for instruments fall somewhere in between. Just how reliable an instrument will be will influence the strength of any conclusions drawn by a study.

To illustrate reliability, we shall carry out a little experiment using a simple physical measuring instrument, only because it is easier to make and use at short notice than a more complex one for an abstract social science concept. Carry out Activity 4.4 at this time.

ACTIVITY 4.4

(a) You need to have:

- a clear plastic 15 cm ruler that measures in mm;
- two rectangular rubber erasers or blocks of wood, at least 1 cm thick (larger is better);
- some sticky tape.

Tape the erasers to either end of the ruler as shown in Figure 4.1, to give it 'legs'.

(b) Now take a piece of paper and cut a strip about 2.5 cm (25 mm) wide. Do not use a ruler, just cut it freehand since there is a need for a little variation in the width to simulate natural (true) variability and to give a true variance.

(c) Draw 10 lines across the strip at roughly equal intervals as shown in Figure 4.1.

(d) Measure the width of the strip at each of these lines with the legged ruler to the nearest whole 1 mm. Do not expect them to be all the same. Do not be too careful in your measures at this time, since this is supposed to be the less-than-perfect measuring instrument.

(e) Now take the erasers off the ruler (it is now 'legless') and repeat the 10 measures with the ruler flat on the paper. Even though this time you can be very careful and measure to the nearest half mm (0.5 mm), do not expect them to all be the same since this was a freehand cut with some variability. In other words, if it is between 2.6 and 2.7, record 2.65.

(f) Save these measures as we will set up a simple spreadsheet to do the number crunching.

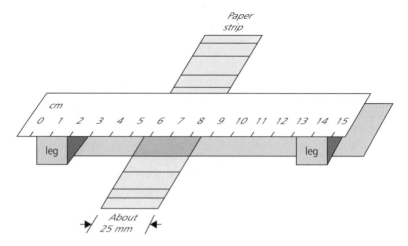

FIGURE 4.1   *A 'legged' ruler for Activity 4.4*

All measuring instruments, whether for physical objects or abstract concepts, will produce a variety of values when applied. This variation in scores or values is called *variability*. In a group of subjects there is going to be a natural variety of scores on a test, a variety of heights, a variety of attitudes. All the measures of the strip of paper were not the same in Activity 4.4, even when measured with the near-perfect legless ruler. Even if you had cut the lines very carefully using a ruler, it would have been possible to find an instrument that would be sensitive enough to find a variety of measures of width along its length. This variability can be quantified for a group of measures on a subject or subjects or objects and represented by the *variance,* S^2, which is calculated as follows:

$$S^2 = \frac{\text{sum of all (the differences with the mean)}^2}{\text{number of measures}}$$

This can be expressed mathematically as

$$S^2 = \frac{(x_1 - \overline{x})^2 + (x_2 - \overline{x})^2 + (x_3 - \overline{x})^3 + \dots}{n}$$

where

   x_1, x_2, x_3, etc., are individual measures
   $\overline{x}$ is the mean (average) of the set of scores
   n is the number of measures

which becomes very tedious when there is considerable data and is usually written in the shorthand of mathematical symbols as follows:

$$S^2 = \frac{\sum_{i=1}^{n}(x_i - \bar{x})^2}{n} \qquad (4.1)$$

where

Σ (sigma)	says 'the sum of whatever follows'
x_i	is an individual measure i, where $i = 1$ to n, thus x_1, x_2, x_3, etc.
$\bar{x}$	is the mean of the set of scores
n	is the number of measures.

If you take the square root of the variance, you get the *standard deviation from the mean*, whose meaning and use will be considered in Chapter 6. Continue with Activity 4.5 where you will use the data that you collected.

ACTIVITY 4.5

(a) Set up the spreadsheet shown in Table 4.1, entering in the trial data shown just to make sure all the equations are entered correctly. If you are unfamiliar with spreadsheets, see Appendix B before carrying out this activity for yourself.

(b) Enter the values for the 'legged' ruler in the spreadsheet shown in Table 4.1 replacing the values shown in column **B**. Everything in cells B15 and B16 will be calculated for you.

(c) Replace the values in column **F** with yours from the 'legless' ruler. Everything in cells E15 and E16 will be calculated for you.

A mathematical footnote About half the differences from the mean, $(x_i - \bar{x})$, will be positive numbers and about half will be negative. If all these were to be added up, the result would be close to zero. But note that after finding the difference from the mean the value is squared (square a negative number and the result is positive) and then they are all added together, so the numerator will *not* be zero after all (see the example in Activity 4.5).

It is generally assumed that most tests or measuring instruments in the social sciences are far from perfect in measuring what they are supposed to measure, somewhat like the ruler on legs. Therefore, we have to imagine that if there were a perfect measuring instrument (like our legless ruler), it would produce a *true score*. What we actually get as a result of collecting data with a test or instrument (analogous to our legged ruler) is an *observed score*. The difference between the two is attributable to measurement error, due to the imperfect instrument.

TABLE 4.1 *A worksheet for entering the data for the trial of the legged ruler*

	A	B	C	D	E	F
1	Activity 4.4					
2		Observed Scores	(nearest 1 mm)		"True" Scores	(nearest 0.5 mm)
3	Line number	Legged measures			Legless measures	
4	1	24			25.0	
5	2	24			25.0	
6	3	25			25.5	
7	4	26			26.0	
8	5	26			26.0	
9	6	26			26.5	
10	7	27			26.0	
11	8	26			26.5	
12	9	27			27.0	
13	10	28			27.5	
14						
15	mean = 25.9		◄─	mean = 26.10		◄─
16	variance = 1.49		◄─	variance = 0.59		◄─
17	Observed = natural + error			True = natural		
18						
19			rxx = 0.40			

=AVERAGE(B4:B13)
=VARP(B4:B13)

=AVERAGE(E4:E13)
=VARP(E4:E13)

=E16/B16

This error is usually expressed in terms of variability, there being more variability for a more imperfect measuring instrument. Thus for the legged ruler, the variability in readings is due to a combination of the imperfect nature of the ruler itself and the varying paper width (remember, there is no such thing as an exact width). In other words, the observed score variability is due to true score variability (varying paper width) and error caused by difficulty in reading the instrument. Similarly, the IQ scores (observed) of a group of people will vary partially because of true variability within the group and partially because of error in the IQ test itself.

Consider the perfect instrument, the legless ruler, where the variability is due only to the varying width of the paper and not the instrument. To quantify this, we say the perfect instrument has a true score variance with no error variance. This can all be expressed as a simple equation for the variance of the real measuring instrument, the legged ruler, which says the variance in the observed scores is the sum of the variance in the true scores plus the variance due to error:

$$S_x^2 = S_t^2 + S_e^2 \qquad\qquad (4.2)$$

where

S_x^2 = observed score variance, of a group of individual's actual scores

S_t^2 = true score variance, of a group of individual's true scores

S_e^2 = error variance, due to instrument error.

From this, a rigorous definition of reliability is defined (thus the use of ≡) as the ratio

$$\text{reliability} \equiv \frac{\text{variance in the true score}}{\text{variance in the observed score}}$$

which is usually written mathematically as

$$r_{xx} = \frac{S_t^2}{S_x^2} \qquad\qquad (4.3)$$

So let us now see what the reliability of the legged ruler is. Carry out Activity 4.6 at this time.

ACTIVITY 4.6

(a) Now examine the spreadsheet in Table 4.2. You have entered data for the 'observed score' for the legged ruler in column **B** and the 'true score' (the less flawed legless ruler) in column **G**. What was the reliability of the legged ruler? Why is it not perfect (i.e. exactly 1.0)? From where does the error variance come in this case?

(b) Since the use of the legged ruler is somewhat dependent upon who is using it, you may want to see if the reliability of the instrument with the strip of paper is different in the hands of a friend or relation. Just get them to make the 10 measurements on the strip, one for each line, and insert their data into the spreadsheet.

(c) Would you expect the reliability to increase with practice? How is this like a social science observational instrument used, say, in a classroom? Is it just the instrument that can introduce error?

Types of reliability

In reality, the true score usually does not exist since we cannot make the perfect measuring instrument. This is particularly true for instruments to measure abstract concepts in the social sciences, and therefore the true score variance can never be known. As noted earlier, even the legless ruler is not perfect. The consequence of this is that all reliability coefficients are estimates, depending on what form of reliability one is using. The following are some of the types of estimates commonly reported (adapted from Mehrens and Lehmann, 1984), which are indicators of:

1 *Stability*. This is often referred to as the test–retest estimate of reliability. This involves administering the instrument to the same group of people on two different occasions. Valid results for the calculation are not easy to obtain, since it is difficult to get subjects to do the same thing twice, there is the possibility that doing the task once will affect the second performance, and there is the possibility of something happening to subjects between applications that would affect the second score. This form is of value for measures aiming at long-term predictions.

2 *Equivalence*. To calculate this involves administering two equivalent forms of the same measuring instrument to the same group on the same day. This approach is most appropriate for tests of content (achievement) where inferences about skills and knowledge at a specific time are to be made.

3 *Internal consistency*. These are really indicators of the homogeneity of questions in a test or questionnaire, or the relative degree to which the responses to individual items correlate with the total test score. This approach allows a reliability coefficient to be calculated on one administration of a test. The most common version of this is the Pearson product moment correlation coefficient, based on splitting the test into two equal parts. If the test has questions scored on a right/wrong basis, the Kuder–Richardson estimates (K–R 20 and K–R 21) are appropriate. Alternatively, if items are not scored dichotomously, then Cronbach's alpha method is appropriate as a generalization of the K–R 20 estimate. There are a number of other tests available, of varying mathematical complexity.

4 *Inter-judge (-scorer) reliability*. This is highly appropriate for such activities where personal judgement is involved, for such situations that require checking the consistency of observations when several observers are collecting data, or to determine the consistency of classification skills across researchers. Data collecting activities like marking essays, classifying test items according to cognitive emphasis, judging a dog show are also typical. For example, if a researcher were recording the types of teacher–learner interaction in a class, then to confirm consistency in classification of the types of activity it would be desirable to have two or more other equally qualified persons carry out a classification of a given class (on video tape) and determine the consistency across researchers. This estimate requires scoring by another (or more) independent judge of a sample of subjects. The correlation between the judges gives an estimate of reliability.

5 *Intra-judge (-scorer) reliability.* This is of value when considerable data has been collected over a period of time by a researcher and the consistency of observations or classifications should be checked. A sample (randomly selected) set of observations is repeated at a later date and the reliability calculated.

As noted earlier, numerous textbooks will provide guidelines for the design of measuring instruments that will assist in maintaining a high reliability. These include the more obvious rules, such as when designing a questionnaire that is the operational definition of a concept, the greater the number of questions that constitute a definition, the more reliable that concept's measurement will be. All too often, single-attitude questions on a questionnaire are used as an operational definition of individual abstract concepts, resulting in considerable, highly unreliable data. This, unfortunately, is encouraged by the fact that computer programs will take individual responses to questions and process them as if they were scores on a set of questions, a prime example of the old computer saying, 'garbage in, garbage out'. In other words, there is nothing to stop a researcher from doing this, since the computer will not know any better.

Take the example used earlier, where one of the variables to be investigated in a study was perception of the quality of television. The response to the direct question 'Rank the overall quality of television on the five-point scale' might depend strongly on which day of the week subjects were asked this. The morning after an evening consisting of a series of second-rate reruns could produce a low rating, whereas after an evening of very good programmes, the rating would be higher. A better approach would involve asking a set of questions that would enquire about different types of programmes to help the respondent focus on a cross-section of television offerings. Such an approach would produce more consistent results across time and thus be considered more reliable.

If you are interested in finding out what the resulting equations are for the above reliability estimates, you are referred to standard texts (e.g. Thorndike and Hagen, 1977; Mehrens and Lehmann, 1984; Cronbach, 1990; Black, 1999). What is of primary importance at this point is that a report describing research that used a measuring instrument should provide some indication of its reliability, appropriate to the instrument and its application. Commercially produced or professionally developed test and other instruments should provide such information as part of the package. Researchers designing their own should carry out their own calculations of reliability and report the results.

CALCULATING CRONBACH'S ALPHA RELIABILITY COEFFICIENT

As an example, the calculation of one of the most commonly used coefficients will be considered. Earlier, reliability was defined as the ratio of variance in true score to variance in observed score, in equation (4.3),

$$r_{xx} = \frac{S_t^2}{S_x^2}$$

The difficulty is that except in rare cases, we do not have any data on the true score. It is just not possible in most cases to have a perfect measure for comparison as we did with the legless ruler. Therefore, it is necessary to devise estimates for reliability. The basis for most estimates combines equation (4.2) with the definition, by first solving it for the true score variance, the one that is hardest even to estimate, giving

$$S_t^2 = S_x^2 - S_e^2 \qquad (4.4)$$

Substituting this into the definition in equation (4.3) gives

$$r_{xx} = \frac{S_x^2 - S_e^2}{S_x^2}$$

Dividing both terms in the numerator by the denominator provides the following simplified expression:

$$r_{xx} = 1 - \frac{S_e^2}{S_x^2}$$

This makes life a little easier, since S_x^2 is the variance of the scores from the instrument and S_e^2 is the error variance which can be estimated. One such estimate has resulted in a commonly used coefficient, Cronbach's alpha, α, an indicator of internal consistency across questions in an instrument. It has the equation

$$\alpha = \frac{N}{N-1} \left(1 - \frac{\sum\limits_{i=1}^{N} S_i^2}{S_x^2} \right) \qquad (4.5)$$

where N is the number of questions and $\sum_{i=1}^{N} S_i^2$ is an estimate of the error variance, made up of the sum of all the variances for all the questions across the subjects. This is best seen by looking at a spreadsheet which allows one to enter raw scores for each subject, say in a trial, and automatically calculate alpha, as shown in Table 4.2.

Note that each subject's scores for each question is in the columns, and the responses for a given question can be seen by looking across the appropriate row. In columns **L** and **M**, the standard deviation and variance for each question is calculated. When summed in cell **M12**, this is used in the

TABLE 4.2 Worksheet for determining Cronbach's alpha and item–total correlations for a trial group for the piloting of a questionnaire

	A	B	C	D	E	F	G	H	I	J	K	L	M	N
1	Quest	Albert	Bill	Carla	Denis	Eddie	Fred	Greg	Hanna	Irene	Jack	S_i	S_i^2	Item-total correlation
2	1	5	1	1	1	1	5	3	3	1	1	1.60	2.56	0.79
3	2	4	2	3	2	2	4	4	4	3	2	0.89	0.80	0.91
4	3	1	5	5	2	3	3	5	5	5	1	1.63	2.65	0.23
5	4	4	2	3	3	2	4	1	4	3	2	0.98	0.96	0.70
6	5	5	2	4	2	3	5	3	3	2	3	1.08	1.16	0.62
7	6	4	3	3	4	2	4	4	4	3	2	0.78	0.61	0.78
8	7	5	2	5	3	3	3	3	3	1	1	1.30	1.69	0.48
9	8	3	1	3	4	2	4	2	5	3	2	1.14	1.29	0.68
10	9	3	1	4	3	1	5	5	3	4	3	1.33	1.76	0.64
11	10	1	5	1	2	2	3	1	3	5	3	1.43	2.04	-0.18
12	Totals:	35	24	32	26	21	40	31	37	30	20	$\sum S_i^2 =$	15.52	
13	Mean =	29.60												
14	$S_x =$	6.41				$n =$	10							
15	$S_x^2 =$	41.04				$\alpha =$	0.69							

= STDEVP(B2:K2) & **Copy down**

= VARP(B2:K2) & **Copy down**

= PEARSON (B2:K2,B$12:K$12) & **Copy down**

= AVERAGE(B12:K12)
= STDEVP(B12:K12)
= VARP(B12:K12)

= (G14/(G14–1))*(1–M12/B15)

= SUM(K2:K11) & **Copy** across left

= SUM(M2:M11)

numerator in the fraction in equation (4.5) as the estimate of the error variance. The denominator is just the observed score variance of the total scores, found in cell **B15**. In this example, the reliability coefficient is not too bad for a trial group.

Now the real value of such a process is for piloting an instrument and identifying where the weaknesses lie. Therefore, the last column gives the researcher a clue. It provides the correlation between the responses for each question and the corresponding totals. Thus, those questions for which the individual responses are high when the totals are high, or low when the totals are low, will have a high item–total correlation, a desirable trait. Those with low or negative correlations need attention, though it is not possible to tell exactly what is wrong with them from this data. The researcher still needs to be a detective to identify what exactly the deficiency is (e.g. due to the wording of the question it is not interpreted in the same way by all.) Carry out Activity 4.7 at this time.

ACTIVITY 4.7

(a) Which questions would you suspect need attention in this set of 10? Can you see why from looking across the rows?

(b) Are there some subjects who seem to be answering the questions consistently along one part of the scale, while others are all over the scale? What might this indicate is the source of the problem with the questions?

(c) You can set this table up on a worksheet and try changing some of the data (i.e. the subject's responses) to see how they affect the reliability.

(d) This worksheet can be used for any trial by changing the data in the shaded cells. If more cells are needed, just add more rows for more questions or more columns for more subjects. If fewer are needed, just erase the contents of unneeded cells.

The recognition of the non-trivial problems associated with developing highly reliable and valid instruments has resulted in complete research projects being committed to the development, trialling and improving of instruments to provide dependable operational definitions of specific constructs. Other studies, as you will find, do not dedicate sufficient resources, and sometimes it becomes very apparent when reading the report that the lack of quality of the instruments has weakened the validity of the outcomes.

OBJECTIVITY

Objectivity is of particular importance when human judgements are involved, for example when classifying pupil behaviour using an observation schedule, the wording of individual questions in a questionnaire, or marking an essay looking for certain points. Instruments designed in such a way that they have clear, unambiguous questions tend to be rated as highly objective. Objectivity often depends on how questions, verbal or written, are presented to a subject. Even tone of voice can reduce the objectivity in a situation, such as an interview or when questions or statements are read to a group. Low objectivity can affect adversely both the reliability and validity of any measuring instrument.

It is very difficult to determine the level of objectivity from a report; therefore it probably would be necessary actually to see a written instrument or be there to watch data being collected, hear an audio tape or see a video tape, when there is verbal interaction between a researcher and the subjects. Ideally, a reader would expect some mention of steps taken to ensure objectivity, particularly when the intent of the research is to investigate contentious issues. A common example is telephone surveys to determine political preference. Even this does not solve all the problems of data quality, as will be seen in the next section.

The subjects: how well do they cooperate?

Human beings can be perverse, doing the unexpected and almost inexplicable. Very often even the personal interaction skills of the researcher are not enough to elicit valid and reliable responses from subjects. Historically various polling organizations have endeavoured to collect opinions from samples of the voters to predict the outcome of the elections. As a consequence of the misprediction of the outcome of the 1949 Presidential contest in the United States between Truman and Dewey, many newspapers announced the day after the election that Dewey had won (based upon polling samples), when in reality he had lost. Subsequently, polling organizations have invested considerable resources to ensure more representative samples since their results, and livelihood, depend on a high predictive validity, one that can be checked! Over the years, these organizations seem to have become more accurate in their predictions.

Then more recently, there arose a new factor that seems to have had a significant affect on these predictions. The national election for Members of Parliament in the United Kingdom in the spring of 1992 produced the usual output of predictions, right up to the day of the election. It was predicted that the Conservative Party would not gain the majority of seats in Parliament and therefore would not be the party in power and select the Prime Minister. The predictions were wrong! It was a close election, but the Conservatives eventually had a comfortable majority of 21 seats (down from 78). What went wrong? Introspection and investigation over the following weeks produced the hypothesis that a sizeable number of voters in the samples who were verbally asked said they would vote for Labour, when in reality they voted for the Conservative candidate. Why, one might ask, when assured of anonymity would they do this? It seems that the campaign tended to emphasize the point that the Conservatives, who were in power, were supporting somewhat selfish, monetarist policies, to the detriment of the poor and unemployed.

Some people questioned about voting intentions seemed not to wish to admit supporting policies furthering self-interest rather than the more altruistic ones of the Labour Party, so guilt generated a small lie. In an endeavour to overcome this anomaly, one polling organization has subsequently used written questionnaires, anonymously returned, rather than telephone or doorstep interview. Time will tell whether this overcomes the problem.

People do not answer questions honestly for a whole host of reasons. Researchers too often underestimate the intelligence of their subjects. There is the story of the man who had a flat tyre on a road next to a mental institution. As he removed the wheel, he accidentally kicked the wheel nuts off the edge of the road into a river. He became very agitated, not knowing what to do next, when an inmate on the other side of the fence, who had been watching the events, suggested: 'Why don't you take one nut off each of the other wheels and put them on that one? That will get you to a garage.' The man said, 'What a good idea!', thought a minute, and then said, 'Excuse me for asking, but what are you doing in there?' The inmate's reply was: 'I may be crazy, but I'm not stupid.' Organizations have used screening tests to identify mental problems in potential employees, and yet these do not always serve their intended function. Human subjects are often capable of identifying what the operational definition of a set of questions might be and answer accordingly. If the instrument is perceived as a threat, then the truth may not prevail. More subtly, some subjects want to be overly helpful and provide information that is not wholly true, but they feel it might help the researcher, so they exaggerate, over- or underemphasizing (see the case study).

A CASE STUDY

There is the tale of the anthropologists who heard of a tribe living in a remote place that performed a most hideous cannibalistic dance before eating their defeated enemies after battle. They travelled day and night to get there and, after considerable negotiation with a tribal representative, were able to witness this spectacle. They returned home and generated several fascinating journal articles on cannibals.

Years later, another anthropologist related the following, having contacted the same group. The report back to the village leader, Henry, after the meeting between the great anthropologist, Farlander Jones-Smithersbothom, and the tribal representative, Fred, went something like this:

Fred: I've just met another pale-skinned eccentric who wants to come and visit us.
Henry: I suppose he will have to be entertained, any requests?
Fred: Yes, he says that he and his colleagues would like to see the funny dance that we did for those 'explorers'.

continued

> *Henry*: You mean the one they described and had us do where John jumps about with a cow bone in his teeth, you kick the coconut that looks like a head, and I wear a pile of sheep guts as a hat?
>
> *Fred*: That's it.
>
> *Henry*: That's disgusting. They didn't want to see the one about happy flowers? Who are these guys anyway?
>
> *Fred*: They call themselves 'anthropologists' and claim just to want to watch us for a while. They must be bored.
>
> *Henry*: Well I gave old Melvin a clip around the ear for peeping in my hut at my wife the other day, I hope they aren't like him. Anyway, they are our guests and we must be hospitable. Do have Mary make those nice chicken kebabs on sticks, the ones that look like fingers, but tell her not to put so much pepper on them, the 'explorers' didn't seem like them much. Forget the tomato juice, that didn't go over well either. And do arrange to have the children go off to pick fruit, I wouldn't want them to see such a degrading spectacle.

Surveys among captive audiences, like school children, may produce results that are highly unreliable and do not necessarily contain the truth, depending on their age and attitudes towards education. Numerous reported research projects use students in the academic institution of the researchers, simply because they are convenient. Ignoring the problem of representativeness of the sample, can undergraduates be convinced to answer or participate honestly? Some instruments have been cleverly designed to detect inconsistencies or exaggerations in responses, but this is not a simple task.

In summary, the best planned scheme for data collection may not be as good as hoped because of fickleness of a significant number of members of the sample. Sometimes this is avoidable through sufficient insight into the characteristics of the sample and how the instrument will be perceived. Such problems do emphasize the need for researchers to be very sensitive about how the data is collected.

CRITERIA FOR RELIABILITY, VALIDITY AND OBJECTIVITY

The criteria for Data Quality II in the Profiling Sheet are as follows.

Commercially produced and tested with high validity, reliability and objectivity (V, R, O) Commercially produced tests that are sold usually have published values for reliability and strong rationale for their validity. It is up to the researcher to justify the use (validity) for the situation at hand.

Project produced and tested with high V, R, O If the research project has designed an instrument, ideally the researcher(s) will have gone to the trouble of assuring the validity and enhancing the reliability through trials, plus appropriate coefficients will be presented in the paper.

Commercially or project produced with moderate V, R, O   This level is for instruments that have published coefficients that are not terribly high, but at least the values and justification have been produced.

Commercially or project produced with low V, R, O, or no information provided   Occasionally, a report does not justify or defend the validity and objectivity, and/or produce any indication of the reliability of the instrument(s).

Inappropriate instrument for this application   This judgement may require some detailed knowledge or experience of the actual instrument, but it does happen that researchers do not use appropriate instruments.

Finally, carry out Activity 4.8.

ACTIVITY 4.8

In light of the above discussions, evaluate two or more articles or reports using the criteria Profiling Sheet at the end of the chapter. You may want to use new articles or ones used for activities in previous chapters. Photocopy the portion of the Profiling Sheet as needed.

MODEL ANSWERS AND COMMENTS

Activity 4.3

1   *Successful person*

   (a)   Personal annual income might provide an indicator that changes with time: will they be successful next year?
   (b)   Attitude towards job and career: depends on whether focus of the research is about peoples' own perceptions which may affect motivation, or some external criteria. The choice will depend upon the research question.
   (c)   Investment portfolio, if success is considered best defined as the accumulation of wealth.

2   *Effective teacher*

   (a)   Success rate of class: there is no guarantee that the teacher is the only contributor to high or low scores; others include social class, school resources, parents, etc.
   (b)   Self-evaluation: what is the aim of the research? This could be related to self-confidence, willingness to innovate, etc.

continued

(c) Student evaluation questionnaires are like the question on what constitutes good television: some teachers entertain and keep the students happy but do not stretch them, others get students to accomplish more but induce stress, while some seem to accomplish both. This would depend on what is meant by *effective*, a difficult concept to define in any situation.

3 *Quality of long-term memory*

(a) Nonsense syllables presented to a group allow for control over what might be previously learned, but people do not tend to memorize nonsense, and most long-term memorization occurs within some context.

(b) Trivial Pursuit may test one's memory within a realistic context, but the researcher has no control over the content and how it was acquired, and, depending on the version, the content can be culturally biased.

(c) IQ tests do test knowledge and to some extent memory, but they test other things as well.

Profiling Sheet: *Understanding Social Science Research,* © Thomas R. Black, 2001

Article: _____   **Type of Study:** ☐ Descriptive, ☐ Survey/correlational, ☐ *Ex post facto,* ☐ Experimental/quasi-experimental.

Questions/ hypotheses	Representativeness	Ethics and Confidentiality	Data Quality I	Data Quality II
Valid question or hypothesis based on accepted theory with well-justified referenced support	Whole population	Ethical standards met and data sufficiently confidential that no individuals or institutions can be identified	Educationally, sociologically, psychologically, etc., significant and manageable number of concepts	Commercially or professionally produced/tested with high validity, reliability and objectivity(V, R, O)
Valid question or hypothesis based on own theory, well justified	Random selection from a well-specified population		Limited academic significance, very narrow perspective	Project or personally produced/tested with high V, R, O
Credible question/ hypothesis but alternative possible, or too extensive/global, or support missing	Purposive sample from a well-specified population, with justification for representativeness	Ethical issues not addressed or confidentiality not discussed when it should have been	Large number of concepts, potentially confusing	Commercially or project produced with moderate V, R, O
Weak question/ hypothesis, or poorly stated, or justified with inappropriate references	Volunteers or convenience, with no justification of representativeness	Ethical issues not addressed and/or some loss of confidentiality	Too many concepts and variables investigated to provide meaningful results	Commercially or project produced with low V, R, O, or no information provided
No question or hypothesis stated, or inconsistent with known facts	Unidentified group	Ethical standards violated and/or subjects endangered owing to no confidentiality	Trivial concepts, not academically significant	Inappropriate instrument for the variables/concepts described

Comments and rationale for classification:

5

Descriptive Statistics

Graphs and Charts

The term *statistics* usually conjures up a vision of great tables of numbers. What we want to consider here is not the collection of numerical data, but how this data will be presented to a reader of a report hopefully to enhance the meaning of what has been collected. There are two types of statistical procedure that can be employed, the choice being dependent upon the function or use of the statistics. Procedures that describe a set of data for a group to enlighten one of the characteristics of that group alone are referred to as *descriptive* methods. Translating tables of relatively meaningless numbers into forms that actually provide some information about a group requires the employment of a variety of techniques; a number of these will be examined in this chapter. Alternatively, there are other techniques that are used to make inferences about larger groups (populations) based upon the data collected on the identified representative sample; these are referred to as *inferential* procedures, which will be introduced in later chapters.

There is a certain amount of satisfaction in having collected data and having lists of numbers, but even mathematicians do not get much joy out of just looking at piles of figures. In the world of computers, raw numbers are referred to as *data*, with the implication that they lack any intrinsic meaning. Processing the data should result in *information*, something that mere mortals can look at and readily understand. Descriptive statistical procedures will allow the researcher to use the data to provide general information about the group investigated, regardless of whether or not inferences about a population are to be made. These procedures involve intellectual 'tools' to generate carefully organized tables of numbers, graphs and calculated indicators of group characteristics, such as the mean (arithmetic average). But as for any set of techniques, there are rules and not all researchers seem to be aware of them, as will be seen when evaluating reports. Computer software often makes the mechanics of generating tables and graphs easier than producing them by hand, but even these powerful tools must be kept under a tight reign so that they are not used inappropriately.

This chapter will introduce two aspects of descriptive statistical procedures: frequency distributions, and graphs and charts. The next chapter will describe measures of central tendency and indicators of variability. Some procedures will be described in detail so as to assist in understanding the basis for deciding when they are used appropriately; graphs and charts will be examined to ensure that they are presented correctly. First, we shall look at classifying numerical data in a way that is based upon how constructs are quantified and how the data is collected.

TABLES, GRAPHS AND CHARTS

Initially, a researcher must organize the raw data into some meaningful form. This data often consists of a large collection of numbers, such as scores on a test or other measuring instrument. In many cases, displaying data in a more organized manner can be done by using a computer program, which will save considerable time. It is necessary to understand what the program does and how it carries out the task, so that what is wanted is actually achieved. Modifying the computer adage 'garbage in, garbage out', there is always the danger of 'data in, garbage out'. Basically, it is not wise to assume that the computer programmer who wrote the program knows best. These are sophisticated tools, but still require the researcher to make decisions, and it is not too difficult to find reports where decisions about how data is displayed or graphs are plotted have been left to the 'default' decision of the software package used: the results are not as informative as they could have been.

The most basic technique possible for organizing data will result in summarizing the data in frequency tables, which list the frequency of occurrence of specified characteristics or ranges of scores. Tables 5.1, 5.2, and 5.3 provide examples showing the major types of frequency data, each of which will be discussed briefly. The type of data collected will eventually determine which kinds of graphs best illustrate the results.

Measurement scales

Starting with the most basic type of data, Table 5.1 gives the number of schools in each category for a survey. The variable on the left, type of school, is considered to be a *nominal scale*, as would be any variable which involved name value only. The order of presentation of the schools in Table 5.1 intends no implication of relative quality and the order presented is not the only one possible. Even numerals can constitute nominal data, such as postal codes (a table showing how many people in each code area), or numerals on football players' shirts (a table showing frequency of penalties for each player designated by his number). The order of the numerals has nothing to do with the data since they are simply a convenient replacement for names.

If the order in which something is ranked is important, such as shown in Table 5.2, showing numbers in each social class in a study, then it is considered an *ordinal scale*. In such a situation, the order does make a difference, but there is no suggestion that the difference between A and B is the same as that from B to C. In some sense, A is better or higher than B, but how much is not

TABLE 5.1 *Frequency table for types of schools (nominal scale) in Bloggsmoor Local Education Authority, England*

Type of school	Frequency
Boys Comprehensive (BC)	16
Girls Comprehensive (GC)	14
Mixed Comprehensive (MC)	20
Boys Private (BP)	8
Girls Private (GP)	6
Mixed Private (MP)	10

TABLE 5.2 *Frequency table showing numbers of subjects in each social class (ordinal scale) in a study sample*

Class	Frequency
A	21
B	44
C	32
D	55
E	16

quantified. Ordinal data can also result from measuring instruments in the social sciences that require ranking of behaviour or events, such as attitude scales in a questionnaire. For example, consider the following question:

	Usually		Occasionally		Rarely
Television news broadcasts are informative.	1	2	3	4	5

There is no guarantee that the difference between rank 1 and rank 2 will be perceived as the same as the difference between rank 2 and rank 3, and so on. It is like a race – the horse that comes in first may have won by a whisker, and the third place horse may be a long way behind.

When measurement becomes more refined, then individuals are scored, that is assigned numerical values on an *interval scale* with equal intervals, though where true zero is on the scale is not known. Examples of such scales include temperature (degrees Celsius, zero is just the freezing point of water and not a lack of temperature) and IQ scores. Table 5.3 provides an example of a frequency table (or frequency distribution) of IQ test scores for a school. As would be expected, each interval is the same size, covering the same range of numbers.

The *ratio* scale has equal intervals as well, but zero does mean something: a total lack of the characteristic. For example, distributions of such characteristics as height, weight and percentage of questions at a specific cognitive level on a test are ratio scales, since zero does mean a total lack of the attribute. Do not be misled by the fact that IQ scores (interval data) were originally a ratio:

TABLE 5.3 *Frequency distribution of IQ test scores (interval scale) for a school, as shown on a worksheet*

	A	B
	Scores	**Frequency**
1	Scores	Frequency
2	61–65	1
3	66–70	1
4	71–75	0
5	76–80	3
6	81–85	8
7	86–90	10
8	91–95	25
9	96–100	55
10	101–105	53
11	106–110	27
12	111–115	11
13	116–120	7
14	121–125	5
15	126–130	1
16	131–135	2
17	136–140	1

the actual mental age score divided by the chronological age (it is now more complex; see Kline, 1991). It is the actual score that is important and only the unconscious (hopefully a transient condition) or the uncooperative in a population for which such a test is designed would ever get zero.

The type of scale that is used will determine how the data can be displayed graphically and which statistical tests will be appropriate. There is a certain amount of discussion on just how much restriction a type of data should impose on the choice of statistical tests. For example, most inferential tests assume that the scales are interval or ratio, but some researchers (e.g. Chase, 1985) argue that one does not have to be too rigorous. For example, a questionnaire that uses a five-point ranking as in the above example on each of 25 questions would provide total scores that could be considered as ordinal. Alternatively, one could argue that since there are 100 possible rankings, the total score is approximately interval in nature, since the total score range is 25 to 125. If a research report does use data that has its origins in ordinal scales as interval data, then it should say so and justify this usage. It would then be up to the reader to determine the validity of such an argument in that situation.

Planning frequency distributions

Frequency tables for nominal and ordinal data are usually the result of a fairly straightforward exercise in classification: in which category does each subject fit? Tables 5.1 and 5.2 are typical examples. Frequency tables for interval and ratio data present the questions how many intervals and how big? In some cases, each score constitutes an entire interval because there is a small range of scores, but often it is necessary to have *grouped* data because of the large number of potential scores, as shown in Table 5.3. In such situations, one could apparently group the data in any number of different sizes of intervals, starting at a variety of places, but there are some rules of thumb. Chase (1985) maintains that 15 intervals are best but no fewer than 10 and usually no more than 20 intervals should be used. Outside this range, the shape of the distribution can be distorted, and for some considerations, the shape of the distribution will be very important. Therefore, it is worthwhile looking carefully at any graphs of interval data presented in a report and counting the number of intervals. Carry out Activity 5.1 to see how this is done on a spreadsheet.

ACTIVITY 5.1

(a) Enter the data in Tables 5.1 to 5.3 on separate worksheets in an Excel spreadsheet. We will use these shortly.

(b) Copy Table 5.3 onto a new worksheet (call it Table 5.3a) and make a new table by combining the frequencies in adjacent intervals. For example, the new interval 66–75 would have 1, 76–85 would have 11, etc. Repeat the process to make another table (call it Table 5.3b) by combining three intervals at a time from Table 5.3, making new intervals each having a spread of 15. Save these, because you will use them in the next activity.

Creating a frequency table from raw data requires a few simple decisions, including deciding on the limits for each interval. Examining Table 5.3, it has intervals of five score points, and the process of making this frequency distribution would have been a simple matter if IQ scores had been only whole numbers. The researcher would have just counted up the number of scores that were in each of the sets of five numbers, for example if 25 persons had scores that were 91, 92, 93, 94 or 95. The limits 91 and 95 are called the *apparent* limits. This would be all that was necessary to consider if the data were whole numbers or integers, or in statistics terminology, a *discrete* variable.

Many scores will not necessarily be a whole number, since they are the ratio of two numbers times 100. Such a calculation can produce virtually any numerical value, with fractional parts of a whole number, and are considered to be *continuous* variables. For example, a student correctly answering 58 questions on a mathematics test with 64 equally weighted questions would have a score out of 100 of

$$\frac{58}{64} \times 100 = 0.90625 \times 100 = 90.625$$

Thus, it is necessary also to identify the *real* limits of each interval. If we were to use apparent intervals of five points each ending in 100, then in the case above the real limits are 90.50 to 95.4999.... In other words, the interval would be from 90.50 to just below 95.50 (up to but not including 95.50), as shown in Figure 5.1, simply 0.5 points above and below the apparent limits. This derives from the fact that we traditionally round up to the next whole number if the fractional part of a number is 0.500 or above, and round down to the next whole number if it is 0.499999... or below. Thus our score of 90.625 would also fall in this interval and not in the one below, even though it is less than 91.

To determine how many intervals there should be requires a bit of trial and error. First take the total range of scores the study found and divide by 15 (the 'ideal' number of intervals), and adjust from there. For example, the range of IQ scores in Table 5.3 was 64 to 136, or 72 points; divided by 15 this gives 4.8 or, rounded up, 5 points per interval. Now it is possible to begin with 64, but that would provide intervals that are difficult to read since people expect to start with a one, so it is best to drop back to the apparent limit of 61 (real limit 60.5) and go up to apparent limit 65 (real limit 65.5), then 66–70 (65.5–70.5), then 71–75 (70.5–75.5), and so on. As you can see, $65.5 - 60.5 = 5.0$ points for an interval that would allow the grouping of decimal numbers as well as whole numbers, in intervals of five. This results in 16 intervals that are fairly easy to read, as can be seen from Table 5.3.

Drawing graphs and charts

It has been said that a picture is worth a thousand words, and when it comes to trying to understand numerical data, this is very true. At the same time, if you want to deceive someone, pictures (or graphs and charts) are quite good as well. To see the true potential for deception it is worthwhile referring to the short and entertaining text by Huff (1954). In this section, some guidelines will be provided to help you determine the quality of graphical presentations.

Most computer spreadsheet packages, like Excel, and statistical packages, SPSS for example, have built-in graphics facilities. The user enters the data as a frequency table, chooses various options and the program displays (and usually can print out) the graph or chart chosen. Some are better than others from the viewpoint of offering appropriate graphs as well as displaying a high-quality visual representation.

The most basic question to ask is whether or not the most appropriate type of graph has been used. As noted earlier, the type of data (nominal, ordinal, interval or ratio) will influence the types of graphs and charts that are appropriate for displaying data. Figure 5.2 summarizes appropriate usage dependent upon data type, with each graph and chart illustrated in figures below.

The most basic graph is a *bar chart* (or block diagram), which is used for nominal and ordinal data. It is a graphical frequency diagram where it is the height of the bar that conveys the message. Each bar does *not* touch the next

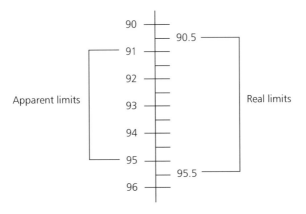

FIGURE 5.1 *Real and apparent limits*

	Bar chart	Pie chart	Histogram	Frequency polygon
Nominal	X	X		
Ordinal	X			
Interval			X	X
Ratio			X	X

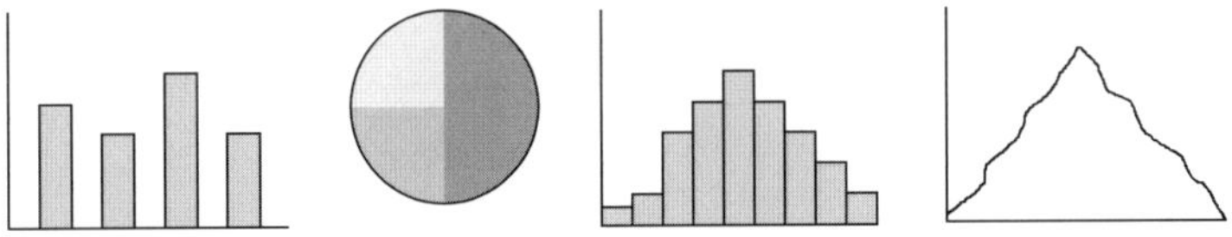

FIGURE 5.2 *Appropriate usage of different charts and graphs for frequency data*

since for nominal data the order of the bars is irrelevant, and for ordinal data the intervals are not necessarily the same size. This avoids any implication that the graph is displaying interval data. To illustrate these, data from Tables 5.1 and 5.2 are displayed as bar charts in Figures 5.3 and 5.4.

Pie charts are picturesque, but not very informative except for nominal data, when the frequencies are converted to percentages. Thus, if the frequencies for each type of school in Table 5.1 were converted to percentages of the whole sample of 74 schools, then one could draw a pie chart, as shown in Figure 5.5. Again, the pattern for the slices of the pie will be selected on the basis of what is most meaningful, since there is no implied order or ranking. Each percentage is a proportion of the circle, a fraction of 360°; thus the area of each pie slice is proportional to the percentage.

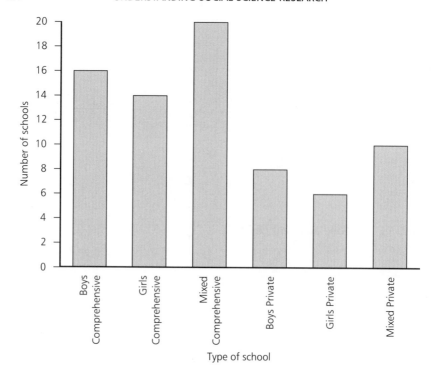

FIGURE 5.3   *Bar chart for numbers of different schools in a study using data from Table 5.1*

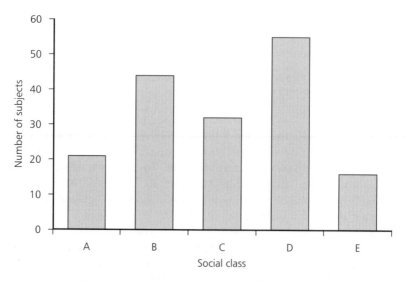

FIGURE 5.4   *Bar chart for numbers in each social class in a study using data from Table 5.2*

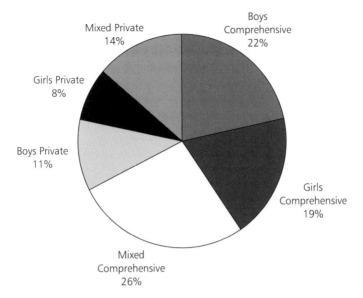

FIGURE 5.5   *Pie chart showing percentages of each type of school using data from Table 5.1*

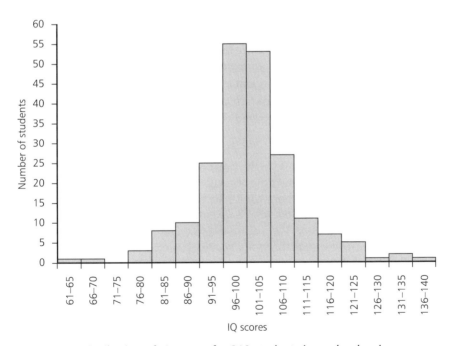

FIGURE 5.6   *Distribution of IQ scores for 210 students in a school, using data from Table 5.3*

Histograms are special bar charts where adjoining bars touch, thus indicating interval or ratio data, where each interval is the same size as the next and the data is considered to be continuous. The area under each bar, as well as its height, is indicative of the number of subjects in that interval. This interpretation for area on a graph will become more important as we consider other ways of displaying interval and ratio data. Figure 5.6 is a histogram of the data from Table 5.3, showing the distribution of IQ scores for a group of students.

Plotting graphs

Plotting graphs in Excel is quite easy using the Chart Wizard, a built-in guide that takes you through each step. This puts over 100 different types of charts and graphs at your finger tips using only the mouse. You do have to make decisions about which is most appropriate for the data collected and to adjust the charts and graphs beyond the default settings. Not always do these provide the best picture of the results. Appendix B provides a detailed guide to the Chart Wizard. Consider this first and then try Activity 5.2.

ACTIVITY 5.2

(a) Using Chart Wizard, plot each of the charts in Figures 5.3 to 5.6 from the frequency tables you entered in Activity 5.1. You can display these on the worksheets next to each frequency table.

(b) In Activity 5.1(b), you were to combine intervals to create new frequency tables for the data in Table 5.3. Plot these two sets of data as histograms. What do you notice about the shape of these new distributions compared with the original?

In Figure 5.6, the intervals on the horizontal axis have been labelled using the apparent intervals. Some authors will use the real interval limits to mark the edges of each bar. Others prefer to use the number that is the centre value for an interval (e.g. 63, 68, 73, 78, etc.), which might affect the choice of intervals. Thus to use the values 60, 65, 70, 75, etc., as interval labels which look nice, the real intervals would have to be 57.5–62.5, 62.5–67.5, 67.5–72.5, etc.

There are alternatives to histograms that make the shape of the distribution more apparent. *Frequency polygons* are just line graphs that join the centres of the tops of the bars on histograms. Figure 5.7 is the equivalent frequency polygon for the histogram in Figure 5.6 and the data in Table 5.4. Note that the horizontal axis is labelled with the numbers of the centres of the intervals. Now carry out Activity 5.3 to see how to plot one using Excel.

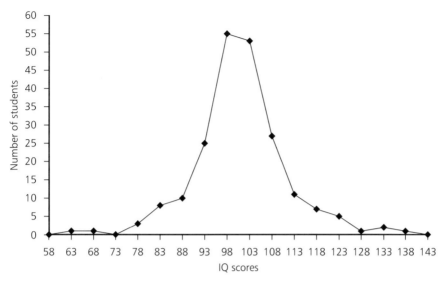

FIGURE 5.7   *Frequency polygon for data in Table 5.4*

TABLE 5.4   *Data from Table 5.3 with interval centres added*

	A	B	C
1	Scores	Centres	Frequency
2	56–60	58	0
3	61–65	63	1
4	66–70	68	1
5	71–75	73	0
6	76–80	78	3
7	81–85	83	8
8	86–90	88	10
9	91–95	93	25
10	96–100	98	55
11	101–105	103	53
12	106–110	108	27
13	111–115	113	11
14	116–120	118	7
15	121–125	123	5
16	126–130	128	1
17	131–135	133	2
18	136–140	138	1
19	141–145	143	0

=B2+5 and **Copy** down the column

ACTIVITY 5.3

(a) Copy the data from Table 5.3 and add a new column between the two data columns. Also add a row at the top and enter one more interval. Add another interval at the bottom with a zero value. These will anchor the ends of the following graph on the horizontal axis.

(b) Enter the midpoints as shown in Table 5.4. This can be done easily by putting the number for the first, 58, $= B2 + 5$ in cell **B3**, and then just **Copy** it down the column: it will change accordingly so that each cell is five points more than the previous one.

(c) Now using Chart Wizard, plot columns **B** and **C** to make a frequency polygon like the one in Figure 5.7.

There will be occasions when researchers want to show a smoothed version of a frequency polygon, the implication being that if one had the data for the whole population, it would not be so jagged (Chase, 1985). A *smoothed frequency polygon* is achieved by averaging sets of adjacent intervals: add up the values and divide by 3. It is somewhat easier to identify the shape of a distribution from a smoothed graph. The shape of a distribution is of greatest importance when the choice of measures of central tendency is made, as will be seen in the next section. Rather than doing this by hand, all one has to do is tick the appropriate box in Excel and it is done automatically. The data has been plotted as the graph in Figure 5.8 and you will see how to do it in Activity 5.4.

ACTIVITY 5.4

(a) Using the worksheet in Table 5.4, plot a second frequency polygon like the one in Figure 5.7.

(b) Activate the chart and double click on the data points to activate them, which will bring up the **Format Data Series** window. Select the **Patterns** tab and in the lower left-hand corner, tick the box for ❑ **Smoothed Line** and click on the [OK] button. The graph should then look like the one in Figure 5.8.

Little deceptions

There are a number of interesting distortions resulting from transgressions of the rules that can be introduced when plotting a graph or drawing a chart. Huff (1954) has the best catalogue of sins, particularly relating to the world of advertising, but the few presented here are the most common violations

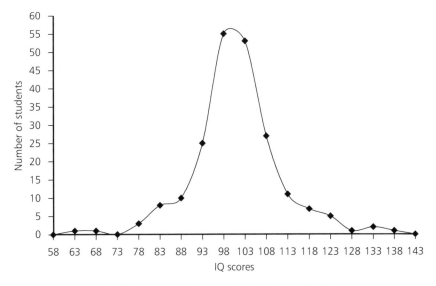

FIGURE 5.8   *Smoothed frequency polygon for data in Table 5.4*

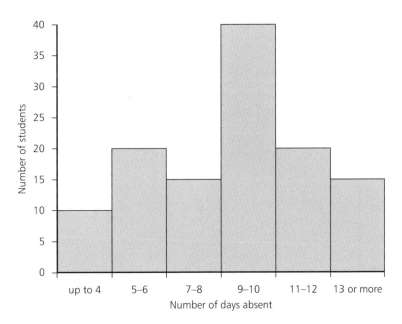

FIGURE 5.9   *Histogram with unequal interval size and too few intervals*

seen in research papers. One that appears all too frequently is histograms with unequal numerical intervals, but showing equal physical size on the graph. More often, histograms are produced with too few intervals. Figure 5.9 provides an example containing both errors. At the other extreme, too many intervals used with small samples can provide flat, uninformative graphs.

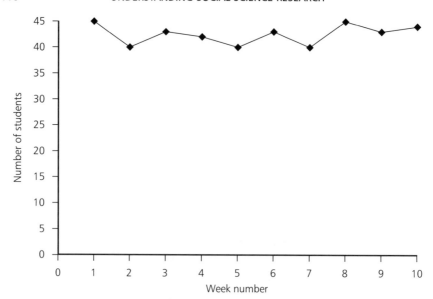

FIGURE 5.10   *Number of students absent in each week over a term.*
                Does there appear to be much variation?

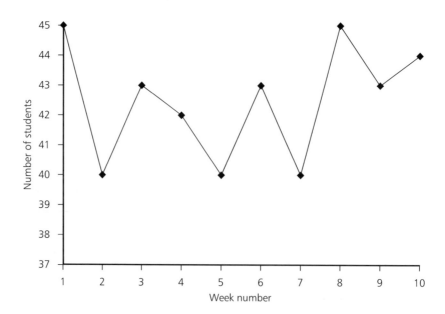

FIGURE 5.11   *Number of students absent in each week over a term.*
                Now does there appear to be much variation?

Presenting a graph where the vertical frequency axis does not start at zero is an approach commonly used to exaggerate differences. While this is acceptable for the horizontal variable axis (since often we use interval data where zero has no real meaning), it is deceptive on the vertical, as seen when comparing Figure 5.10 with Figure 5.11 and considering the different meanings they potentially convey. Now look at Activity 5.5.

ACTIVITY 5.5

Find an example of a distorted graph in your daily newspaper; you should be able to find at least one in either the advertisements or the financial section without too much difficulty.

What follows are some more exercises in plotting graphs for you to try in Activity 5.6, with model answers.

ACTIVITY 5.6

1   Enter each of the data sets shown in the exercises on the next page on a separate worksheet in a workbook.
2   Use the Chart Wizard guide provided in Appendix B to initiate a chart in an area to the right of the data on each worksheet.
3   When you reach Step 2 where a choice of charts is required, use the criteria summarized in Figure 5.2 to select the most appropriate type of chart for the data.
4   Complete the processes in Steps 3 to 5; you can return to the various choices later and change them for each chart.
5   Edit the chart using the menu bar to change the chart. You will have to do this, for example, to obtain a proper histogram.
6   Try editing the charts using the mouse as suggested. This takes a bit of practice if you are not used to using a mouse.
7   You will find that some data sets can be used to illustrate more than one type of chart. Copy the data to a new worksheet to show the second type of chart. *Hint*: You may find it is better to change the data ranges and/or horizontal axis points.

SUMMARY

Presenting numerical results as graphs and charts can enhance communication with readers of a report, but this assumes that these have been generated with care. Computer packages make it relatively easy to present very professional looking graphs, but still require the user to 'make key' decisions.

Worksheet Exercises Data

a. Survey of 6th form students' career
    preferences.

	A	B
1	Career choices	Frequency
2	Banking	12
3	Commerce	22
4	Industry	32
5	Small business	12
6	Social service	25
7	Teaching	12

b. Survey of highest qualifications
    among staff in a school.

	A	B
1	Qualifications	Frequency
2	PhD/EdD	3
3	MPhil	2
4	MSc/MA/MEd	4
5	BAEd/BEd or BSc/BA w/PGCE	13
6	BSc/BA	3
7	Cert Ed	2

c. Survey in a. above with frequencies changed to
    percentages.

	A	B	C
1	Career choices	Frequency	Percent
2	Banking	12	10.4%
3	Commerce	22	19.1%
4	Industry	32	27.8%
5	Small business	12	10.4%
6	Social service	25	21.7%
7	Teaching	12	10.4%
8	Total:	115	100.0%

d. Survey of sample of graduates to find typical starting salaries.

	A	B
1	Salary (×1000)	Frequency
2	4–5	1
3	5–6	3
4	6–7	2
5	7–8	5
6	8–9	8
7	9–10	13
8	10–11	16
9	11–12	15
10	12–13	12
11	13–14	9
12	14–15	7
13	15–16	5
14	16–17	3
15	17–18	1
16	18–19	1

Model Answers

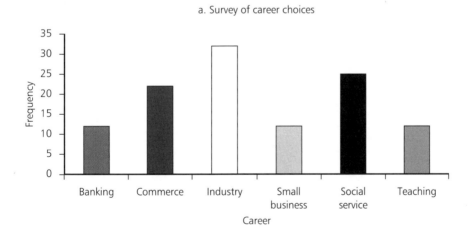

a. Survey of career choices

b. Qualifications of staff

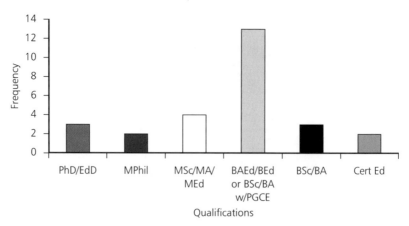

b. Qualifications of staff with order reversed

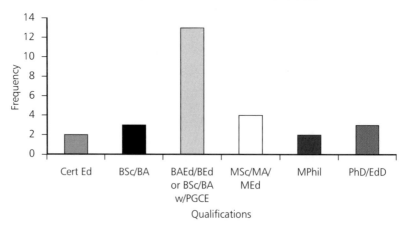

c. Percentages of career choices among students

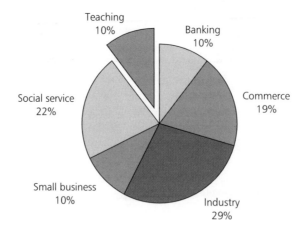

d. Starting salaries for sample of new graduates

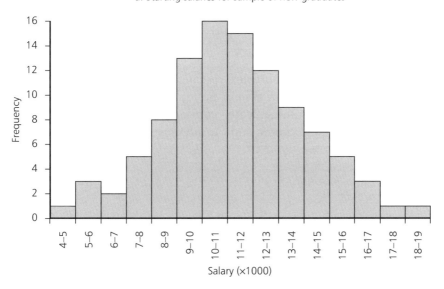

d. Starting salaries for sample of new graduates

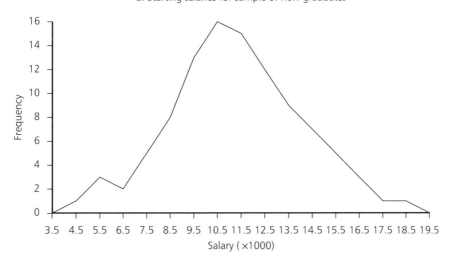

Now try Activity 5.7.

ACTIVITY 5.7

Find one or more journal articles, research papers or reports that use
charts or graphs to display results. Evaluate the use of these in terms
of their ability to communicate, considering both criteria for the
design of graphs and charts, and the inferences or conclusions drawn
from them. Are they justified?

6

Descriptive Statistics

Indicators of Central Tendency and Variability

Graphs and charts are often very good at giving us a picture of group characteristics, but often journals do not publish them, either because of demands for space, or because it is assumed that a few numerical characteristics for groups will conjure up images of these graphs in the minds of the readers. This chapter will not only introduce these numerical indicators, but draw links to the graphs that they imply to help you to visualize them when reading articles.

In order to describe characteristics and tendencies of groups, researchers use several techniques, the most visual being that of graphs and charts. For histograms and frequency polygons, it is not just the immediate knowledge of the height of specific bars or points that is of interest, the overall shape of the graph will also convey important information. When the graphs themselves are not provided in research reports, but left to the reader's imagination, visualizing a graph will depend upon understanding some statistics that tell where the centre is and indicate its width and general shape. First, some common shapes of distributions will be introduced.

SHAPES OF DISTRIBUTIONS

Natural variation in performance for a number of human traits will ideally result in a bell-shaped curve, the 'normal' distribution, when data from a frequency distribution is plotted as a histogram or frequency polygon. Recall that this variability was quantified as the *variance* that was a contributing factor in defining and calculating reliability in Chapter 4. A wide variety of human characteristics, such as height and weight at a given age, will demonstrate this variability by forming a normal distribution for the whole population or a truly representative sample. Adolphe Quetelet is considered to be the mathematician who, in the late 1800s, fathered the theory that human traits follow the normal curve.

As a consequence, mental measuring instruments have often been designed specifically to generate a normal distribution of scores, particularly for cases where the designers argue that the underlying trait being measured is normally distributed in the population being considered. Intelligence as

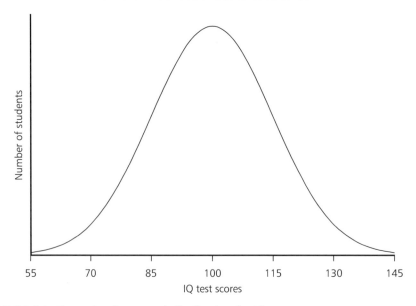

FIGURE 6.1 *Example of a normal distribution for IQ test scores*

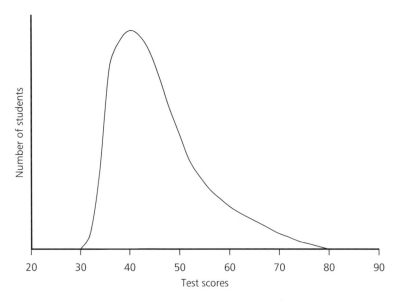

FIGURE 6.2   *Example of a positively skewed distribution for a
                    measured trait*

measured by an IQ test will provide such a distribution for representative
samples of an age group, such as the one shown in Figure 6.1, but this is only
because the tests have been designed to produce results that form such a
curve. In fact, many of the early US Army Alpha Intelligence Tests (*c.* 1921)
generate positively skewed distributions, with a long tail at the high end of

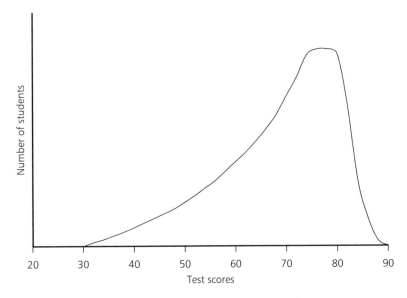

FIGURE 6.3   *Example of a negatively skewed distribution for a measured trait*

the graph (Dorfman, 1978), such as illustrated in Figure 6.2. In other words, intelligence is not necessarily normally distributed just because IQ tests produce a normal distribution. At present, with no means of measuring intelligence other than tests from which we infer its level from scores, the argument about the true underlying distribution in the population of all humans rages on.

Most psychologists still argue that intelligence is normally distributed and as a consequence, psychometricians ensure that IQ tests produce normal distributions of results. It is processes employed during test construction that make it highly probable the instrument will generate scores forming such a distribution for representative samples of the population. This involves selecting questions that provide the optimal amount of spread in scores.

Alternatively, tests designed by teachers and examination boards may well be *criterion referenced* (actual grades are determined by comparing scores against specific predetermined criteria) rather than *norm referenced* (designed to produce a normal distribution with grades based on how examinees perform relative to each other). The design of such tests makes no assumptions about the shape of the distribution of scores and, therefore, the choice of the questions does not force the shape one way or another. There has been a tendency for criterion-referenced tests to produce negatively skewed distributions (with long tails at the low end) such as the one shown in Figure 6.3. Since the objectives and criteria for success for such tests tend to be well defined and well understood by the examinees, they tend to be better prepared for them, and consequently scores tend to bunch towards the high end.

While other shapes will appear, these three basic categories of distributions will suffice for the following discussion on choice of statistics (numbers) that would best describe a group characteristic. Some other shapes will be discussed later. Frequently in social science research, it is *assumed* that the distribution of scores on questionnaires or other instruments is normally distributed, without showing any evidence. This is based upon similar arguments for assuming intelligence is normally distributed and often presented without corroborating evidence. As a reader, you may not have recourse to the raw data and must trust that the researcher has checked it, but rest assured not all traits or characteristics are normally distributed. For example, income across most societies has a long tail containing a relatively few high-income people and would produce a graph with a shape like that of Figure 6.2.

Measures of central tendency

Usually researchers use a numerical characteristic to describe a group as a whole, rather than presenting lists of individual scores, frequency tables or even graphs, as noted earlier. A number that gives a typical score or measure for the group, one that indicates what the members of the group tended to do, provides a means of communicating and even comparing groups to each other. These *measures of central tendency* identify the point on a distribution around which all the other scores tend to group. There are several and the process of deciding which is most appropriate involves looking at the shape of the distribution, since some measures are more appropriate than others for certain shapes of graphs.

The best indication of how a group as a whole has performed on a trait that is normally distributed (the scores produce the bell-shaped curve of Figure 6.1) is given by the measure of central tendency called the arithmetic average or the *mean*. This is found simply by adding all the scores and dividing by the number being measured, tested or examined. For example, IQ tests have been designed so that the 'average' IQ score for a population is 100. The mean is the most appropriate for a normally distributed characteristic if for no other reason than half the scores will be below the average and half above. This definition of the mean is more specific than that possibly implied by the everyday usage of the term, average. Having an 'above-average' or 'below-average' IQ tells little except that one is in the upper half or lower half of a normal distribution. To say that someone is 'average' is basically meaningless, at least in the world of statistics.

The word 'average' is not very specific either, since it can apply to other measures of central tendency. Another one, the *median*, divides a distribution of any shape in half: in other words, half the subjects' scores in a skewed distribution, such as shown in Figure 6.4, will be below the median (but now *not* below the mean) and half above. Consequently, half the area under the graph will be below the median and half above. Thus it is a better indicator of central tendency for non-normal distributions than the mean.

The *mode* is nothing more than the score interval with the highest frequency: the interval of the peak. It is most appropriately used for ordinal data, where means and medians cannot be calculated. For example, the shoe

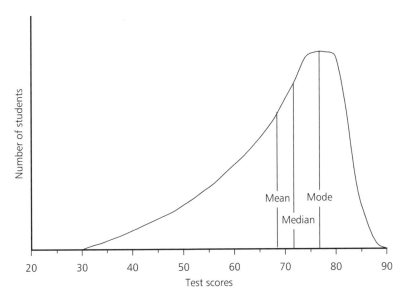

FIGURE 6.4   *A skewed distribution showing mean, median and mode*

shop may use the mode for shoe width when ordering a new variety of shoes to try to sell, since this is the width most people have. For a perfectly normal (bell-shaped) distribution, the mean, median and mode are all at the same place. For distributions of interval or ratio data, the mean or median will tell where the dividing line is such that half are above and half are below, but neither number alone tells much about the shape of the graph. If both have the same value, then it may be a normal distribution, whereas if the median were greater than the mean (as in Figure 6.4), then it might be negatively skewed, and if the mean were greater than the median, then it might be positively skewed. But another value is needed to give a more accurate indication of the shape of the graph, particularly when it has not been provided and the reader has to imagine what it will look like.

Indicator of variability for normal distributions: the standard deviation

When a graph is presented, additional meaningful information can be readily extracted by looking at its shape. The width of the curve indicates by how much scores for a trait vary round the mean and the area under the total curve gives the number of persons being measured. The relative width of a normal distribution, and consequently the degree of trait variance, is indicated by its *standard deviation* from the mean. The calculation of this statistic was carried out in Chapter 4 by finding the square root of the variance (Activity 4.3) and is relatively easy to carry out using many pocket calculators and spreadsheets.

Since the normal distribution is based upon a curve generated by a mathematical equation, it has well-understood characteristics, such as the distribution of the area under the curve. The standard deviation provides a

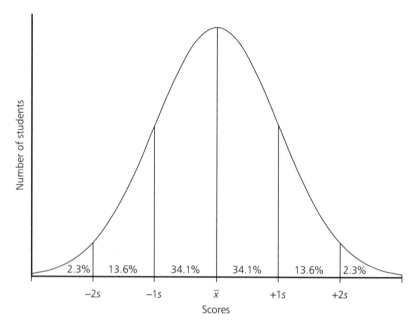

FIGURE 6.5　*Areas under the normal distribution for each standard
deviation*

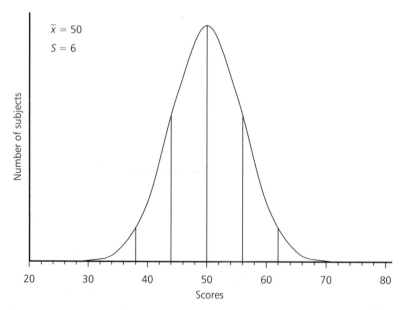

FIGURE 6.6　*Normal distribution of scores, with a mean of 50 and standard
deviation of 6*

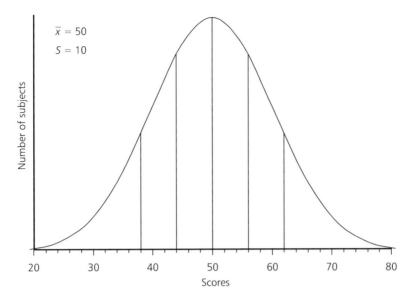

FIGURE 6.7   *Normal distribution of scores, with a mean of 50 and standard deviation of 10*

mechanism for describing this ideal distribution, attributes which tend to be applied to any normal-appearing distribution. In particular, a true normal distribution will have about 34% of the area (or 34% of the scores) fall within each of the first standard deviations on either side of the mean. Thus about 68% are within one standard deviation from the mean, as shown by the *area under the curve* of the marked section in Figure 6.5. Each of the second standard deviations contains about 13.6% and the third about 2.3%. Thus 95.6% of the area (or scores) of a true normal distribution will fall within two standard deviations from the mean.

The standard deviation also provides a clue about the shape of the curve: the larger it is, the broader the bell-shaped curve, as seen by comparing the two distributions in Figures 6.6 and 6.7. Thus with the mean and standard deviation, it is possible to picture a bell-shaped curve with centre at the mean and bulge about the size of the standard deviation. This may be of value to a reader of reports, since often graphs are not provided and only the statistics are presented.

ALGEBRAIC SYMBOLS

Various systems of symbols are used in articles, reports and textbooks on statistics, so it is best to define what will be used in this book. In figures and tables, as well as the formulae in the text, the following will be used:

continued

a	the sample group designation (it could be b, c, d, ...)
$\bar{x}_a$	the mean score for sample group a
x_i	individual scores, such that $i = 1, 2, 3, \ldots , n$; thus x_1 is the score for subject 1, x_2 is the score for subject 2, etc.
S_a	standard deviation of scores for sample group a
n_a	sample size of group a
$\sim$ or $\cong$	means approximately equal to
μ	population mean score
σ	population standard deviation
Σ	shorthand for 'add up all that follows'. An example of a more detailed version of this is

$$\sum_{i=1}^{n} x_i$$

which is shorthand for 'add up all n values for x_i as i goes from 1 to n; in other words, $x_1 + x_2 + x_3 + \cdots + x_n'$.

CALCULATING MEANS AND STANDARD DEVIATIONS

Of the measures of central tendency and variability, means and standard deviations are the ones most often presented in reports, having been calculated from raw data. This can be done by hand or on a calculator but there are functions built in on spreadsheets that make the task much easier.

Mean

The mean was defined as the sum of all the scores of a set of subjects divided by the number of subjects. Mathematically, the mean represented by $\bar{x}$, is defined as

$$\bar{x} \equiv \frac{\sum_{i=1}^{n} x_i}{n} \tag{6.1}$$

where each x_i is an individual score for subjects 1 to n, and n is the total number of subjects. This equation simply says:

Add together all the individual scores, x_i, where i goes from 1 to n, and then divide by the total number of subjects, n.

In Excel, this is the =AVERAGE(range of scores) function.

Standard deviation

There are two commonly used calculations for standard deviation that depend upon to whom one is referring. First, there is the calculation that simply gives the value for groups, either samples, S, or whole populations, σ. This is expressed as the square root of the variance, which was the sum of the squares of the difference between each subject's score and the mean, divided by the number of subjects. Expressed mathematically for a sample group as

$$S = \sqrt{\frac{\sum_{i=1}^{n}(x_i - \bar{x})^2}{n}} \qquad (6.2)$$

where there are n subjects in the sample that has a mean $\bar{x}$. This equation says, starting from the inside and working out:

Find the difference for each score x_i and the mean of all the scores, $\bar{x}$, and square this difference. Then add all of these squared differences together and divide the total by the number of subjects, n. Finally, find the square root of this number.

As can be seen, the sum is not dependent on whether each sample score is larger or smaller than the mean. If the differences had not been squared each time, then the sum would likely have been close to zero with some subjects above the mean and some below. In Excel, this is found using the =STDEVP(range of scores) function.

Sometimes it is desirable to provide an *unbiased estimate of the population standard deviation, s,* from sample data. This requires dividing by $n-1$ instead of n, as shown:

$$s = \sqrt{\frac{\sum_{i=1}^{n}(x_i - \bar{x})^2}{n-1}} \qquad (6.3)$$

Which is presented will depend upon the point the report is trying to make: describe a group or make an inference about the larger population. Some statistical tests require the use of equation (6.3) rather than (6.2), as we will see later. This is calculated in Excel using the =STDEV(range of scores) function (note that the other function has a P for population). Carry out Activity 6.1 at this time.

TABLE 6.1 *Sample data for students answering a set of questions*

	A	B
	A	**B**
1	**Subject**	**Score**
2	Mary	34
3	John	22
4	Henry	37
5	Albert	43
6	Sam	26
7	Anne	41
8	Sue	33
9	Jane	29
10	Fred	39
11	Albert	30
12	**Mean =**	
13	**Std Dev =**	
14	**Est Pop SD =**	

ACTIVITY 6.1

Using the data from a questionnaire shown in Table 6.1, enter it on a new worksheet and find the sample mean, sample standard deviation and the unbiased estimate of the population standard deviation using the Excel functions. (Answers are at the end of the chapter.)

Comparing distributions

Since it is not easy mentally to compare a real distribution with the ideal one implied by the mean and standard deviation, a visual technique is useful. Spreadsheets have functions that make this task relatively easy and allow you to overlay one graph on the other. Carry out Activity 6.2 at this time.

ACTIVITY 6.2

Using an Excel worksheet, this activity will allow you to generate an ideal normal distribution and then plot the raw data on top of it to see how close the two curves are.

(a) Set up the worksheet shown in Table 6.2 below. Note that you will enter numbers only in the shaded cells. In the other cells, enter the equations as shown. When you change the numbers in the shaded cells, these values will change automatically.

continued

(b) Block off cells **A6:C25** as your source of data, and call up the Chart Wizard:

    Step 1: Choose **XY Scatter** and the graph that is the smoothed lines without markers, and then click on **Next>**.

    Step 2: Presents a graph so you can confirm your choice; if acceptable, click on **Next>**.

    Step 3: Allows you to change the graph (e.g. remove gridlines, add chart and axis titles) and then click on **Next>**.

    Step 4: Allows you to save it on a separate sheet or next to the data.

This will initially plot one curve as shown in Figure 6.8.

(c) Now in column **C**, under **Real** in the shaded cells, type in the data from Table 5.4, using the centres of the intervals. How close is this second curve to the ideal? It should look like Figure 5.7 overlaid on the ideal curve below (though narrower due to the different x-axis).

Diseases of the curve

Earlier, three basic categories of curves were described: normal, positively skewed and negatively skewed. If researchers are rigorous, they will not use means and standard deviations as the measures of central tendency and variance for groups whose data is too skewed. This should also influence the types of statistical test chosen, as will be seen in later chapters. How much is 'too skewed' is an issue that will be addressed later.

To add to the complexity, not all normally appearing distributions are truly normal. Figure 6.9 illustrates what is meant by *kurtosis*, distributions that are somewhat normal in appearance, but do not really fit the ideal, mathematically generated normal distribution. A curve that is more narrow and peaked than an expected normal distribution is referred to as *leptokurtic* and one that is more short and rounded is referred to as *platykurtic*. While the calculation of the mean and standard deviation for each of these three curves from their respective raw data produces the same mean and standard deviation, only the areas under the normal distribution correspond to the percentages shown in Figure 6.5. As with skewness, this can affect the types of statistical tests that can be used with a set of data, and the issue will be addressed later.

There are mathematical ways of describing skewness and kurtosis (a perfectly normal curve will be 0.0 for both), but the calculations of these indicators are beyond the scope of this book (see e.g. Ferguson, 1976; Blalock, 1979).

In the real world of research, raw data for a sample may not suffer from skewness or kurtosis, but may have other shapes. Figure 6.10 shows a few

TABLE 6.2 *Worksheet for generating an ideal normal distribution*

	A	B	C	
1	mean =	101		
2	Std dev =	10		
3	n =	210		
4	Interval width =	5		
5				
6	Scores	Ideal	Real	=B$4*B$3*NORMDIST(A7,B$1, B$2,0) & **Copy** down to line 22
7	63.0	0.03 ◄		
8	68.0 ◄	0.18		
9	73.0	0.83		=A7+$B$4 & **Copy** down to line 22
10	78.0	2.97		
11	83.0	8.29		
12	88.0	17.99		
13	93.0	30.42		
14	98.0	40.05		
15	103.0	41.06		
16	108.0	32.79		
17	113.0	20.39		
18	118.0	9.88		
19	123.0	3.72		
20	128.0	1.09		
21	133.0	0.25		
22	138.0	0.04		
23	*138.0* ◄			=A23
24	*101.0*	0.00		
25	*101.0*	55.00		=B$1
26	Total =	209.99	0.00 ◄	=SUM(C7:C22) & **Copy** to B26

possibilities, such as a nearly flat distribution, a bi-modal (having two modes or peaks) distribution, U-shaped and J-shaped. Like those characteristics that produce skewed distributions, these may result from the situations where the true traits simply are not normally distributed, the sample is not representative of the population for a normally distributed trait, or the measuring instrument is faulty. Bi-modal distributions are interesting in that they might indicate the presence of *two* distinct groups in a sample; in other words, an uncontrolled extraneous variable may have had an affect on the scores.

Interpreting normal distribution data

It is possible to glean a certain amount of information when provided with the mean and standard deviation alone. For example, as mentioned earlier,

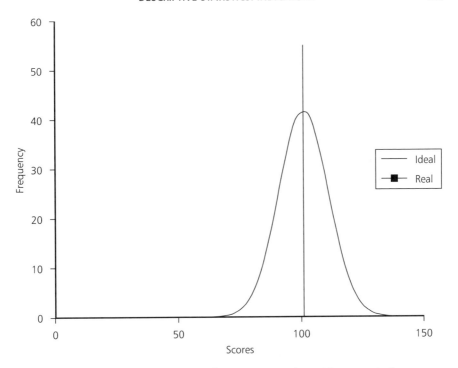

FIGURE 6.8   The 'ideal' normal curve for x̄ = 101, and s = 10, generated
              from the worksheet in Table 6.2

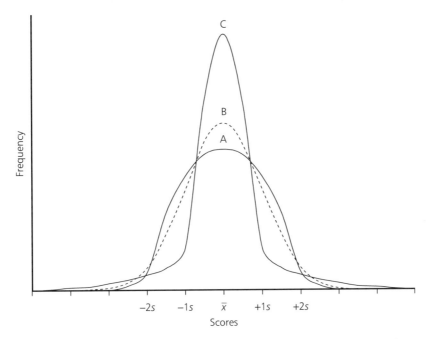

FIGURE 6.9   Three graphs whose data would generate the same mean and
              standard deviation, but A is platykurtic, B is normal and C is
              leptokurtic

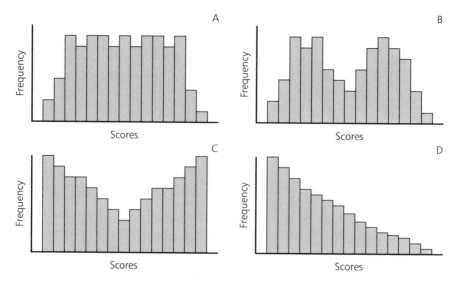

FIGURE 6.10   *Non-normal distributions: A, flat; B, bi-modal; C, U-shaped;*
D, J-shaped

IQ tests are actually designed to have a mean of 100 and a standard deviation of 15. Thus, about 68% of all persons taking an IQ test should have an
IQ of between 85 and 115. One way of indicating an individual's performance is by stating his/her position on the horizontal axis in terms of percentage of examinees performing below this position, the *percentile group*. In
other words, if John did better than 67% of the other people taking an exam,
then John was in the 67th percentile group. If you have an IQ score of 115,
one standard deviation above the mean, then your score is better than 84%
of all persons taking that examination (50% below the mean plus 34% up to
the first standard deviation). This also means that, visually, 84% of the area
under the curve is to the left, as shown in Figure 6.11.

One can identify where in a distribution an individual score lies when the
mean and standard deviation are known. It is relatively easy to convert a
raw score into a number of standard deviations, called *z-scores*, which can be
found in a table to see exactly what percentile group that score falls in:

$$z\text{-score} = \frac{\text{raw score} - \text{mean}}{\text{standard deviation}}$$

which can be written mathematically as

$$z = \frac{x_i - \bar{x}}{s}$$

For example, an IQ score of 92 would be

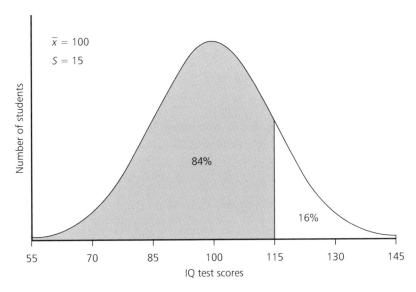

FIGURE 6.11 *The 84th percentile group for IQ test scores*

TABLE 6.3 *Abridged z-score table for determining percentiles for (area under) a normal distribution (generated in Excel)*

z-score	% between mean and z	z-score	% between mean and z	z-score	% between mean and z
0.00	0.00	1.10	36.43	2.10	48.21
0.10	3.98	1.20	38.49	2.20	48.61
0.20	7.93	1.30	40.32	2.30	48.93
0.30	11.79	1.40	41.92	2.40	49.18
0.40	15.54	1.50	43.32	2.50	49.38
0.50	19.15	1.60	44.52	2.60	49.53
0.60	22.57	1.70	45.54	2.70	49.65
0.70	25.80	1.80	46.41	2.80	49.74
0.80	28.81	1.90	47.13	2.90	49.81
0.90	31.59	2.00	47.72	3.00	49.87
1.00	34.13			etc.	etc.

$$z\text{-score} = \frac{92 - 100}{15} = \frac{-8}{15} = -0.53$$

or 0.53 standard deviations *below* the mean. Looking this up in Table 6.3 reveals that the score corresponds to a percentage score of between 19.15% and 22.57%, or about 20.0% (estimate) below the mean. (A longer unabridged table would give you this percentage directly.) Subtracting this from the 50% total below the mean results in this score being in the 30th percentile. In other words, this person scored higher than 30% of the persons taking this test. This simply tells how a person with this score performed with respect to all the others. What decisions are made based upon such results is the domain of the researchers or other persons using this data. Now try Activity 6.3.

ACTIVITY 6.3

Find the percentile group for IQ test scores of 110, 98 and 120, using Table 6.3. The answers are at the end of this chapter.

Treating diseased curves as normal

What are the consequences of a researcher using the mean and standard deviation for distributions that are not normal, curves that have kurtosis, skewness, are bi-modal, etc.? It really does depend on just how far they deviate from being truly normal and this is an issue that will be raised again in later chapters when considering various statistical tests that assume normality. It is of interest, though, to consider just how the basic interpretation of information can differ depending on whether raw data is used or a distribution generated from a calculated mean and standard deviation.

Several years ago, a colleague who introduced an independent learning (individualized instruction) programme in his A-level physics class (roughly equivalent to American first-year university physics for engineering/science students) gave an end-of-year examination that produced a definite bi-modal distribution. Though the original data has long been lost, it was something like that in Table 6.4. From this ratio data (percentage of correct questions), the mean and standard deviation shown have been calculated. The fifth column shows the z-scores based upon these, and the sixth column shows the equivalent interval frequencies that would exist if this were a truly normal distribution with the mean and standard deviation given. Note how the frequencies in the third and sixth columns begin to diverge. This is even more clearly illustrated when the data from the two columns is plotted as a frequency polygon using the midpoints of intervals, as shown in Figure 6.12. If one were to use the mean, standard deviation and z-scores to interpret placement of individuals having taken this class test, the interpretation would deviate considerably from reality.

My colleague did suggest an interesting hypothesis to explain the distribution. While the top mode was higher than past means, the bottom mode was lower, suggesting that two groups of students existed: those that actually enjoyed using independent learning materials and those that did not, their attitudes tending to affect their commitment and subsequent performance. An interesting hypothesis, but unfortunately one that was not followed by a rigorous research study. Now carry out Activity 6.4.

TABLE 6.4 *Data for a bi-modal distribution that has a mean, $\bar{x}$ = 59.2, standard deviation, S = 18.0, and sample size, n = 143*

Midpoint	Interval	Raw data interval frequencies	Cumulative frequencies	z-scores (based on mean and s.d.)	Interval frequencies based on z-scores	Cumulative frequencies based on z-scores
13	11–15			-2.57	0.6	0.7
18	16–20	0		-2.29	1.2	1.6
23	21–25	1	1	-2.01	2.1	3.2
28	26–30	5	6	-1.73	3.5	5.9
33	31–35	8	14	-1.46	5.5	10.4
38	36–40	12	26	-1.18	7.9	17.1
43	41–45	19	45	-0.90	10.6	26.3
48	46–50	11	56	-0.62	13.1	38.2
53	51–55	8	64	-0.34	14.9	52.2
58	56–60	6	70		15.8	67.7
63	61–65	9	79	0.21	15.5	83.5
68	66–70	12	91	0.49	14.1	98.3
73	71–75	21	112	0.77	11.8	111.3
78	76–80	14	126	1.04	9.2	121.8
83	81–85	9	135	1.32	6.6	129.7
88	86–90	6	141	1.60	4.4	135.2
93	91–95	2	143	1.88	2.7	138.7
98	96–100	0		2.16	1.6	140.8
103	101–105			2.43	0.8	141.9

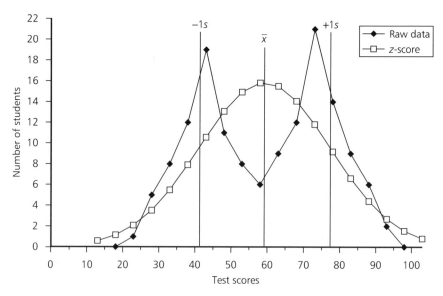

FIGURE 6.12   *Bi-modal distribution from raw data frequencies and an*
implied normal distribution based upon calculated mean
and standard deviation, using data from Table 6.4

ACTIVITY 6.4

Consider the data in Table 6.4 and Figure 6.12 and let us examine some of the consequences of assuming that this is a normal distribution. In Table 6.4, one standard deviation each side of the mean corresponds roughly to the real intervals 40.5 and 75.5 (marked with the square bracket [on the table).

(a) Using these limits, find the sums of all the 'Raw data frequencies' and the 'Frequencies based on z-scores' between +1 and −1 standard deviation.

(b) Divide each of these two numbers by n_a = 143 and multiply by 100 to get the percentage in the interval of $1s_a$ either side of the mean.

(c) How do these compare with what one would expect (see Figure 6.5)?

(d) On the graph in Figure 6.12, note the dashed vertical lines at −1s and +1s. Visually compare the areas under each of the two curves for the intervals of one standard deviation either side of the mean. How close is the actual bi-modal distribution to the normal distribution in terms of area?

(Answers are at the end of the chapter.)

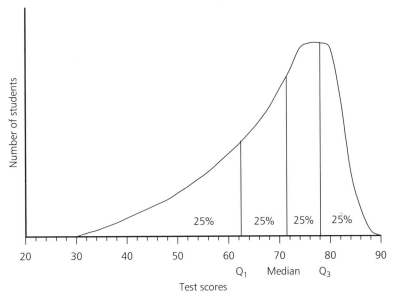

FIGURE 6.13   *Median with first (Q_1) and third (Q_3) quartiles for a negatively skewed distribution*

Alternative measures of variability for non-normal distributions

If the distribution of scores deviates considerably from the bell shape, then the standard deviation will not be the best indicator of variability. Since not all traits or the operational definitions of traits produce normal distributions, then means and standard deviations are not always appropriate. Alternatives, therefore, may be more appropriate.

Quartiles are an extension of the median, which together break up a distribution into four equal areas under the curve, each section containing 25% of the subjects. This indicator of variability is more appropriate for non-normal distributions, giving a better indication of the spread of scores, and makes no assumptions about the shape of the distribution. Figure 6.13 shows the median and quartiles for a skewed distribution.

The least informative indicator of variability is the *range*, simply describing the maximum and minimum scores for the measured trait. It is appropriate for distributions that have strange and unusual shapes, for small sets of data for which there is not a sufficiently large set of numbers even to plot a graph. The range does not tell us anything about the shape of a distribution, just its limits.

Finally, some studies require only descriptive statistics and consequently present just means and standard deviations, tables, graphs and charts, carrying out no statistical tests. As Lehmann and Mehrens (1979) note, a descriptive study is one that is primarily intended to describe existing conditions and not to make predictions or establish causal relationships. Surveys are often attempting to find out what exists in a large population through sampling, while case studies investigate a small population in greater depth. In both cases, the potential problems associated with the measurement of traits plus displaying and interpreting results must be considered. The following criteria should provide a means of rating studies according to their use of these tools.

CRITERIA FOR DESCRIPTIVE STATISTICS

This section of the Profiling Sheet will require you to integrate more complex concepts and ideas when judging a report. You will find that with graphs and charts, aesthetics even comes into the decision. Thus, the levels listed below are related primarily to correctness of use; how effective a graph or chart is in communicating results is something you will want to note in your comments.

Appropriate display of data and results   Appropriate choice of graphs and charts, measure of central tendency, and indicator of variability for the type of data (nominal, ordinal, interval or ratio) and the shape of the distribution of raw data.

Some inadequacies, incorrectness in data/results display   You may want to include just plain poor displays under this level, since most inappropriate choices of graphs produce misleading information (see below).

Other methods of displaying data/results would be more appropriate
For example, histograms have been used instead of bar charts for ordinal data, means and standard deviations have been used instead of medians and quartiles for very skewed or other non-normal distributions.

Serious misconceptions through use of descriptive statistics   For example, graphs with no vertical axis zero, exaggerating fluctuations or distribution shape.

Intentionally misleading use of descriptive statistics   By now, you should be able to tell when they are trying to deceive you! While this category will apply frequently to advertising that purports to use statistics, it is not often applicable to professionally produced research reports. Most of the sins manifest in academic research are due to ignorance or poor judgement rather than malice.

In some situations when judging the quality of descriptive statistics, it will be the lack of graphical representations that will impede understanding. There is also the danger that the substitution of means and standard deviations for graphs of raw data will cover up the true non-normality of the shape of the distributions. As will be seen in the following chapters, there is an underlying assumption that all the distributions are (nearly) normal, and have roughly the same variance (and consequently the same standard deviation, i.e. shape) for specific tests, and when they are not, alternatives should be used. Unfortunately, what is 'near enough' is not always simple to determine! Finish this chapter by doing Activity 6.5.

ACTIVITY 6.5

Select several articles that use descriptive statistics, including graphs and charts where possible, and evaluate them using the Profiling Sheet at the end of the chapter. Duplicate it as needed and add comments where appropriate.

ANSWERS

Activity 6.1

Mean = 33.4; std dev. = 6.41; est. pop. std dev. = 6.75

Activity 6.3 (approximate)

110: z-score = +0.667, thus 24.72% above the mean or 74.72 percentile

98: z-score = –0.133, thus 5.30% below the mean or 44.70 percentile

120: z-score = +1.333, thus 40.85% above the mean or 90.85 percentile

Activity 6.4

(a) Actual for bi-modal distribution = 86; z-score generated = 95.7.
(b) Actual for bi-modal distribution = 60%; z-score generated = 67%.
(c) Expected = 34.1 + 34.1 = 68.2%, thus the z-score percentage is close; the actual for the bi-modal distribution percentage is not so close.
(d) The area under the actual bi-modal distribution is obviously much smaller than what is expected for a normal distribution for 1s either side of the mean. This simply illustrates the weakness of using mean and standard deviation to describe a non-normal distribution.

Profiling Sheet: *Understanding Social Science Research,* © Thomas R. Black, 2001

Article: _____   **Type of Study:** ❏ Descriptive, ❏ Survey/correlational, ❏ *Ex post facto,* ❏ Experimental/quasi-experimental.

Questions/ hypotheses	Representativeness	Ethics and Confidentiality	Data Quality I	Data Quality II	Descriptive Statistics
Valid question or hypothesis based on accepted theory with well-justified referenced support	Whole population	Ethical standards met and data sufficiently confidential that no individuals or institutions can be identified	Educationally, sociologically, psychologically, etc., significant and manageable number of concepts	Commercially or professionally produced/tested with high validity, reliability and objectivity (V, R, O)	Appropriate display of data and results as statistics or in tables and/or graphs, clearly labelled
Valid question or hypothesis based on own theory, well justified	Random selection from a well-specified population		Limited academic significance, very narrow perspective	Project or personally produced/tested with high V, R, O	Some inadequacies in presentation of tables/graphs
Credible question/ hypothesis but alternative possible, or too extensive/global, or support missing	Purposive sample from a well-specified population, with justification for representativeness	Ethical issues not addressed or confidentiality not discussed when it should have been	Large number of concepts, potentially confusing	Commercially or project produced with moderate V, R, O	Other methods of displaying statistics, graphs or charts would have been more appropriate
Weak question/ hypothesis, or poorly stated, or justified with inappropriate references	Volunteers or convenience, with no justification of representativeness	Ethical issues not addressed and/or some loss of confidentiality	Too many concepts and variables investigated to provide meaningful results	Commercially or project produced with low V, R, O, or no information provided	Serious misconceptions encouraged owing to nature of graphical display of results
No question or hypothesis stated, or inconsistent with known facts	Unidentified group	Ethical standards violated and/or subjects endangered owing to no confidentiality	Trivial concepts, not academically significant	Inappropriate instrument for the variables/concepts described	Intentionally misleading use of descriptive statistics

Comments and justification for classification:

7

Statistical Inference

One way of looking at the human condition is to consider life as a continuous series of probabilistic events, most often having multiple causal factors. Insurance companies actually calculate premiums based on the probabilities that certain events will occur. Thus if the insurance premium for the contents of your house is higher than a friend's who lives in a different town in a comparable house, then this more than likely reflects the difference in frequency of burglaries over the past year in the two areas. Your health insurance rates will increase dramatically if you ski, hang-glide or parachute for a hobby, since the probability of being injured is higher.

On a more mundane level, consider the common cold. What causes a cold? A virus, you say. Well then, why is it you are the only one in your family not to get a cold when everyone else in the house has it? Whether or not you actually suffer from the cold virus depends on a number of factors, or variables, such as which cold virus it is (apparently it mutates all the time) and whether or not you have a resistance to that one, your relative health, including getting enough sleep and eating a well-balanced diet, proximity to a sneezer, the quality of the ventilation in the house, the relative humidity of the air (air-borne viruses like it damp), etc. It would be virtually impossible to determine why you, as an individual, at a specific time, did (or did not) get a cold when others did. Our knowledge of the factors involved in the spread of other diseases varies in terms of our ability to determine total causality, covering all possible variables. History is littered with plagues that decimate sizeable portions, but not all, of populations. While it often is not possible, nor in the long run profitable, to identify causes with respect to individuals, it is possible to determine *tendencies of groups* to respond to carefully isolated factors, even when it is suspected that there is multiple causality. The difficulty is determining whether the occurrence of an event has happened by chance, as the result of uncontrolled factors, or as the result of the factor(s) under consideration.

What can a statistical test tell a researcher? It can *not* prove that one variable caused another, but it can tell whether the observed result generated by a group experiencing one variable is likely to have occurred as a random event due to natural variability, or not. If the test says that it is unlikely that the result occurred by chance alone, it is still up to the researcher to prove that the one variable was the only possible cause. Statistical tests are like the 'idiot lights' on the dashboard of your car: they only tell you that *something* has happened, for example that there is a difference between groups, but not exactly what caused it. If the OIL light comes on, it could mean the engine is low on oil, the engine bearings have worn out, the signal-sending device on the engine is broken, or a wire has shorted out to the light. The motorist obviously checks the oil level first, but if that is adequate, then it is time to call the mechanic, who will try to find the reason for the light being on. In the social sciences, the researcher should plan a study such that when the light comes on (the statistics indicate that something probably happened), then there are predicted, defensible relationships, links or causes.

As noted earlier, inferential statistics involve using data collected from samples to make inferences about a larger population or populations. The complication is that most research employs samples (which are *probably* representative) and *includes* the collection of data that provides measures of group characteristics or tendencies, often means and standard deviations. Using this information, there is a desire to compare groups to determine whether differences really exist. If so, then this difference will ultimately extend back to the original populations, however they are defined. All of this depends heavily upon probability, and it is never possible to speak about relationships with absolute certainty, a fact that causes a distinct amount of mental anguish for most people who feel that events should have a high degree of certainty. But this is just part of the process of building evidence to support the validity of hypotheses and theories.

Thus, to succeed in making one's case in the world of inferential statistics, it is necessary to be in as strong and defensible a position as possible, basically so that the results and conclusions will withstand the onslaught from the competing alternatives hypotheses. These include ones that say there is no relationship, or that other variables are the primary cause of the observed effect. Therefore, a researcher conducting an experimental study should be able to defend any suggestion that a cause and effect relationship exists by undertaking to prove that there are probably no other possible causes than the one(s) identified. In other words, a study must strive to eliminate any competing variables: put simply, there is a high probability nothing else could have done it.

Ex post facto studies using the same statistics will tell whether or not any differences between groups with different life experiences are large enough so that they are considered to be from different populations. While such studies that do find significant differences will not be able to justify causal relationships (the variables tend to be too general and there is insufficient control over components), they will confirm the existence of the differences, assuming the samples are representative of the populations with those life experiences for the trait in question. For example, if there were a significantly lower reading ability for assembly line workers than management personnel, it would *not* mean that being an assembly line worker caused them to have this lower reading ability. What could be said is that assembly line workers do have a lower reading ability, determining *why* would require further research.

Correlational studies, another approach, strive to establish the existence of relationships among variables that are not directly causal in nature; instead there may be a third unknown causal variable for two observed related changes, or a common cause for the two observed variables. For example, as children become older, they gain weight and increase in height, though not necessarily at constant rates. There is a correlation between these two phenomena, gaining in height and weight, but one does not cause the other. The question also arises, is the correlation large enough for the sample size to establish that it is not just a chance occurrence (i.e. it really is not zero) and that the results indicate a relationship in the population?

Ultimately, there arise four interrelated concerns that will influence the validity of inferences made about the population(s) and their characteristics:

1 formulation of the hypothesis
2 representativeness of the samples
3 choice of statistical test(s)
4 interpretation of 'significance'

As seen in Chapter 2, there is a need to state the expected outcomes of inferential statistical research in terms of the null hypothesis: that there will *not* be any statistically significant difference. In other words, it is expected that any differences or changes or relationships found will be attributable to chance alone, natural variation. Even if the null hypothesis is rejected, it only means that the difference or occurrence witnessed *probably* did not occur by chance alone, but was bigger than what would be expected as a result of natural variation within a sample. This probability level traditionally has been set at 5%, which basically means that if a statistical test says that the probability of this event occurring by chance alone is less than 5%, less than 1 chance in 20, then it probably did *not* occur as a random event. At this level, there is something probably influencing the event(s), or at least the event(s) has(have) occurred as the result of some external influence other than natural random fluctuation. Exactly what this influence is, is not made clear by the statistical test. As noted before, it is still up to the researcher to justify that what he/she did, or the variables identified, were the only possible influences, which is the function of the research design.

This chapter will bring together ideas introduced in Chapter 2 on research questions and hypotheses, Chapter 3 on research designs, and the introduction to the normal distribution in Chapter 6. Before the actual choice of statistical tests can be considered, it is necessary to take a brief mathematical look at what underlies statistical inference and significance. This will be done graphically as much as possible, since most decisions are made on the basis of where the means of sets of data are in a normal distribution. Correlational studies and issues related to interpretation of results will be introduced in Chapter 8, and Chapters 9 and 10 will continue the review of inferential statistics by considering experimental and related designs, and some of the tests that are used to decide the acceptability of stated hypotheses.

PROBABILITY AND STATISTICAL INFERENCE

While it is beyond the scope of this book to present probability theory, it is not difficult to see how the concept of probability applies to inferential statistics. In the previous chapter, the possibility that many human characteristics are normally distributed was introduced. For traits that have such distributions, the mean is the most appropriate measure of central tendency and the standard deviation is the most appropriate indicator of variability in that distribution. There is a distinction made when using these to describe populations and samples of populations: the whole population mean and standard deviation are referred to as *parameters*, whereas these values for a sample are referred to as *statistics*.

It is rare, if ever, that we know the population parameters, unless the population is very small, as in a case study. Consequently, sample statistics are used as estimates, which naturally stimulates the question: how good are these? Just as individual scores for a trait vary round a mean forming a normal distribution, the means of samples themselves will vary if a large number of representative samples are taken from a population. If the frequency of these means is plotted on a graph, not surprisingly we find yet another normal distribution. This *distribution of sampling means* will be quite useful in making inferences about the population. Figure 7.1 shows all three distributions for IQ scores: A, an exemplar population distribution with parameters provided; B, a single sample distribution with its statistics; and C, a distribution of sampling means. The IQ score is used here simply because it is one distribution for which the parameters are known, since the tests are designed to produce a mean of 100 and a standard deviation of 15 for all age groups.

Remember that when the term population is used, it refers to a group in which all share a limited range of common characteristics. In social sciences, these are often not obvious to the casual observer and require some form of detailed observation, measurement or questioning of the subjects. So, initially, the question is whether or not a sample as a group is similar enough to the population for the trait or characteristic in question to be considered representative. A statistical test should be able to resolve what is enough.

The first thing to notice in Figure 7.1 is that it is not easy to tell from the low curve B whether or not the sample is typical of the population. The second thing to notice is the standard deviation (and width of the bell-shaped curve) for the distribution of sample means is relatively small compared with the standard deviations for the population and any single sample. Thus it is very unlikely that a truly representative sample will have a mean very different from that of the population. This fact is used in the most basic of inferential statistical tests, deciding whether a sample is to be considered part of a defined population, or part of some other unknown population. To distinguish this standard deviation from that of a sample of the population, the standard deviation of the distribution of sampling means is used, which is known as the *standard error of the mean* (SEM). This will be designated by $\sigma_{\bar{x}}$ if it is calculated from the population parameter, the population standard deviation, σ, and found by

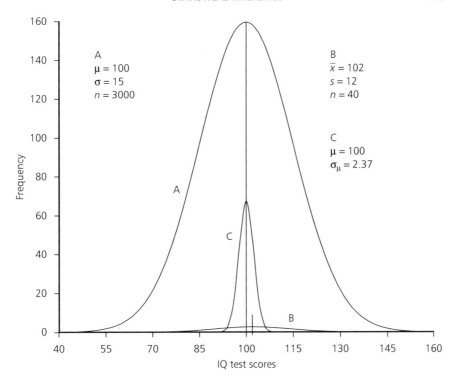

FIGURE 7.1   A, the population distribution of IQ scores for all
3000 11 year olds in a local education authority (LEA); B, a
single exemplar sample distribution of IQ scores of a random
selection of 40 11 year olds in the LEA; and C, the distribution
of sample means for a large number of such random samples
of 40 students

$$\sigma_{\bar{x}} = \frac{\sigma}{\sqrt{n}} \qquad\qquad (7.1)$$

for sample sizes, n.

If an estimate of the standard error of the mean is calculated using statistics, a sample standard deviation, then it will be designated as $s_{\bar{x}}$ and calculated from

$$s_{\bar{x}} = \frac{s_a}{\sqrt{n_a}} \qquad\qquad (7.2)$$

where s_a is the estimate of the population standard deviation of sample group a whose size is n_a. Obviously, the standard error of the mean depends on the size of the samples: if they are very large then the standard error of the mean, and consequently the width of the curve, will be very small.

It is illustrative to consider an example. In order to carry out a study, a researcher selects a sample of 40 students from the LEA population of 3000 11 year olds described in Figure 7.1. They are given an IQ test: the group mean is found to be 106. Is this group typical? Let us first state this question as a null hypothesis:

H_0:   There is no significant difference between the IQ of the sample group and that of any other random sample of 40 taken from the population.

In normal English, we would say that we expect that the sample *is* representative of the population for this trait. Here the sample mean will be used to resolve the issue. To make the decision, it is necessary to zoom in on distribution C in Figure 7.1, the sampling means, which is shown enlarged in Figure 7.2. The question now becomes one that is stated in terms of probabilities:

What is the probability that a sample of 40 with a mean of 106 would be randomly chosen from the population?

Recall that the area under the distribution for a range of scores represents the percentage of people (or sample means) having scores within that range (see Figure 6.5 in Chapter 6). Using Table 6.3 in Chapter 6, the number of standard deviations from the mean (SEMs) can be used to determine what percentage of sample means that one would expect below this group's. Using $\sigma_{\bar{x}}$ from Figure 7.2,

$$z = \frac{106 - 100}{2.37} = 2.53$$

Therefore, a sample mean of 106 is 2.53 standard deviations (SEMs) above the population mean, as marked on Figure 7.2. From Table 6.3, this tells us that 49.43% of the sample means would be expected to be between this score and the population mean. Add to this the 50% below the population mean and we find that 99.43% of the sample means should be below this. Stated positively ($100\% - 99.43\% = 0.57\%$), the probability of this event occurring as an expectedly random event as shown in Figure 7.2 is

0.57 of a chance in 100

5.7 chances in 1000

57 chances in 10,000

Thus this sample mean does seem to be a highly unlikely event, but what is *unlikely enough* for researchers?

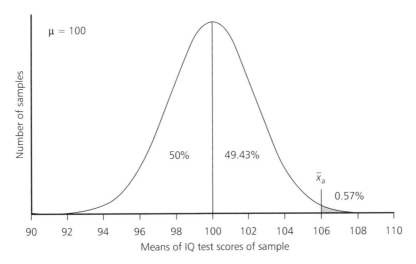

FIGURE 7.2   *Distribution of sampling means (each sample size = 40),*
showing the position of the mean of a single sample, $\bar{x}_a$ = 106

Testing the null hypothesis

For normally distributed traits, those that produce sample means out in either of the tails are highly unlikely. Social science researchers commonly accept that events which occur less frequently than 1 in 20 (5 in 100) are unlikely to have occurred by chance alone and consequently are considered statistically significant. To apply this to a normal distribution would mean that the 5% must be divided between the top and bottom tails of the distribution, with 2.5% for each (there are occasions when all 5% would occur in one tail, but that is the exception, to be discussed later). From Table 6.3 in Chapter 6, the top 2.5% is from 47.5% onward, or (interpolating) 1.96 standard deviations (SEMs) or more from the mean. The ranges of sample means that would be considered *statistically significant*, and result in the rejection of the null hypothesis since they probably did not occur as part of the natural chance variation in the means, are shown in Figure 7.3, as shaded areas.

Thus for the situation above involving the mean IQ of the sample of 11 year olds, the cutting point of 1.96 standard deviations (SEMs) would correspond to 1.96 x 2.37 = 4.64 points above or below the mean. Thus a sample mean IQ of less than 95.36 or greater than 104.64 would be considered significant and the sample not typical of representative samples of the population. Therefore, the sample mean of 106 in the example of the group with a mean IQ of 106 would be considered statistically significant and the group not typical, and it is unlikely that they are a representative sample of the whole population, for IQ. Now momentarily return to Figure 7.1 and imagine where our sample with a mean of 106 would appear on the graph: just to the right of the one with a mean of 102. It is not obvious from comparing a sample mean with that of the population that the sample would not be

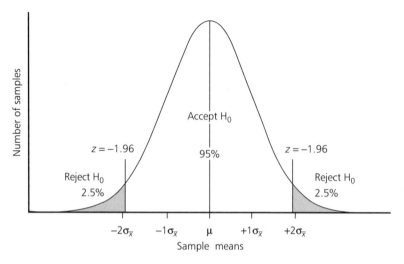

FIGURE 7.3   *Normal distribution of sample means with 5% significance levels, where μ is the population mean and $\sigma_{\bar{x}}$ is the standard error of the mean*

considered typical – hence the need for a separate test comparing the sample mean with that of the distribution of *means of all possible samples*.

Carrying out the z-test

It is not necessary to draw a graph of sample means to resolve such questions. This can be done by simple calculations and checking the results against a table or using a function on the spreadsheet. The z-test allows us to resolve this more quickly by finding the z-score for the mean of the sample group and directly find out where in the distribution it is. The equation is quite straightforward:

$$z = \frac{\bar{x} - \mu}{\sigma_{\bar{x}}} \tag{7.3}$$

where $\bar{x}$ is the sample mean of interest, μ is the population mean, and $\sigma_{\bar{x}}$ is the standard error of the mean. To calculate the z-score for the question of the sample group of 40 with a mean IQ of 106,

$$z = \frac{106 - 100}{2.37} = 2.53$$

As above, if we were to look in a table of z-scores and corresponding area, such as Table 6.3, we would find that the total area below this is

49.43% + 50% = 99.43%. This is usually expressed as the opposite, 0.57% or 0.0057. If we had selected 5% as our 'goal post', beyond which we reject the null hypothesis H_0 that there is no difference between this sample and any other sample, then we would reject H_0. In other words, since this is less than 0.05 and the results are stated in shorthand as $p < 0.05$, the probability that this sample has a mean that is typical of all similar samples of the same size is less than 5%. Thus this is said to be statistically significant.

If the sample were larger or smaller, then the standard error of the mean would be different. For example, if the sample were half the size, only 20, then

$$\sigma_{\bar{x}} = \frac{15}{\sqrt{20}} = 3.35$$

This would be in the denominator of equation (7.3) and if the mean of the sample were the same, then the value of z would be

$$z = \frac{106 - 100}{3.35} = 1.79$$

Again, looking at Table 6.3, we find that this time the area up to this mean is 50% + 46.32% = 96.32%. Thus the probability of it belonging is 5.68%, greater than the cut-off of 5%, and we accept the null hypothesis H_0 that it is not significantly different from any other sample of 20. In other words, it is typical of samples of 20 for this trait of IQ.

Now carry out Activity 7.1 to test other groups.

ACTIVITY 7.1

(a) Our researcher, having learned his lesson about sampling, now takes a larger random sample of 80 11 year olds, finding the mean IQ for the group to be still 102. Is this group representative of the population? Why or why not?

(b) Our researcher thinks that he can increase the IQ of children by improving their blood circulation through physical exercise. The subjects jog 5 miles (8 km) a day for three weeks and are then given another IQ test. This time the mean for the group of 40 is 104. Are they still typical of all children at this age? Why or why not? (This is *not* a good design, but it provides a simple exercise!)

(Answers are at the end of the chapter.)

TABLE 7.1 *Worksheet for carrying out a z-test when given sample and population means and standard deviations*

	A	B	C
1		Population	
2	mean =	100	
3	s.d. =	15	
4		Sample	
5	mean =	106	
6	n =	40	
7	SEM =	2.37	
8		Sample > Pop	Sample < Pop
9	z-score =	2.53	-2.53
10	probability =	0.0057	0.9943

Callouts:
- =B3/SQRT(B6)
- =(B5–B2)/B7
- =(B2–B5)/B7
- =NORMSDIST(–B9)
- =NORMSDIST(–C9)

Instead of calculating *z* by hand and looking up cut-off values in a table, we can set it out on a worksheet. Table 7.1 shows a simple worksheet for carrying out the *z*-test when the population and sample means are provided, with the standard deviation. Carry out Activity 7.2 to set this up.

ACTIVITY 7.2

(a) Set up a worksheet as shown in Table 7.1, to calculate automatically a *z*-test for a sample from a population with a known mean and standard deviation. Start by using the population values for the IQ test for rows 1 and 2. Insert the formulae shown in the callouts in rows 7, 9 and 10. Then you can change the values in the shaded cells in rows 5 and 6 and these values will be automatically calculated for you. There are two values for *z*-scores and probabilities to take into account which end of the distribution is being considered.

(b) The worksheet has the values for the sample illustrated in Figure 7.2 in the text for a sample having a mean IQ of 106. From row 9, it can be seen that it is unlikely that this sample is typical of all possible samples.

(c) If the sample were smaller, would you still expect it not to be representative of the population for this trait? Try changing *n* to 30 and 20. What is the probability in each case? Would you consider these samples to be typical?

continued

(d) What would be the minimum sample size needed to find a significant difference between a sample with a mean of 97.5?

(e) The previous two steps seem to indicate that all one needs is a large enough sample to find a significant difference, but is this true? What have we assumed when we have changed the sample size and would it necessarily be a valid assumption?

There will be occasions when the raw data for the sample is available, instead of just the means. Activity 7.3 provides another worksheet for such a situation.

ACTIVITY 7.3

(a) To carry out a z-test starting from raw data, set up the worksheet shown in Table 7.2. Cells **13A** to **22C** can be **Copy**ied from the worksheet in Table 7.1. Replace the values in **B17** and **B18** with the formulae shown, the first to calculate the sample mean and the second to count how many scores there are. This allows you to expand the number of subjects by **Insert Rows** between row 2 and 11 without having to change the formulae. They change automatically to accommodate the new rows of data.

(b) The scores are for students on a standardized test where the mean and standard deviation are known, as shown. Change some of the individual scores and see what it takes to make this small group no longer 'typical'.

Research errors

Since all of inferential statistics results in probabilities and not certainties, it is not difficult to accept that there is a finite probability that, using the above 'rules', it is possible to reject wrongly the null hypothesis when using the 5% level as the cut-off, specified as α. In other words, there is still a 5% probability that the group with the significantly different mean does belong to the population. It is possible to make it more difficult to prove that a group does not belong to the population by changing the level to 1% or even higher, but there would still be a finite chance that such a group would belong to the population. On the other hand, what if a researcher accepts the null hypothesis that there is no difference between the sample and the population, using the 5% (or 1%) level? There is still a finite probability that the decision is not correct and that the sample does not belong to the population. Thus, what level a researcher chooses for deciding is a difficult one and will depend upon the type of decision that will be made as a consequence.

TABLE 7.2 *Worksheet with raw sample data for a z-test*

	A	B	C
1	Subject	Score	
2	Mary	39	
3	John	52	
4	Henry	47	
5	Albert	43	
6	Sam	56	
7	Anne	41	
8	Sue	33	
9	Jane	60	
10	Fred	39	
11	Albert	50	
12			
13		Population	
14	mean =	50	
15	s.d. =	10	
16		Sample	=AVERAGE(B2:B11)
17	mean =	46	
18	n =	10	=COUNTA(B2:B11)
19	SEM =	3.16	
20		Sample > Pop	Sample < Pop
21	z-score =	−1.26	1.26
22	probability =	0.8970	0.1030

This is where *academic* or practical significance is important. Sometimes authors do not distinguish between these and only report statistical significance. This is compounded by authors who report different levels of significance for different outcomes; that is some are described as $p < 0.05$, while others are $p < 0.01$, and so on. Setting the level of significance before the study is essential for two reasons:

1 The consequences of the decision to accept or reject H_0 should determine the minimum level for significance. Not considering why a level is chosen can lead to the question 'So what?' In other words, the results are statistically significant, but so small a difference as to have no practical or academic significance.
2 Like gambling, you place your money before the dice are thrown, the ball released on the roulette wheel or the cards are revealed. Otherwise, it is cheating.

Let us return to the question of probabilities of wrong decisions. Referring back to the previous example of selecting representative groups of children, the group with a mean IQ of 106 was considered not to be representative of the whole population. While this is a perfectly reasonable decision, this is not proof that the group is not representative. In other words, the group could all belong to the same class through events not under control of the schools and may even be the only group with a mean IQ this high. Remember that the bell-shaped normal curve ideally never touches the x-axis and there is always a finite probability that some group will exist quite naturally out in the tails. But the criterion here is that the group or groups selected must be seen to be representative and not deviate from the population group by too much. So for the purposes of this study, the researcher rejected the null hypothesis and this group as being typical. Yet there will be other situations where rejection probably would not be the best action.

As we have seen, if a researcher rejects the null hypothesis because he/she has chosen for a study, a probability of less than 5% as statistically significant, then there is a finite probability that the conclusion is wrong. In fact, there is a 5% probability that the researcher will be wrong to reject the null hypothesis, or, stated differently, there is a 1 in 20 chance that the sample *was* part of the population. To make this type of erroneous decision is described as making a *Type I error*, and the probability of making a Type I error is simply equal to the level of significance chosen, α. The chance of making a Type I error can be reduced by lowering the level of significance to, say, 1% (i.e. less than 1 in 100 chance, or $z = 2.58$). The less likely one is to find significance, at the 1% instead of the 5% level, the stronger the support for any conclusions. Sometimes this is phrased as relative confidence: 95% confident or 99% confident that a sample does not belong to the population. Also, one will often find the significance level stated as a probability (of something occurring by chance) less than a value, such as $p < 0.05$, or $p < 0.01$.

Unfortunately, this raises the other problem that, by reducing the probability of rejecting a null hypothesis (increasing the confidence level) when it is really true, the chance of accepting the null hypothesis when it is false increases. To accept the null hypothesis when it is really false is known as making a *Type II error*. The probability of making a Type II error can be reduced primarily by increasing the sample size. Assuming the sample has been selected randomly, the greater size increases the probability that the sample will be truly representative. This provides some insight into why researchers are keen to have large samples. These two types of error and the alternative correct decisions are summarized in Figure 7.4. You will also note that correctly rejecting H_0 is labelled as *power*, the probability of making a correct decision, which will be discussed later.

As Rowntree (1981) notes, resolving the above question is analogous to the following dilemma that arises in courts of law: if weak evidence is accepted, there is a danger many innocent people will go to prison (a Type I error, rejecting the null hypothesis that there is no significant difference between these people and innocent people, when it is true). Alternatively, by

Possible realities

		H_0 true	H_0 false
	H_0 accepted	Correct decision	Type II error
Decisions			
	H_0 rejected	Type I error $(p = \alpha)$	Correct decision (*power*)

FIGURE 7.4   *Possible consequences of decisions based on two possible alternative realities*

increasing the demands on the quality of evidence, the probability of more guilty persons not being convicted would increase. This is parallel to raising the significance level to 1%, thus risking a Type II error, accepting the null hypothesis that there is no difference between these people and the innocent, when it should be rejected. Maybe it is fortunate that the conclusions of a single piece of social science research are rarely used as the basis of a radical decision affecting vast numbers of people! How do other professions that use statistics as a decision-making tool, like the pharmaceutical industry testing new medicines, protect themselves? They replicate the study using different samples of persons. Getting the same results time after time reduces the probability of making a decision error.

In summary, the sample size and choice of significance level will affect the probability of drawing the wrong conclusions. Usually, researchers do not know which type of error is made, but they are concerned about which type to risk making. This means that a decision should be made as to which type of error a researcher can best tolerate in a study and this in turn will determine the choice of significance level and influence the sample size. To play the game of statistical inference honestly, the decision about the significance level should really be made *before* the statistical test is carried out, when the null hypothesis is stated. Though widely practised, reporting just the most significant level found as the statistical tests are performed is not proper, since this implies that the criterion for acceptance/rejection of the null hypothesis was not set ahead of time.

There are a large number of statistical tests that will allow the comparison of pairs of groups, whole sets of groups, etc. All of these tests share basically the same characteristic: a test of some null hypothesis stating no difference across groups. The same issues as identified above will apply when interpreting the results. The tests only tell whether or not the differences are statistically significant: did they occur by chance alone as a result of natural variation, or was there probably some outside influence? The same questions as to which type of error, Type I or II, is to be risked must be considered. What *should* the significance level be? How small a sample can the study withstand? As you were warned, while this book treats the issues and stages in individual chapters, in reality the necessary decisions are all interrelated and consequently will often need to be made considering several of the issues together. Carry out Activity 7.4 at this time.

ACTIVITY 7.4

Below are two descriptions of research projects. For each, consider the type of error the researcher has possibly made, a Type I or a Type II (model answers are at the end of the chapter):

(a) A researcher gave a class an IQ test and found the mean to be 108, and rejected the null hypothesis that they were not different from representative samples from the population; in other words, he concluded that they were not typical of the population. Later the teacher told him that this was the third time that they had taken an IQ test in a month and were probably becoming test-wise. Which type error has he possibly made? Why? What could be done to avoid this error?

(b) A researcher selected 200 adults from 8 randomly selected rural adult education classes on local history in his county to participate in a test of knowledge about banking. Their mean score was not significantly different from those from the whole county, and thus the null hypothesis that rural adults were no less knowledgeable was accepted. Subsequently it was found that six of the adult education centres selected were in commuter areas for the main city. Which type of error has possibly been made? Why? What could be done to avoid this error?

Type I and II errors and choosing α

How should researchers choose a value for α? Too often it is simply a matter of using 0.05 because 'this is what everyone else does'. More disturbing is the fact that many researchers do not seem to understand statistical significance. First they do not declare and justify a value for α at the beginning of the report. Second they report a variety of significance levels for tests. Therefore you may find some are $p < 0.05$ while others are $p < 0.01$ or $p < 0.001$. Since the value of α really only has meaning if stated as the criterion for making the decision as to accept or not accept H_0, then choosing a convenient value later is not logical.

As noted above, the choice of α should be based upon the consequences of making Type I and Type II errors. If it is simply a matter of inadvertently pursuing a line of research that does not cost too much, or of exploring tentative variables, then to be wrong is not disastrous and a high value for α may be appropriate. But if the outcome of the research is to contribute to a larger decision-making process that might affect the well-being of people, then a more conservative, lower value for α may be more appropriate. When reading articles, it is worthwhile looking for a statement that says α was set *before* the data was collected and statistical tests conducted, and *why* that level was chosen.

Power

Calculating the probability of making a Type II error (usually referred to as β) is not trivial and is beyond this text, though it is reasonably straightforward on a spreadsheet (see Black, 1999) and is a statistic provided by many packages such as SPSS. What is of interest, however, is its opposite, *power*, the probability of correctly rejecting H_0. It is defined simply as

$$power \equiv 1 - \beta$$

Referring to Figure 7.4, this is what researchers strive for, to reject H_0 correctly, to find that the hypothesized difference is real. It is possible to describe power graphically and the logic goes as follows:

1 If one rejects the null hypothesis H_0 that a sample belongs to the distribution of samples from the specified population, then it can be assumed that it belongs to a different population.
2 For the sake of estimating β and power, we assume that the mean of our non-typical sample is a good estimate of the mean of the alternative population, which for argument's sake will have the same standard deviation (SEM) as the original.
3 We then draw a second distribution of sample means around this mean, as shown in Figure 7.5.
4 Now this second distribution of sample means overlaps with the first and using the cut-off score for α/2, we can also divide this second distribution into two parts: the area to the left gives us an estimate of β and to the right an estimate of power. In this example, the area is about 72% of the total right-hand distribution, so power is 72% and β, the probability of making a Type II error, is about 28%.

Obviously, the greater the difference between the population and sample means (for the same sample size), the further right the second distribution will be and the greater the area for power, since α/2 remains in the same place. Power is also influenced by the size of the SEM (how wide the curve will be) which is in turn influenced by the standard deviation, which is in turn influenced by the reliability of the instrument. Recall that reducing the error results in increasing the instrument's reliability. Therefore, the higher the reliability of the measuring instrument, the narrower the distributions and potentially power will be higher. Thus a study with an instrument that is not very reliable may not find the results that are there. Since power is the

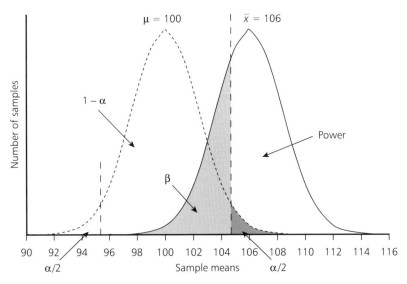

FIGURE 7.5 *A graphical representation of the relationships across α, β,
and power for a z-test of whether a sample is representative
of all possible samples from a population*

likelihood of correctly rejecting H_0, this provides a strong motivation for
ensuring that the measuring instrument is as reliable as possible.

It was also noted that increasing sample size is a major contributor to lowering the probability of making a Type II error. Since the SEM is smaller (distributions are narrower) for larger samples, this also increases the power of
a test. Error (and consequently wider distributions) can also be introduced
by poor procedures (e.g. observers becoming a variable by influencing outcomes, poor sampling, loss of subjects that have scores predominantly in a
certain range). On the other hand, it is possible that through inappropriate
sampling one could select groups that are not representative of the declared
population and consequently find differences that do not exist (a Type I
error). This is where procedures and statistical tests interact. As you read
articles and reports, consider the processes carefully and look for situations
where they could generate misleading results. Providing a value for power
is a better way of demonstrating the strength of the significance, since α
should have been established as a result of possible consequences of decisions to be made.

One-tailed or two-tailed test

Occasionally, a study will state that it has used a one-tailed test. As seen
above in Figure 7.3, the null hypothesis could be rejected because of a sufficiently low or sufficiently high mean score for the sample; thus this is a two-
tailed test. If, however, there were some evidence that the only likely
outcome would be in one direction, for example if the sample mean were

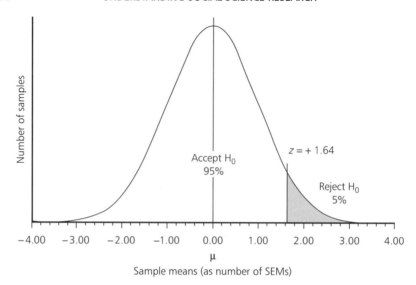

FIGURE 7.6 *Rejection area for a one-tailed test when the expected difference is the sample mean will be greater than that of the population:* α = 0.05

TABLE 7.3 *Approximate probability levels,* α, *and corresponding z-scores for a normal distribution of sampling means (two-tailed and one-tailed)*

α	$z(\alpha)$ two-tailed	$z(\alpha)$ one-tailed
0.10	±1.64	1.28
0.05	±1.96	1.64
0.02	±2.33	2.05
0.01	±2.58	2.33
0.001	±3.29	3.10

different it would be greater than the population mean, then the researcher could declare a one-tailed test. What is the advantage? Such a test only has a rejection area in one tail, so the cut-off score for α = 0.05 for a one-tailed test would be equivalent to that for α = 0.10 for a two-tailed test. In other words, it is much easier to find a difference, as shown in Figure 7.6, and an obvious way is to increase the power of the test. The equivalences for values of α are shown in Table 7.3, to illustrate this as well.

When is it justified for a researcher to declare a one-tailed test? Since this should have been stated *before* the statistical test was carried out, there should have been some evidence that the direction of difference could only be one way. For example, if the sample group were to have some learning experience that conceivably would only improve its performance with respect to the population or reduce the strength of an attitude, then the one-tailed test may be justified. It is up to the researcher to justify the choice and not report it simply because no significance could be found with a two-tailed test. Such 'data snooping' is not in the spirit of statistical tests and likely to incur doubt on the legitimacy of a report.

Finish this chapter by doing Activity 7.5.

ACTIVITY 7.5

(a) Suggest one reason for increasing the probability of making a Type I error by changing α from 0.05 to 0.10 for some research in your area.

(b) Suggest one reason for decreasing the probability of making a Type I error by changing α from 0.05 to 0.001 for some research in your area.

(c) Give three ways of increasing the power of a study.

This chapter has introduced statistical significance using the z-test, checking whether a sample is 'typical' of all possible samples. In the next chapter, tests will be presented that determine whether two or more groups are typical of samples from one or more populations. These analogous tests allow us to check whether score differences for groups are large enough to be considered more than what could be expected from natural variation alone. In other words, these tests are just variations on the same theme.

MODEL ANSWERS

Activity 7.1

(a) $z = 1.19$, which is still less than 1.96, so the answer is yes.

(b) $z = 1.68$, which is still less than 1.96, so the answer is yes, and he has no proof that physical exercise increases IQ. Even if z were greater than 1.96, there is not sufficient control of other contributing factors for such a study to provide sound support for the hypothesis.

MODEL ANSWERS

Activity 7.4

(a) Type I. The familiarity with the measuring instrument has confounded the results, and thus they may not accurately reflect the group's mean IQ. Possible solution: use an earlier result, if the test is acceptable.

continued

(b) Type II. The members of the sample groups were not necessarily typical of rural adults. Two possible solutions: either the definition of 'rural adults' needs to be clarified and may be subdivided by occupation, or a more 'typical' county should be selected. Alternatively, the results could be extended to rural adults in that county, which may have a larger proportion of rural resident commuters than nationally.

8

Correlational Studies

The three fundamental ways of analysing and presenting the results of measurement-based studies using inferential statistics that will be used here are based upon designs introduced earlier: surveys, *ex post facto* and experimental studies. Correlational analysis stemming from surveys will be considered below as the main statistical tool used with survey data and the statistical tests for the other two approaches will be introduced in Chapters 9 and 10.

WHAT DO CORRELATIONS TELL US?

Correlations are a method by which we describe the relationship between pairs of variables resulting from a survey of a single group. This does *not* mean establishing cause and effect relations, since correlations only indicate the strength of relations between variables in a single sample of subjects and regression equations tell how one variable changes with respect to another. For example, there is a high correlation between age and height for a range of ages of children, but neither one causes the other. In this case, growth determined by genes and nutrition are the most likely causes. Correlations should be tested to see if they are statistically significant, to determine whether the value for the sample allows us to say that it is really different from zero for the population or the difference is so little as to be attributable to chance. Even if the correlation is statistically significant, this still has nothing to do with proving causation. Occasionally a report will state or imply causal relationships on the basis of correlations, but it requires a much more structured study to determine the true causal chain and begin to justify such claims.

How can we visualize what is meant by correlation and regression? Data for such calculations comes from single samples and consists of pairs of numbers for each subject. For example, for each child, what is his/her height and weight? If we plot these pairs of numbers for all the members of our sample, a *bivariate distribution* can be produced: two variables plotted against each other, as opposed to a frequency distribution with one variable against frequency of occurrence. This looks like numerous points on a graph, for our example of weight versus height, which is usually referred to as a *scatter diagram*.

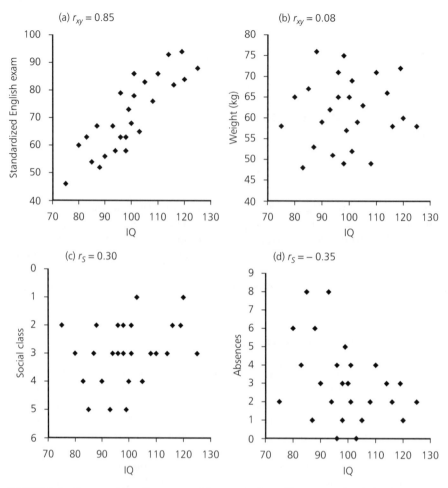

FIGURE 8.1 *Four scatter diagrams with correlations (from contrived data)*

A high correlation (indicating a strong relationship) might come from a scatter diagram that looks like Figure 8.1(a). A weak relationship and a low correlation would have a scatter diagram like Figure 8.1(c). If we had *no* correlation, it would look something like Figure 8.1(b), since $r = 0.08$ is nearly zero. And occasionally, the situation arises where one variable decreases as another increases, producing a negative correlation, such as shown in Figure 8.1(d). The larger the value (either positive or negative), the more closely packed are the points around an imaginary best-fit straight line. The closer to zero, the more the points will look like a round cloud.

By implication from examples (a) and (b) in the figure, it appears that correlations can be calculated for interval or ratio (continuous) variables, a common occurrence. It is also possible to find correlations for interval and ranked (ordinal) data, as seen with social class in (c) and absences in (d). It is even possible to show the relationship between two ordinal variables,

TABLE 8.1 *Some common coefficients of correlation and association*
for combinations of data pair types

	Interval/ratio (continuous)	Ordinal	Nominal
Interval/ratio (continuous)	Pearson product moment, r_{xy}		Point biserial correlation, r_{pb}
Ordinal		Spearman's *rho*, rank order correlation, ρ	Cramér's C
Nominal	Point biserial correlation, r_{pb}	Cramér's C	Coefficient *phi*, ϕ (dichotomous)

for example to show how closely the rankings of children with learning disabilities determined by a classroom teacher compare with those of a visiting psychologist.

It is even possible to have combinations of interval, ratio or ordinal data, *and* dichotomous (nominal) groupings. For example, one could find the degree of association between attitudes towards science and sex of the students (ordinal versus nominal). It is even possible to determine the level of association between two dichotomous variables, such as a voter's sex and choice of two candidates (nominal versus nominal).

DIFFERENT TYPES OF MEASURES OF CORRELATION AND ASSOCIATION

Most commonly we see correlations between quantified variables, measures that result in continuous numbers. This usually provides Pearson product moment correlations, which, as we will see later, allow us to generate quantitative predictions. But there are other coefficients that describe relationships between variables that are reported as ranks or only as categories. Table 8.1 provides a cross-section of the ones most likely to be encountered in the literature. These are (with examples):

- *Interval–interval:* Weight versus height, both variables are interval data, they can be any value (within a reasonable range), thus collecting weight and height data on each member of a sample would result in using Pearson product moment correlation to determine the strength of relationship. While one might rightfully expect that for a random sample of children this would result in a high positive correlation, this might not be true of a sample of persons suffering from some hormonal or genetic defects.
- *Ordinal–ordinal:* Social class and number of children a family has. This requires a coefficient that treats the data as ordinal values (class is ordinal

and children come in whole numbers, with not all children being the same for many traits), and thus will require Spearman's rho.

- *Nominal–nominal:* Male and female versus voting for a specific political party or any of the other parties (dichotomies). Categorical relationships that consist of dichotomous variables such as these require the use of the phi coefficient. If the question required comparing several parties and included another category for gay persons (multiple categorical levels for each variable), then this would require Cramér's C.
- *Interval–ordinal:* Speed in completing assembly task (time to assemble a circuit board: interval) versus number of trials (ordinal) required to reach criterion of quality in production (less than 5 rejects per 100). Here, the interval data would be turned into ranks as well and Spearman's rho employed.
- *Interval–nominal:* Time to run a kilometre versus gender. This special situation can be best described using the point biserial coefficient.
- *Ordinal–nominal:* Income range versus original university degree subject. Again, this is a case where the data needs to be reduced to a simpler form and the ordinal data, income range, is considered to be nominal, so that Cramér's C can be used.

Some examples

Table 8.2 provides some examples of correlations from research. From this list you can see that the range of values between −1.00 and +1.00 is considerable, and that the relative strength can vary as well. These all describe *linear* relationships; thus as one variable increases, so does the other at a constant rate. Negative correlations tell us that as one increases the other decreases, again at a constant rate. There are other types of relationships where there are non-linear correlations, but these are very uncommon. How important or *academically significant* a correlation is depends on its size. This indicates the strength of the relationship between the two variables. Table 8.2 provides a selection of examples and later we will see how the relative strength can be quantified.

Guilford and Fruchter (1973) suggest the following four combinations of predictions that can be made, each presented with examples:

1 *Attributes from other attributes* – predict incidence of divorce from social class, political party affiliation, or religious creed.
2 *Attributes from measurements* – predict divorce incidence from scores on an achievement test.
3 *Measurements from attributes* – predict probable test scores from gender, socio-economic, or marital status.
4 *Measurements from other measurements* – predict academic achievement from aptitude test scores.

How do we use correlations? Primarily there are two practical ways to employ these:

TABLE 8.2   *Some real exemplar correlational relationships (after Black, 1999)*

Potential relationship	Typical r	Relative strength
IQ score and elementary school grades/achievement tests (Atkinson et al., 1990)	0.60 to 0.70	Strong
Grade in mathematics and mathematics self-concept in a sample of Flemish primary school children (Muijs, 1997)	0.50 to 0.60	Moderate
Scholastic Aptitude Test (SAT) and freshman (first-year) university results (USA): predictive validity (Atkinson et al., 1990)	0.31 to 0.50	Weak to moderate
IQ scores and graduate school achievement (Atkinson et al., 1990)	0.30 to 0.40	Weak
A-level results and first-year university results: predictive validity (Bourner and Hamad, 1987)	0.00 to 0.28	Very weak to negligible
Liking for electronic voice response systems and age of US respondents (Katz et al., 1997)	− 0.29	Weak
Authoritarianism and aestheticism among US high school seniors (final-year secondary) (Minium et al., 1993)	− 0.42	Weak to moderate

1   To determine the amount of variance that is shared by the two variables, found simply by the square of the correlation coefficient (this is an indication of academic significance). For example, as in Figure 8.1(a) if the correlation between IQ scores and an achievement test in English were 0.70, then 0.49 or 49% of the variance is shared. In other words, although there is not a causal relationship, there is a shared influence on their variances.
2   To make predictions using regression lines.

We will return to these functions shortly, but first let us see how we can find correlations easily from data using a spreadsheet.

CALCULATING CORRELATIONS

The formula for calculating Pearson product moment correlation can appear daunting, but it is a built-in function in Excel and all statistical packages,

$$r_{xy} = \frac{\sum_{i=1}^{n} (x_i - \bar{x})(y_i - \bar{y})}{nS_x S_y} \qquad (8.1)$$

where x_i and y_i are the matched pairs of scores, $\bar{x}$ and $\bar{y}$ are the means of the two tests or instruments, S_x and S_y are the standard deviations, and n is the total number of subjects. As an example, carry out Activity 8.1 to set up some data and find the correlation.

ACTIVITY 8.1

(a) On a worksheet, enter the two columns of data shown in Table 8.3 and select **CORREL** (or **PEARSON**, they produce the same result) from the Function Wizard. Sweep the two columns as shown to calculate the correlation as shown. The number of decimal places on the spreadsheet has been adjusted to two.

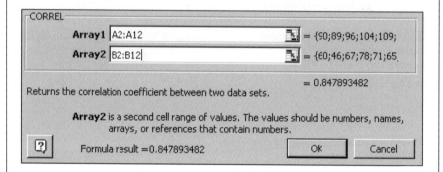

(b) Use the Chart Wizard to plot an **(XY) Scatter** diagram. Change the scale on each axis of the graph to what is shown in Figure 8.2. What does this correlation coefficient tell us?

(c) Find or collect some new data to enter in the worksheet and find the correlation.

The first thing to notice is that the tighter the cluster around an imaginary line, the higher the correlation and the more variance the two variables share. In fact the amount of shared variance is simply the correlation squared, so in Table 8.3, where $r_{xy} = 0.85$, then $r^2 = 0.72$ which says IQ scores and maths test scores have 72% shared variance. The remaining variance not attributable to the other variable is assumed to be 'error', whose source is basically anything not accounted for, including sampling errors and even other variables. Table 8.4 shows this relationship for a range of correlations. As you can see, the percentage of shared variance drops very quickly as the correlation goes down. Go back to your worksheet and change some of the data to see the effect on the correlation (e.g. take the first maths score and reduce it to 40).

The second way that correlational relationships are used is to make predictions. For example, given a scatter diagram of weight versus height, would it be possible to predict the weight of someone knowing their height by using such a graph of a sample of a number of people? Is it possible to predict height from weight? Figure 8.3(a) is just such a plot for a larger sample than shown before with a high correlation, each dot representing

TABLE 8.3   *Pairs of scores for each student on two tests in a school*

	A	B
1	IQ	Maths
2	90	60
3	89	46
4	96	67
5	104	78
6	109	71
7	112	65
8	97	56
9	93	59
10	85	51
11	115	78
12	120	80
13		
14	Correlation =	0.85

=CORREL(A2:B12)

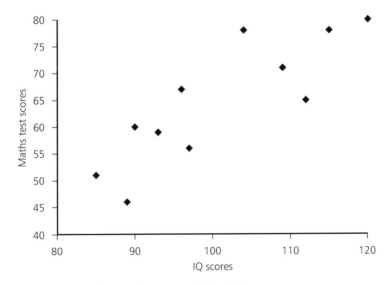

FIGURE 8.2   *Scatter diagram for data in Table 8.3*

persons having that combination of weight and height. Taking a value of weight, such as 50 kg, there is still a wide range of possible heights, ranging from roughly 1.0 to 1.6 m, some more likely than others. But just looking at scatter plots and trying to make predictions would be a frustrating task. As seen for the variety of scatter plots in Figure 8.3(a), even for a high correlation there is a spread of data points. To be able to make reasonably consistent predictions of height using weight (accuracy is something that will be considered later), best-fit straight lines will be drawn through the data: the regression lines, as shown in Figure 8.3(b).

TABLE 8.4   *A selection of correlation coefficients and corresponding impact on the proportion of variance in x attributable to the variance in y, when making predictions*

r_{xy}	Percentage attributable, $r_{xy}^2 \times 100$
0.10	1
0.20	4
0.30	9
0.40	16
0.50	25
0.60	36
0.70	49
0.80	64
0.90	81

REGRESSION

Taking the process of analysis in correlational studies one step further involves calculating a *regression coefficient* (for interval/ratio data) which tells us the slope (angle with respect to the horizontal axis) of the best straight line through the scatter diagram for predicting height from weight. But because of the scatter of the points (the correlation is not 1.00), there is actually a second possible best straight line for predicting the reverse, weight from height. These two regression lines are shown in Figure 8.3(b). How these are calculated is beyond this text (see e.g. Chase, 1985), but as we will see it is easy to generate them separately in Excel. What is more important, though, is that we know how these values are used. For example, trying to make 'exact' predictions from regression equations when the correlation is very low will result in very uncertain results. The correlation basically indicates the *strength* of the prediction. Thus, the lower the correlation, the greater the angle between the two regression lines; consequently, this would result in wildly different predictions. Now carry out Activity 8.2 to see how these predictions differ.

ACTIVITY 8.2

In Figure 8.3(b), find the predicted height for someone weighing 60 kg using the 'Height from weight' line by drawing a line up from that point on the weight axis, and then drawing another line to the height axis. Then take this height and predict the weight by extending your horizontal line until it intersects the 'Weight from height' line, then dropping a vertical line to the weight axis.

(a) Do you get 60 kg again? If not, how much difference is there?
(b) Would there be more or less difference if the angle between the lines were greater (i.e. if the correlation were smaller)?
(c) Repeat the above process by starting with different weights.

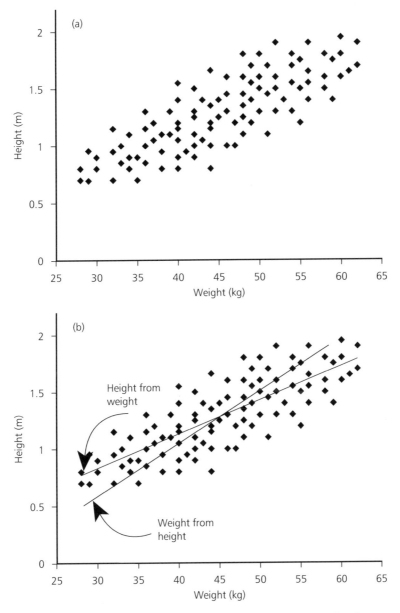

FIGURE 8.3   *Scatter diagrams for weight versus height for a sample of 100 school children, where the correlation $r_{xy} = 0.80$: (a) raw data; (b) with regression lines*

HOW ACCURATE CAN PREDICTIONS BE?

Ferguson (1976) summarizes the problem of interpreting the meaning of correlation coefficients by noting that these are *not* proportions: thus 'a coefficient of 0.60 does not represent a degree of relationship twice as great as a

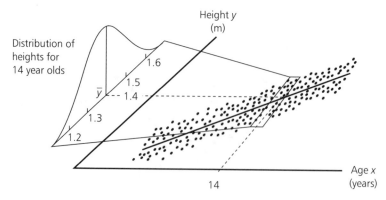

FIGURE 8.4   *Scatter diagram for height versus age for a group of children*
8–18 years old, used to find the most likely height for
14 year olds

coefficient of 0.30'. Also, he observes that the difference between 0.40 and 0.50 is not the same as the difference between 0.50 and 0.60. So what does the magnitude of a correlation mean? One approach is to consider variances and the shapes of distributions, which will be done visually, keeping the mathematics of the arguments to a minimum.

A scatter diagram with a correlation of 1.00 would consist of a perfect line of dots which would correspond to the regression line, but this rarely (if ever) exists when looking at correlations between human characteristics. As Guilford and Fruchter (1973) note, it is possible to think of a regression line as a set of mean scores with the dots on either side showing the amount of variance in the sample at a given point. If you can find variance, you can find a standard deviation, and if you can find a standard deviation, you can imagine a normal curve. Figure 8.4 shows a scatter diagram for height versus age for a large group of children between the ages of 11 and 18 years, with a high correlation, $r_{xy} = 0.90$. If one were to use this graph to predict the height of a group of 14 year olds, it would be 1.4 m, going up to the regression line and over to the y-axis. Yet even the raw data draws attention to the fact that this might not be the only possible value. Remember that the researcher is making inferences about the whole population based upon this sample. There will be natural variability within the sample and there will potentially be some error due to sampling. It is best to consider the predicted value as the most likely value, but not the only possible height. The same would be true for any other prediction, be it for 13.5 year olds, 16.7 year olds, etc.; the predictions will be the *most likely height*. Personal experience confirms the fact that children of a given age are not all the same height.

The reverse is true as well. It is possible to predict the age of a child by looking at his/her height, but again there will be a range of possible values with a most likely one for a given population. This is illustrated in Figure 8.5

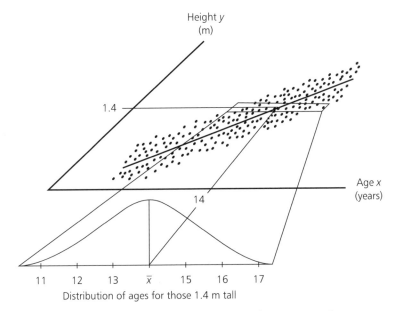

FIGURE 8.5   *Scatter diagram for height versus age for a group of children 8–18 years old, used to find the most likely age for a child of height 1.4 m*

where the scatter diagram is approached from the opposite direction: taking a height of 1.4 m, what is the most likely age? If the standard deviation of this distribution were known, then even the certainty of the prediction could be stated: 95% certain that it is between ±2 standard deviations. Such data (along with other techniques) might be used by an archaeologist or forensic scientist trying to determine the age of a child from his/her skeleton, though knowledge of the growth rate in the population might not be very accurate, adding to uncertainty in the estimate of age at death.

The standard deviation of these distributions (which are assumed to be the same anywhere along the regression line) is called the *standard error of the estimate*. If can be found by considering data in a given interval, say between 13.5 and 14.5. Obviously, the smaller the correlation, the greater the scatter of data points and the larger the standard error of the estimate. This means that for large correlations, the 95% confidence interval, roughly ±2 standard deviations either side of the prediction (i.e. the interval in which there is a 95% probability that the predicted value will fall), will be small. For small correlations, the standard error of the estimate will be larger, the 95% confidence interval will be larger, and the relative accuracy of the prediction lower.

To illustrate this let us recall the example in Table 8.3, the scores on two tests taken by a group: an IQ test with scores x, and a mathematics achievement test with scores y. Since both tests produce a mean and standard deviation, these can be used along with the correlation between the two sets of scores to produce values for the standard error of the estimate:

$$s_{xy} = s_x \sqrt{1 - r_{xy}^2} \qquad \text{(predicting } x \text{ from } y\text{)} \qquad (8.2)$$

$$s_{yx} = s_y \sqrt{1 - r_{xy}^2} \qquad \text{(predicting } y \text{ from } x\text{)} \qquad (8.3)$$

The first is for predicting mathematics scores, y, from scores on the IQ test, x, and the second for predicting IQ scores, x, from scores on the mathematics test, y. This shows the effect of the correlation coefficient on the accuracy of any prediction directly: the larger r_{xy}, the smaller the standard error of the estimate, and vice versa. Therefore, for the following values from the data in Table 8.3,

(IQ)	$\bar{x} = 100.9$	(maths)	$\bar{y} = 64.6$
	$s_x = 11.7$		$s_y = 11.4$

the distributions around any predictions would have standard deviations of

$$\text{(IQ from maths)} \qquad s_{xy} = 11.7 \sqrt{1 - 0.85^2} \cong 6.2$$

$$\text{(maths from IQ)} \qquad s_{yx} = 11.4 \sqrt{1 - 0.85^2} \cong 6.0$$

But before making any predictions, we need to have the regression equation.

Generating regression lines

Without assistance from computer programs, this can be a time-consuming task. Now most statistical and many spreadsheet packages have such a facility built in to make the task very easy indeed. Carry out Activity 8.3 to find out how to do this in Excel.

ACTIVITY 8.3

(a) Return to the worksheet in Table 8.3, and the resulting Figure 8.3, that you set up. Double click on the scatter diagram to activate it. Click on one of the data points so they are all highlighted.
(b) With the mouse, click on the **Insert** option on the menu at the top of the sheet.
     From the list, select **Trendline** and you should get the following window:

continued

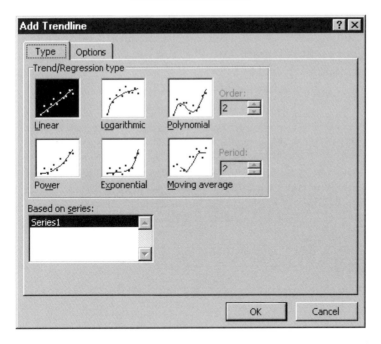

(c) If the **Linear** graph is not black, then click on it now. Then click on the **Options** tab to get the following window:

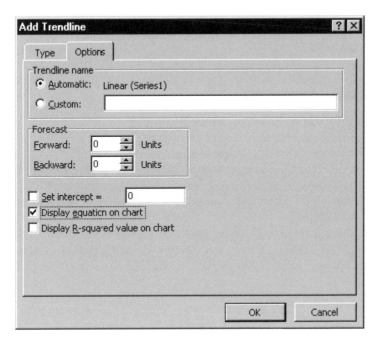

continued

> (d) Click on the small box next to **Display equation on chart** and then click on **OK**. You should find a best-fit regression line on your scatter diagram with the corresponding equation, like that shown in Figure 8.6.
> (e) Now predict what the likely Maths test score would be of someone with an IQ score of 105.

To refine our prediction, we can now use the standard error of the estimate. In Activity 8.3, you should have found that someone with an IQ score of 105 is likely to have a mathematics test score of

$$y = 0.824(105) - 18.517$$

$$y \cong 68.0$$

From above, $s_{yx} = 6.0$, and therefore we could say that

$$y = 68.0 \pm 1.96(6.0)$$

$$y = 68.0 \pm 11.9 \qquad\qquad \text{with 95\% confidence}$$

Alternatively, we could say that there is a 95% probability that y is between 56.1 and 79.9, the 95% confidence interval. Thus we can see that even with a moderately high correlation, 0.85, there is considerable margin for error in any prediction.

STATISTICAL SIGNIFICANCE

Some studies will include all correlations for all combinations of variables. While this may seem to be a way of identifying possible relations, there is an increased danger that statistically significant correlations will occur by chance alone. This increased risk of a Type I error would involve rejecting the null hypothesis that the correlations occurred by chance alone, when it was really true that they were a random occurrence, and thus not indicative of any relationship.

The significance of a Pearson product moment correlation is checked using a special version of the t-test (which we will consider in detail in the next chapter):

$$t_r = \frac{r_{xy} \sqrt{n-2}}{\sqrt{1 - r_{xy}^2}} \qquad\qquad (8.4)$$

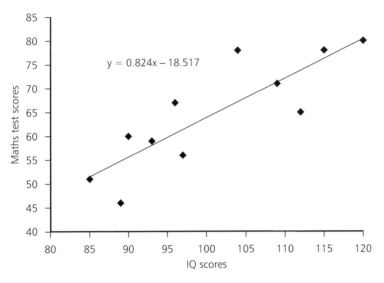

FIGURE 8.6   *The scatter diagram from Figure 8.3 with regression line added using* **TRENDLINE** *in Excel*

This value is checked against the minimum for the chosen level of significance, which varies somewhat with the sample size. Thus the smaller the sample, the larger the minimum value. This is easily carried out on a worksheet, as you will see in Activity 8.4.

ACTIVITY 8.4

To check the significance of a correlation, all you need is the simple worksheet shown in Table 8.5. This includes equation (8.4) in cell **B4** and the equation for determining the minimum *t*-score for significance level designated in cell **B2** and the sample size in cell **B3**. Thus any of the values in the shaded cells can be changed and a new *t*-test will automatically be carried out for you.

Now we have seen two uses of the word 'significant':

1 one pertaining to academic or practical significance (recall Table 8.2), which can be expressed as the strength of the relationship by R^2 (i.e. how much variance is shared between the two variables, recall Table 8.4);

2 the other describing the likelihood that the correlation was really different from zero or whether it was likely to be just a chance occurrence (dependent greatly on sample size).

Remember that just because a study reports a statistical significance does not necessarily mean that it has found anything of educational, sociological

TABLE 8.5 *Worksheet for testing the significance of a correlation*

	A	B	C
1	Pearson r =	0.85	
2	alpha =	0.05	
3	n =	26	
4	t-ratio =	7.90	=B1*SQRT(B3-2)/SQRT(1-B1^2)
5	$t_{critical}$ =	2.06	=TINV(B2,B3-2)

or psychological significance. For example, for large samples, it is possible to have statistically significant correlations (the population value is really not zero) that are numerically very small. Sear (1983) found correlations ranging from 0.17 to 0.35 between A-level grades and subsequent university degree classification, using results for (apparently) all 1979 graduates. A correlation of this size means very little in practical terms, except to other researchers looking for ideas for more research.

Up to this point, it may have seemed that all relations are linear: an increase in one variable resulting in a direct increase (or decrease) in the other. Though less common, there are non-linear (curvilinear) relationships as well, such as that for the age of mothers versus number of children born: not all age groups are equally likely to have babies, nor does the frequency necessarily increase consistently with age. Correlation and regression coefficients can be calculated for such non-linear relations as well, the details of which can be found in more advanced texts. Again, such correlations can be checked for statistical significance. Carry out Activity 8.5 now.

ACTIVITY 8.5

(a) Sketch a scatter diagram for the suggested non-linear relationship between ages of mothers and number of children born for a sample of mothers.

(b) A report states that the correlation between teachers' assessments and examination board examination results was found to be 0.70. What might this suggest?

FACTOR ANALYSIS

Finally, *factor analysis* is a method of analysing a large number of measures to identify underlying common variables for a larger set in a study (see Kerlinger and Lee (2000: Chapter 34) for a good in-depth introduction to this topic). Because of the rather complex nature of the calculations, factor analysis has only become popular as a research tool since the advent of computer-based statistics packages. While it is a very powerful process, it is also one that is subject to abuse. The process identifies specific 'factors' or constructs in a measuring instrument that belong together and measure virtually the

Table 8.6 *Correlational table for a mythical factor analysis on test scores for various tests given to a group of pupils (after Kerlinger and Lee, 2000)*

	Vocab.	Reading	Synonyms	Numbers	Arith. (std)	Arith. (teach.)
Vocabulary		0.72	0.63	0.09	0.09	0.00
Reading		CLUSTER 1	0.57	0.15	0.16	0.09
Synonyms				0.14	0.15	0.09
Number					0.57	0.63
Arithmetic (std)					CLUSTER 2	0.72
Arithmetic (teach.)						

same thing. For example, it has been found through this process that verbal ability, numerical ability, abstract reasoning, spatial reasoning, memory, etc., all underlie intelligence.

The results of a factor analysis appear as a square matrix table of correlations among potential contributing factors. For example, Kerlinger and Lee (2000) present the correlations among the results of six (mythical) tests given to pupils, showing how common traits manifest themselves (see Table 8.6), though as they note, usually the clusters are not so obvious. Further manipulations and more objective tests are usually needed to highlight clusters and determine the statistical significance of the results, which would establish the soundness of contributions to a common factor(s), if they were to exist. The number is not restricted to two, and in fact most studies produce more than two clusters, but the more there are, the more difficult it is to make any sense of the results.

The main problem of use, and the primary source of abuse, originates in the choice of potential factors. This analysis is based on the assumption that each factor is a valid and reliable measure of a trait, such as the scores from a test, questionnaire or observation schedule. Because of the nature of the computer programs that carry out the calculations for factor analysis, there have been cases where individual questions on a test or questionnaire have been used. As we saw earlier, this is an extremely poor practice considering the almost total lack of reliability and validity any single question can ever have! The fact that the computer cannot tell the difference between the mean score for a number of respondents answering a single item and the mean of a set of whole test scores for a group, does not mean the program should not be used. Again, here is a case where potential abuse is rooted not in the choice of statistical test or the computer program, but in the design of the measuring instruments that are the basis of the analysis.

CRITERIA FOR EVALUATING CORRELATIONS (INFERENTIAL STATISTICS)

The following are some guidelines for applying the criteria in this column of the Profiling Sheet, with specific notes on correlational studies.

Appropriate choice of design, and sound H_0   This and the next criterion are very difficult to judge. While the null hypothesis can be evaluated as to whether the correlations found were significant, often a study does not tell you enough to know whether or not the design is the best. Also, some studies could have considered the interaction of more variables, but have not done so through oversight. Sometimes the limitations are resources, which influence the sample size and therefore the complexity of the study.

A more powerful test could have been used   This criticism can be levelled at some correlational studies; based upon the research questions asked, an experimental approach or a better structured *ex post facto* design would have produced more profitable results. Until you have covered Chapters 9 and 10, this may be hard to judge. Also, the type of correlation calculated may not take advantage of the level of data collected or available: ordinal or nominal data was collected when interval or ratio data would have been more appropriate, or the test does not match the data type. The possible correlations shown in Table 8.1 that use ordinal and nominal data actually increase the risk of a Type II error (not finding a significant correlation when there was one).

Missing analysis where needed   The data was collected or available (*ex post facto*), but not analysed. Correlations could have been found and hypotheses could have been tested.

Inappropriately analysed, tests performed not appropriate   This involves errors in the other direction: finding correlations using calculations intended for interval and ratio data on data that is only nominal or ordinal. Because of the nature of the statistical tests, there is a greater risk of a Type I error because of such a choice as this (finding significant differences where they do not really exist).

No justification for analysis, post hoc *data snooping*   There are those who are like young stamp collectors – they gather data but for no planned reason. Then there is the magic trip to the computing centre where some kind soul puts the data into a statistical package and, miraculously, out come statistically significant correlations! Articulate researchers can cover up this approach with clever words and conclusions. Reading reports can be a bit like looking for the 'small print' in a legal document. It is necessary to understand the rules of the game to be able to spot the more subtle violations or not meeting the assumptions of a test. This level is appropriate for those who start with no research questions or hypotheses, yet produce correlations and grandiose conclusions.
    Finish this chapter by doing Activity 8.6.

ACTIVITY 8.6

Obtain articles that have used correlations and inferential statistical analysis (often easily identified by the presence of r_{xy} and probabilities, e.g. $p < 0.05$, for significance levels). Evaluate each using copies of the Profiling Sheet at the end of the chapter.

Profiling Sheet: *Understanding Social Science Research,* © Thomas R. Black, 2001

Article: _____ **Type of Study:** ☐ Descriptive, ☐ Survey/correlational, ☐ *Ex post facto*, ☐ Experimental/quasi-experimental.

Questions/ hypotheses	Representativeness	Ethics and Confidentiality	Data Quality I	Data Quality II	Descriptive Statistics	Inferential Statistics
Valid question or hypothesis based on accepted theory with well-justified referenced support	Whole population	Ethical standards met and data sufficiently confidential that no individuals or institutions can be identified	Educationally, sociologically, psychologically, etc., significant and manageable number of concepts	Commercially or professionally produced/tested with high validity, reliability and objectivity (V, R, O)	Appropriate display of data and results in tables and/or graphs, clearly labelled	Appropriate choice of design and statistical tests for resolving H_0
Valid question or hypothesis based on own theory, well justified	Random selection from a well-specified population		Limited academic significance, very narrow perspective	Project or personally produced/tested with high V, R, O	Some inadequacies in presentation of tables/graphs	A more powerful test could have been used
Credible question/ hypothesis but alternative possible, or too extensive/global, or support missing	Purposive sample from a well-specified population, with justification for representativeness	Ethical issues not addressed or confidentiality not discussed when it should have been	Large number of concepts, potentially confusing	Commercially or project produced with moderate V, R, O	Other methods of display of data/results would have been more appropriate	Missing analysis where needed
Weak question/ hypothesis, or poorly stated, or justified with inappropriate references	Volunteers or convenience, with no justification of representativeness	Ethical issues not addressed and/or some loss of confidentiality	Too many concepts and variables investigated to provide meaningful results	Commercially or project produced with low V, R, O, or no information provided	Serious misconceptions encouraged owing to nature of graphical display of results	Inappropriately analysed data, tests performed not appropriate
No question or hypothesis stated, or inconsistent with known facts	Unidentified group	Ethical standards violated and/or subjects endangered owing to no confidentiality	Trivial concepts, not academically significant	Inappropriate instrument for the variables/concepts described	Intentionally misleading use of descriptive statistics	No justification for statistical analysis, just *post hoc* data snooping

Comments and justification for classification:

9

Parametric Tests

Single samples and surveys can only tell us so much. More sophisticated designs involve either a single sample which is randomly divided into two or more groups for experimental studies, or multiple random samples from two or more groups to investigate the consequences of life experiences. Such designs require corresponding tests to tell us whether any difference between groups is large enough to be attributable to something besides what we would expect due to natural variation between samples from one population. This chapter presents the first of these tests which will help to resolve such hypotheses for variables that are measured as continuous numbers.

Correlational studies allow the researcher to see if there is any relationship between pairs of variables in a single group, the correlation indicating the relative strength of the relationship. Usually there is insufficient control in such designs to allow any proof of cause and effect. To determine the possibility of existence of such a relationship the researcher must have much greater control over the possible variables that may influence any outcome, and hypothesize such a relationship before beginning the study. Again, because of the nature of the variables (frequently normally distributed around a mean that indicates the central tendency of the groups), any conclusions usually will be 'probablies'. Ultimately, much of the strength of these conclusions rests on the rigour of the design and its execution.

Returning to our simple classification scheme, when the design requires the researcher to exercise control over variables, either directly or indirectly, such designs are similar to those used in biological studies and are usually referred to as experimental designs. On the other hand, as we have seen there will be many times when we want to compare the characteristics of groups based upon life events that have already occurred, namely *ex post facto* designs. The conclusions from this type of study can justifiably describe associations between variables rather than causality. Confusion can arise since both types of study can employ the same statistical tests. It is appropriate to emphasize here that it is not the statistical test that establishes causality, but the research design. The statistical test can only tell us whether any differences are attributable to chance or natural variation. If they are not, it is up to the researcher to demonstrate through the planning and execution of the experimental design that *only* the independent variables he/she had control over (e.g. type of learning materials, nature of counselling sessions, administrative structure of groups in a business) could have caused the difference. This is why the real challenge in quantitative research is in the research design, not in the choice and use of statistics. The choice is limited and relatively simple, while controlling extraneous variables can be very difficult.

TYPES OF DESIGNS

Obviously, since they must contend with human beings as the object of their investigations, social science researchers rarely have the complete control over variables that the biologist in the laboratory does. Consequently, greater ingenuity is required of the social scientist to compensate for this lack of direct control, in order still to use the powerful statistical tests about to be considered. Therefore, the designs used in the social sciences described below have attracted names, such as *ex post facto* and quasi-experimental, that indicate this lack of absolute control usually associated with truly experimental designs. This does not detract from the potential appropriateness and power of such designs, but does indicate that there are a number of new assumptions that must be met to employ these validly, and limitations that must be recognized. Often it is the lack of rigour in designing a study or the faults in execution, rather than the use of more complex statistical tests, which ultimately weakens or totally invalidates the conclusions made in the final research report.

Quantitative designs do compel the researcher to identify a limited number of potential variables, define them rigorously, propose their relationship, and control all others by one means or another. Herein lies the problem: human activity is subject to a myriad of variables. Before considering the statistical tests that might be used, let us review the different types of designs and conditions that will relate to the choice of statistical tests and the justification of their use.

Ex post facto *studies*

Ex post facto simply means after the fact. As we have seen, this approach uses existing data, such as that which is in statistical records, or depends upon existing characteristics and life experiences of the subjects, like the amount of education they have, what type of school they attend(ed), and the occupation or social class of their parents. Though the goals of identifying causal relationships, the defining operationally of variables, and the employment of statistical tools are often the same as used in truly experimental studies (see below), the difference lies in the degree of control the researcher has over the variables. In reality, it is not possible to have complete control over the independent variables such as educational background, social class or genetic inheritance, since they have already occurred or cannot be manipulated.

Consider a study where the researcher wished to determine if there were any relationship between parental education and children's achievement in school. A truly experimental design to resolve issues would not be plausible since it is simply not possible to arrange for a random selection of children to be assigned to new families. An appropriate *ex post facto* design would go a long way to answering such questions, through representative sampling across families with a range of parental education, measuring and observing, and inferences based on statistical tests. But the results would always lack the maximum amount of certainty since all the possible independent (extraneous) variables could not be totally controlled. This is not to demean the approach, just to point up its potential limitations and the greater demand this places upon the researcher to ensure that his/her sample is representative of the populations, for example here, with respect to differences in parental education. Much social science research that employs statistical tests is *ex post facto*, rather than truly experimental, and potentially valuable in its contribution to knowledge. It is carried out in the real world, rather than in a laboratory. The challenge for the researcher is to ensure maximum control of potential contributing factors that might constitute competing hypotheses, through appropriate choice of experimental design and sampling. The main interest then is to determine whether or not sampling has been appropriate and variables have been controlled. The reader may have to infer the use of an *ex post facto* design if this has not been stated outright.

The choice of design and availability of data will also affect what questions can actually be answered. If measures of the desired variables do not exist or were not collected reliably (such as statistical records not being kept, data not collected properly, samples not being representative), then some questions cannot be answered after the fact. For example, to resolve the issue of whether people are taller today than in past years would require representative data (emphasis on representative) from the past as well as the present. Looking for possible sources going back over time, the question arises, do available military records supply valid data? The answer is, only if it could be proven that conscripts and volunteers constituted a representative cross-section of society. Recognizing that throughout history there has been a tendency for many men to avoid being conscripted, this may not be true. One could argue that those who escaped military service in the past were the better educated and consequently better fed, and would not be proportionally represented among those serving. Thus the overall physical attributes (means and standard deviations) of conscripts and volunteers may not be representative of the whole population at that time. The researcher would have to establish the representativeness of the data through (historical) research. This is indicative of the type of questions that would have to be considered if existing data were to be used for an *ex post facto* study.

Experimental and quasi-experimental studies

These differ from other types of research in that there is the possibility of manipulation and control of the hypothesized independent variable (the treatment) by the researcher. Also, there tends to be the requirement that subjects should be randomly assigned to treatment groups so as to eliminate the influence of mediating and extraneous variables. Though this approach has the potential of providing more meaningful data, it tends to be costly and not always possible, as seen earlier with the impossibility of assigning children to new families. Also, there has been the criticism made that true experimental research in education often lacks realism, relevance to class-room problems, and rigour (Lehmann and Mehrens, 1979).

As a consequence, studies frequently have been conducted comparing, for example, the effectiveness of different teaching and learning methods using available groups and the effects of various variables on memory, using undergraduate student volunteers. The last point is simply a reflection of the general difficulty of carrying out research involving human beings and controlling all the possible variables in their lives. Such studies are labelled as quasi-experimental to reflect the lack of control over such factors as sampling. While the use of convenience samples can sometimes jeopardize the validity of outcomes, there will be times when purposive samples of intact groups will enhance the validity of the results. For example, whole existing classes of 30 children are less likely to incur unwanted extraneous variables than artificial classes made up of 30 children who were randomly selected and do not know each other.

Keeping these potential problems in mind, both approaches, experimental and quasi-experimental, employ common designs and statistical tests to resolve hypotheses. What differentiates these is how many variables will be considered in a given study, which usually means how many different groups of subjects (each differing on one or more variables) will be used.

TYPES OF DESIGNS: NUMBER OF GROUPS

Using inferential statistics to determine the acceptability of hypotheses requires an understanding of the limitations of this tool. Quantitative designs have a variety of different statistical tests from which to choose, the choice depending on how many groups are involved. Basically the possible questions that can be answered are whether:

- one sample group belongs to a well-defined population;
- two unrelated groups belong to the same population (not necessarily well defined);
- two related groups belong to the same population; or
- three or more groups belong to the same population for some given trait.

The actual design of the study and how the hypothesis is phrased will be related to how many groups are involved. This will provide a convenient way of viewing different types of design that employ statistical tests.

One-sample group

In Chapter 7, the case of a single group was used as the example when explaining statistical inference. The question was asked, with respect to IQ, does this sample of 40 children appear to be typical of samples randomly drawn from the population of all 11 year olds? In other words, even though the mean IQ score for the sample (in this case, 106) is not the same as the population mean of 100, is it close enough to the population mean for the group to be considered representative of the population, or is it so far away as to consider the sample group to be part of another population? In other words, is it considered an example of the natural variation in IQ scores or not? This example used interval data, but the question can also be asked and answered for situations which lead to an operational definition of the trait that results in the collection of ordinal or nominal data, as will be seen later.

Two independent groups

This class of test involves comparing two groups on some trait and simply asking: do these two groups belong to the same population, or are they so different as to be from two different populations? Basically, if the test decides that the two probably do not belong to the same population, there is no indication as to what populations they do belong. The question is a simple one: do the two groups belong to the same population, whatever that may be? Often, the questions that are resolved by such tests are stated in terms of causal relationships between variables: whatever is being measured (like height, income, IQ) being the *dependent variable* because the scores are hypothesized to depend upon the groups to which subjects belong, the *independent variable* (such as social class, treatment group, age range). Unfortunately, when hypotheses are stated this way, the implication is that if a significant difference is found, a causal relationship exists. As noted time and time again, this is *not* necessarily so. If one has a truly experimental design, then there is a much better chance of proving this than if the design is *ex post facto*, where control over variables is more tenuous. The proof, though, is separate from the statistical test and dependent on adequate control of variables.

There have been an enormously wide variety of applications of tests between two independent groups. Campbell and Stanley (1963) note that the main sources of faults to look for when such a design is employed are:

- how the groups are formed or members selected; and
- whether or not the membership stays constant throughout the experiment or experience.

For example, to answer the perennial question of which are 'better', private schools or state schools, one could compare examination results for representative samples of each. This could be done in the United Kingdom by considering GCSE (General Certificate of Secondary Education) examination results or in the United States by using the SAT (Scholastic Aptitude Test) results. First, the two general issues identified above must be addressed as specific questions: (a) were the groups equivalent in the first place, thus were both groups representative of the whole population of children at entry age for all traits that might affect examination success; and (b) did all those that started in each group finish? If one looks at the children in both types of schools, there tend to be some rather extreme differences for a variety of variables: social class, parental income and race. For criteria (b), most (though not all) in both groups last until the examinations are taken, though the dropout rate tends to be higher in state schools. So while the question could be asked, data collected, and a statistical test used to answer the question, using raw examination results is hardly a valid approach.

Consider a second, but less ambitious study: it would be possible to compare two teaching approaches, if the conditions described above were satisfied by (a) randomly allocating learners to the two groups, and (b) ensuring that there were no 'dropouts'. The problem with this type of study (commonly reported in the literature) is finding truly representative groups: as noted earlier, too often available groups are used without justifying their representativeness of a larger population.

Returning to the first research question, it is impossible to assign pupils randomly to state or private schools, so it would be impossible to eliminate totally the problem of non-equivalent groups. The degree of equivalence in the samples would be determined by sampling techniques. The second issue could be addressed by using gain scores (measure them when they enter and measure them when they leave), and then it matters less who stays or leaves, thus satisfying condition (b). This would require a more explicit definition of 'better' when referring to the relative effectiveness of schools.

The second exemplar research question on teaching approaches raises different problems. For many designs where the question of testing the effectiveness of learning materials or strategies is to be resolved, randomly allocating learners to the two groups and providing pre- and post-tests ensures that most competing hypotheses are eliminated (Campbell and Stanley, 1963). Here the problem has been proving that the original group that was divided in two was truly representative of the whole population of learners. Usually they are not made up of learners randomly selected from a larger population, since they are students who are available to the researcher at the time. Without justification of their being typical, any inferences extended to a larger population would be weak. This does not necessarily totally invalidate such studies, but the reader should be aware of the effect this has on the strength of any inferences.

Similar criticisms have been levelled at studies in other areas. Numerous psychological studies have been conducted using undergraduate volunteers. Sociological investigations have drawn on coherent groups like workers in a specific car assembly factory, a local coal mining community, a suburb of a city, or farmers in one locality.

Sampling problems aside, when comparing two groups, the question being asked with the *t*-test is whether or not the *difference in the means* is significantly different from zero. We would expect the value to be zero (or very close) for all samples if they belonged to a common population. The distribution of differences in sample means has much the same shape as a normal distribution when samples are greater than 30, but becomes increasingly shorter and squatter for samples less than 30. Thus for small groups, it

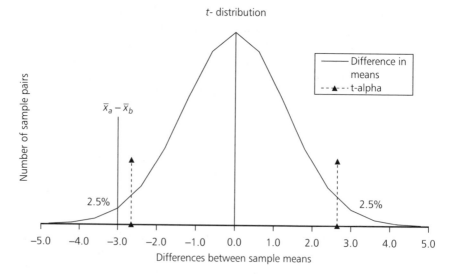

FIGURE 9.1   *A distribution of difference between sample means (t-distribution)*

becomes increasingly difficult to find a significant difference. Since there is essentially a different distribution for each sample size, one example of a *t*-distribution is shown in Figure 9.1. In this example, the difference in the means of the two groups falls outside the critical area and would therefore be considered significantly different. In other words, it is assumed that the two groups are not part of the same population.

As an experimental design, ideally the two groups would have started off as one group randomly selected from a population to ensure the members were representative of that larger population. Then the sample would be randomly divided into two groups. After each received a different 'treatment' (e.g. learning or counselling experiences), the question would be, are the two groups *still* part of a common population? If it were an *ex post facto* design, then the question might be whether two different groups (e.g. teachers of different subjects, different gender groups) have the same attitude. In this situation, random selections from each group would be made and the 'treatments' as such in this case would be the different life experiences.

To use the *t*-test it is assumed that the data is continuous (interval or ratio). The question is answered by comparing the means and using the two standard deviations to generate an estimate of the SEM, now called the *standard error of the difference*, s_{diff} (the standard deviation of the *t*-distribution), as follows:

$$t = \frac{\bar{X}_a - \bar{X}_b}{s_{\text{diff}}} \qquad\qquad (9.1)$$

where

$\bar{x}_a, \bar{x}_b$ = means of the two samples

s_{diff} = estimate of the standard error of the difference found by

$$s_{\text{diff}} = \sqrt{\frac{s_a^2}{n_a} + \frac{s_b^2}{n_b}} \qquad\qquad (9.2)$$

and

s_a^2, s_b^2 = variances (standard deviations squared) of the two samples

n_a, n_b = sample sizes of the two groups.

Typically, a report will provide results in a form similar to those shown in Table 9.1. This simply gives the means, standard deviations and sizes of the two groups, plus the value for the t-statistic and its probability level (if it is significant). The degrees of freedom, df, here equals the total number of subjects, minus two, $n_a + n_b - 2$. The degrees of freedom for a set of data are best described as the number of observations free to vary at one time without affecting the result. The level of significance is dependent upon the degrees of freedom, so a t-distribution is used. Note that most often no graphs or charts will be provided and the reader will be expected to visualize the distributions based upon the means, $\bar{x}_a$ and $\bar{x}_b$, and standard deviations, s_a^2 and s_b^2, presented.

Two related groups

This type of test involves two groups that are related in some way, as described earlier. For example, at the simplest level, a researcher might want to know if a teaching approach were effective by applying a pre- and post-test to his/her class and testing for a significant difference. Since the same students would be doing both tests, they would constitute *related* groups. Unfortunately, there are a number of competing hypotheses even if a significant difference were found. For example, something else may have enhanced learning, the learners matured, they became test-wise, etc. Therefore, using gain scores and two groups (one using a traditional approach and the other the new approach), as described in the previous section on independent groups, would be better, since this approach can eliminate the possibility of competing hypotheses providing better explanations.

The idea of related groups can contribute to an improved design if applied differently. Consider the situation where two teaching methods are to be compared, but for a fair test to be made, the two groups used should be alike and matched on such traits as intelligence, age, social class. The design would wish to determine if a change has occurred in a group, applying a test, a 'treatment' and a retest as above. Comparing the test with the retest involves investigating related traits since the groups have been matched according to traits that might provide competing hypotheses if ignored (Chase, 1985). Other possibilities where groups might be related for potentially confounding traits are if one wanted to compare attitudes, for example towards ethnic minorities, across generations using members of common families. As in the first case, the data gathered from each group will be influenced somewhat by the other. Using related groups can essentially control variables and consequently eliminate competing hypotheses, if used appropriately.

One statistical test for significance in such situations calculates the differences in the means for the pairs and then a mean of the differences for the test, $\bar{D}$, so that

$$t = \frac{\bar{D} - 0}{s_{D\text{-diff}}} \tag{9.3}$$

where

$$s_{D\text{-diff}} = \frac{s_D}{\sqrt{n}} \tag{9.4}$$

and s_D is the standard deviation of the set of differences.

The reader would be presented with a table similar to Table 9.1 again, though the relationship between the groups would be mentioned in the text of the report since the underlying calculations would be different and df would equal the number of pairs less one.

Tails

There are actually two possible ways of reporting significance for two groups. If the researcher has not anticipated which way the difference between the means of the groups will be, then it could be that $\bar{x}_a > \bar{x}_b$ or that $\bar{x}_b > \bar{x}_a$, and it is assumed that it could go either way, so a *two-tailed test* is applied. This means that the difference has to be sufficiently large that the t-score would be in either tail as in Figure 9.1. But if the researcher predicts that the difference could only be one way, for example $\bar{x}_b$ could only be greater than $\bar{x}_a$, then a *one-tailed test* would be applied, where all 5% appears in one end of the distribution, analogous to that shown in Figure 7.6 for a z-score. Obviously it is easier to find significance for a one-tailed test since the 5% level is the same as the 10% level for a two-tailed test. Again, which

TABLE 9.1   *Statistics calculated for testing the difference between two independent groups, df = 22 + 25 − 2 = 45 (H_0 that there is no difference rejected)*

	Group *a*	Group *b*
$\bar{x}$	21.0	18.0
s	4.0	5.0
n	22	25
$t = 2.28, p < 0.05$		

test will be used should have been decided before the test was carried out, and the same problems of risks of Type I and Type II tests apply as noted earlier.

Carrying out t-tests

In Excel, it is quite straightforward to carry out a *t*-test on a set of data. There is a built-in facility that requires you only to type in the raw scores. Carry out Activity 9.1 to see how to do this.

ACTIVITY 9.1

(a)   Start a new worksheet and enter the two columns of data shown in Table 9.2.

(b)   On the main menu, click on **Tools**, then **Data Analysis...**, which should bring up the following:

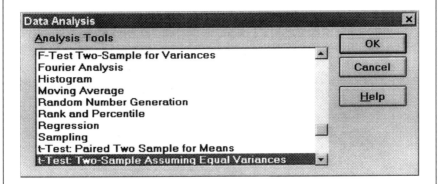

(c)   Use the slider to move down the list and select the test high-lighted. Click on the [OK] button, which should bring up the following window:

continued

---

t-Test: Two-Sample Assuming Equal Variances ☒

Input
Variable 1 Range: `$A$1:$A$11`
Variable 2 Range: `$B$1:$B$11`

Hypothesized Mean Difference:

☒ Labels

Alpha: `0.05`

Output options
⦿ Output Range: `$D$1|`
○ New Worksheet Ply:
○ New Workbook

OK
Cancel
Help

(d) Complete it as shown and click on the [OK] button. You should get the table to the right of the data. I have cleaned mine up by reducing the number of decimal places to two and adjusting the column widths.

(e) If this were a one-tailed test (i.e. it was hypothesized beforehand that Group A would have a higher mean score), was there a significant difference? If no prediction had been made and a two-tailed test was appropriate, would there have been a significant difference?

What if these were matched pairs of subjects, say spouses responding to a questionnaire? This would require the second of the two tests. Carry out Activity 9.2 to see how this is done.

ACTIVITY 9.2

(a) Assume that the data in Table 9.2 is from matched pairs of subjects. Again click on **Tools**, then **Data Analysis...**, and this time select **t-Test: Paired Two Sample for Means**. Use the same settings as before, but make the **Output Range $H$1**.

(b) Do the results indicate a significant difference for a two-tailed test?

(c) Either alter the raw data and repeat the tests, or try some data of your own.

Homogeneity of variance

The *t*-test is what statisticians call 'robust'; in other words, its reliability will not be seriously affected by distributions that are not perfectly normal. The

TABLE 9.2   *Worksheet with raw data and the results of the t-test for equal variances*

	A	B	C	D	E	F
1	Group A	Group B		t-Test: Two-Sample Assuming Equal Variances		
2	56	43				
3	55	38			Group A	Group B
4	50	45		Mean	54.9	47.4
5	58	56		Variance	57.2	73.6
6	64	46		Observations	10	10
7	52	49		Pooled Variance	65.41	
8	48	50		Hypothesized Mean Difference	0.00	
9	51	47		df	18.00	
10	45	35		t Stat	2.07	
11	70	65		P(T<=t) one-tail	0.03	
12				t Critical one-tail	1.73	
13	54.9	47.4	= means	P(T<=t) two-tail	0.05	
14	57.2	73.6	= variances	t Critical two-tail	2.10	

test is less reliable, though, when the two groups have radically different variances. Therefore, if they are different by more than a factor of, say, 3 (i.e. one is three times the other), then it is worth testing for *homogeneity of variance*, using the simple formula

$$F = \frac{s^2_{largest}}{s^2_{smallest}} \qquad (9.5)$$

This can be carried out automatically in Excel, as shown in Activity 9.3.

ACTIVITY 9.3

Table 9.3 provides a set of data for two groups that has a considerable difference in variance. To test whether this difference is significant:

(a) Start a new worksheet and copy the two columns of data from Table 9.1 to Table 9.2, and then change the last two numbers in column A to increase the variance as shown.

(b) On the main menu, click on **Tools**, and then **Data Analysis…**, which should bring up the following:

continued

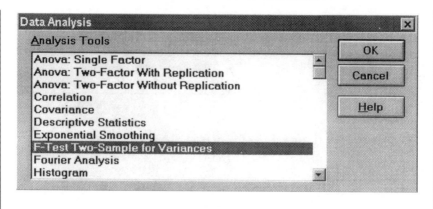

(c) Use the slider to move down the list and select the test highlighted. Click on the [OK] button, which should bring up the
following window:

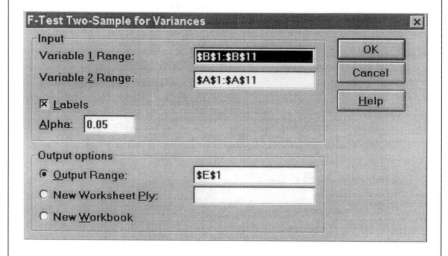

(d) Complete it as shown and click on the [OK] button. Note
that the column with the higher variance is **Variable 1 Range:**,
since that variance will be in the numerator of equation (9.4)
when Excel does the calculation. You should get the table to the
upper right of the data. I have cleaned mine up by reducing the
number of decimal places to two and adjusting the column
widths. The variances are significantly different since F (cell E8) is
greater than F-Critical one-tail (cell E10) on the worksheet.

If it turns out that the two groups have radically different variances,
then there is a separate *t*-test for heterogeneous variances (called 'unequal

TABLE 9.3 *Worksheet with raw data and the results of the t-test for unequal variances, including the test for homogeneity of variance*

	A	B	C	D	E	F
1	Group A	Group B		F-Test Two-Sample for Variances		
2	56	43				
3	55	38			Group B	Group A
4	50	45		Mean	47.4	54.8
5	58	56		Variance	73.6	22.0
6	64	46		Observations	10	10
7	52	49		df	9	9
8	48	50		F	3.35	
9	51	47		P(F<=f) one-tail	0.04	
10	57	35		F Critical one-tail	3.18	
11	57	65				
12				t-Test: Two-Sample Assuming Unequal Variances		
13	54.8	47.4	= means			
14	22.0	73.6	= variance		Group B	Group A
15				Mean	47.4	54.8
16				Variance	73.6	22.0
17				Observations	10	10
18				Hypothesized Mean Difference	0	
19				df	14	
20				t Stat	– 2.39	
21				P(T<=t) one-tail	0.02	
22				t Critical one-tail	1.76	
23				P(T<=t) two-tail	0.03	
24				t Critical two-tail	2.14	

variances' in Excel) that compensates by reducing the degrees of freedom (the calculation is long, but can be found in more advanced texts such as Black, 1999). Try this now in Activity 9.4.

ACTIVITY 9.4

(a) Since the variances are significantly different since F is greater than F-critical one-tailed, when you click on **Tools**, and then **Data Analysis...**, which should bring up the following, you will choose the highlighted version of the *t*-test:

continued

```
┌─────────────────────────────────────────────────────────────┐
│ Data Analysis                                             [x] │
│   Analysis Tools                                              │
│  ┌──────────────────────────────────────────┐   ┌────────┐  │
│  │ Fourier Analysis                      [▲] │   │   OK   │  │
│  │ Histogram                                 │   └────────┘  │
│  │ Moving Average                            │   ┌────────┐  │
│  │ Random Number Generation                  │   │ Cancel │  │
│  │ Rank and Percentile                       │   └────────┘  │
│  │ Regression                                │   ┌────────┐  │
│  │ Sampling                                  │   │  Help  │  │
│  │ t-Test: Paired Two Sample for Means       │   └────────┘  │
│  │ t-Test: Two-Sample Assuming Equal Variances│              │
│  │ t-Test: Two-Sample Assuming Unequal Variances [▼]         │
│  └──────────────────────────────────────────┘               │
└─────────────────────────────────────────────────────────────┘
```

(b) This will produce the following window which should be com-
     pleted as shown. The results are provided to the lower right of
     the data in Table 9.3. Note the reduced degrees of freedom,
     which is how the test adjusts for the heterogeneity of variance.
     Is there a significant difference?

```
┌─────────────────────────────────────────────────────────────┐
│ t-Test: Two-Sample Assuming Unequal Variances            [x] │
│  ┌─ Input ──────────────────────────────────┐   ┌────────┐  │
│  │ Variable 1 Range:    [$B$1:$B$11      ]   │   │   OK   │  │
│  │                                           │   └────────┘  │
│  │ Variable 2 Range:    [$A$1:$A$11      ]   │   ┌────────┐  │
│  │                                           │   │ Cancel │  │
│  │ Hypothesized Mean Difference:  [      ]   │   └────────┘  │
│  │ [X] Labels                                │   ┌────────┐  │
│  │ Alpha:  [0.05]                            │   │  Help  │  │
│  └───────────────────────────────────────────┘  └────────┘  │
│  ┌─ Output options ─────────────────────────┐               │
│  │ (•) Output Range:     [$E$12         ]   │                │
│  │ ( ) New Worksheet Ply: [             ]   │                │
│  │ ( ) New Workbook                         │                │
│  └──────────────────────────────────────────┘               │
└─────────────────────────────────────────────────────────────┘
```

Three or more groups

A more complex type of research question results in comparing three or
more groups, sometimes using complex classification schemes – for example, to determine whether or not the children in three different education
authorities achieved comparable results in their examinations through
gains in scores over a number of years. The measures from a sample from
each could be compared to see if they all basically belong to the same population, which means asking: is there a significant difference across schools

or sex (see Table 9.4)? What sort of data will appear in the cells or boxes will be discussed in the following section. While this is quite straightforward, the challenge for the researcher comes in *proving* which variable(s) (if any of those identified) actually caused the difference: the efforts of the education authority, or was it the ethnic origin of the students, quality of the individual schools, support by groups of parents, student anxiety, water supply, air pollution, number and/or quality of books in the local public library, etc.? Therefore, in most *ex post facto* designs such as this, there is little support for causal relationships and instead the outcomes are described as associations. For example, if it were found that boys in Frogfield LEA performed better than girls in North Noodle LEA, then the results would be presented as that, without any suggestion as to why. It would require additional research, most likely with a qualitative component like interviews, to determine the source of any difference.

Thus the main problem for the reader is not so much in the design, but in the variables chosen and how the results are to be interpreted. The resulting statistical tests to be discussed below will only tell whether there is a difference, not what caused it; thus the real skill comes in selecting a *meaningful* question and identifying educationally, sociologically or psychologically significant variables when first designing the investigation, followed by the use of reliable and valid measuring instruments, as noted in earlier chapters. Almost anyone can put numbers into a computer program and find statistical significance, but it takes a very well-planned study to ask a significant question, and find a meaningful answer using the statistical results. This does not mean that it would not be interesting to know whether there were any differences between groups, but the answer would only be partial: yes or no. The statistical data by itself would not tell why. Often, you will find articles that report the statistical outcome, and then speculate on why. Any follow-up study would provide the researchers with a considerable challenge to determine why, considering the complexity of the variables under which the students have been grouped. Carry out Activity 9.5 at this time.

ACTIVITY 9.5

Consider the following research question and suggested design:

- Question: Do girls perform better in mixed- or single-sex schools?
- Design: Ten schools of each type were randomly selected across the country and standardized achievement tests in mathematics and English were compared (two unrelated groups).

(a) What are alternative hypotheses for the expected outcomes?
(b) Suggest an improved design that would either include or control these.

TABLE 9.4 *An* ex post facto *design to determine whether there is any difference in the examination results across local education authorities (LEAs) (not necessarily a good study)*

	Frogfield LEA	Turnip Green LEA	North Noodle LEA
Boys			
Girls			

Analysis of Variance

The fourth group of statistical tests involves comparing three or more groups, sometimes using complex classification schemes. The test requires the simultaneous comparisons of a number of groups and the parametric test that has been developed is the *analysis of variance*, or ANOVA. This again uses both the means and standard deviations, with all the above assumptions of normal distribution, homogeneity of variance, etc., to make such comparisons, based this time on ratios of variances. Consider, for example, a simpler design than the one outlined above and portrayed in Table 9.4: in this study, the intent was to compare the effectiveness of three approaches to learning. The sample was a stratified random sampling of 3 classes of 14–16 students each from across a local education authority or school district. The results were in the form of gain scores (pre- and post-tests were administered) and the results are summarized in Table 9.5 as means and standard deviations. From this type of results table, usually the reader must try to imagine the distributions, for example the ideal normal distributions that are shown in Figure 9.2 for the data in Table 9.5. Even with these, it is difficult to decide if they are all from the same population.

In this case, the *F*-test, or *F*-statistic, would be used to determine ultimately whether or not groups experiencing the different learning approaches still belong to the same population, based upon how much of an overlap there is among all the distributions. Usually, the reader is only provided with a results table such as shown in Table 9.6, which is not very informative on its own.

The calculation of the *F*-statistic is presented to show how this takes into account the relationships between the three (in this case) 'treatments'. The *F*-statistic is calculated simply by finding the ratios of two separate estimates of the variance for the overall hypothesized common population for all three groups:

1   The numerator is based on the variance of means of the three (in this case) groups with respect to the grand mean, the mean of everyone in the three groups. This is variously referred to as $s^2_{between}$, the mean square between ($MS_{between}$), the mean squares for treatments ($MS_{treatments}$), or the mean square among groups (MS_{among}).

2   The denominator is an estimate of the variance for the whole population based upon the mean of all the variances. This is sometimes referred to as s^2_{within}, the mean square within groups (MS_{within}), or the mean square for errors (MS_{error}).

TABLE 9.5   *A quasi-experimental design to determine whether there*
            is any difference in the performance across the groups
            learning by different approaches, using indicated gain
            scores as the dependent variable

	Approach A	Approach B	Approach C	Overall
Mean of gain scores, $\bar{x}$	12.68	13.53	14.01	13.39
Standard deviation, s	0.90	0.95	0.97	
Sample size, n	15	16	14	45

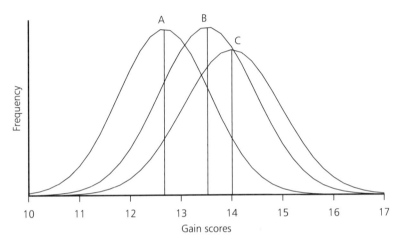

FIGURE 9.2   *Ideal normal distributions for the three treatment groups*
             in Table 9.5, based upon their means, standard
             deviations and sample sizes

TABLE 9.6   *Analysis of variance table calculated for testing the null*
            hypothesis H_0 ($\alpha = 0.05$) that there was no difference across
            the three learning approaches (Table 9.5): to decide, compare
            F with F crit

Source of Variation	SS	df	MS	F	P-value	F crit
Between Groups	13.18	2	6.59	7.45	0.002	3.22
Within Groups	37.16	42	0.88			
Total	50.35	44				

The assumption is that if the groups all belong to the same population, then the two estimates would be the same, and obviously the ratio would be close to one. Therefore, the *F*-test is based upon a distribution of ratios for samples, one that centres around 1.0, as seen in Figure 9.3. The interesting aspect of the family of *F*-distributions is their long tails, the size and shapes depending on a combination of how many groups and how many subjects.

The calculations can be performed as follows:

$$F = \frac{MS_{between}}{MS_{within}} \qquad (9.5)$$

where

$MS_{between}$ = mean square between, treatment, or among groups, found for this situation of three groups, by,

$$MS_{between} = \frac{n_a\,(\bar{x}_a - \bar{x}_T)^2 + n_b\,(\bar{x}_b - \bar{x}_T)^2 + n_c(\bar{x}_c - \bar{x}_T)^2}{3 - 1} \qquad (9.6)$$

where

n_a, n_b, n_c = the group sample sizes

$\bar{x}_a, \bar{x}_b, \bar{x}_c$ = the group means

$\bar{x}_T$ = the grand mean (of all subjects together)

and

MS_{within} = mean square within, or mean square error, found for the situation of three groups by

$$MS_{within} = \frac{(n_a - 1)\,s_a^2 + (n_b - 1)s_b^2 + (n_c - 1)s_c^2}{n_a + n_b + n_c - 3} \qquad (9.7)$$

where

s_a^2, s_b^2, s_c^2 = the group variances (standard deviations squared).

The *df* column indicates degrees of freedom, a concept related to sources of variation in measurements: how many things can you vary and still come out with the same number? As you will note, these are numerically equivalent to the denominators of the respective calculations for mean squares. The F-ratio is then compared with the appropriate table to see if it exceeds the value necessary for significance, and reported as we saw in Table 9.6.

The F-ratio is the basis for deciding whether or not all the groups belong to the same population, and it is a way of mathematically finding what might be determined by considering the overlap of the three distributions in Figure 9.2. In this case, when the F-statistic was compared with a standard

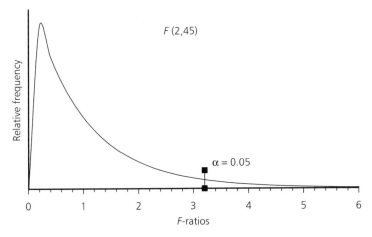

FIGURE 9.3   *An exemplar F-distribution for three groups of 16 each:*
$df_{between} = 3 - 1 = 2$ *and* $df_{within} = 3 \times 16 - 3 = 45$

F-distribution table, it was found that the probability that all three belonged to the same group was less than 5%, and thus stated as $p < 0.05$ (probability less than 5 in 100). This basically means that the differences in gain scores across the three learning approaches could not be attributable to natural variability alone. For this experimental design, the researcher would need to provide some justification that the only possible learning events that occurred for these groups that could have affected the scores were the different experiences that they had during the classes employing the approaches. This would be needed to enhance the strength of any inference about learning approaches causing outcomes that might be made.

Carrying out ANOVA tests in Excel

No one carries out such calculations by hand or even with a calculator. The F-test can be easily carried out in Excel with built-in functions, even when the groups are not of equal size. See Activity 9.6 for an example of how to carry out the analysis of variance for three groups.

ACTIVITY 9.6

(a) Start a new worksheet and enter the data provided in the first three columns of Table 9.7.

(b) On the main menu, click on **Tools**, and then **Data Analysis...**, as in earlier activities, this time selecting **ANOVA Single Factor**, which should give you the following window:

continued

```
Anova: Single Factor                                                    ☒

 ┌─ Input ──────────────────────────────────────────┐    ┌──────────┐
 │  Input Range:              $A$1:$C$11             │    │    OK    │
 │                                                  │    └──────────┘
 │  Grouped By:          ⦿ Columns                  │    ┌──────────┐
 │                       ○ Rows                      │    │  Cancel  │
 │                                                  │    └──────────┘
 │  ☒ Labels in First Row                            │    ┌──────────┐
 │                                                  │    │   Help   │
 │  Alpha:  0.01                                     │    └──────────┘
 │                                                  │
 ├─ Output options ─────────────────────────────────┤
 │  ⦿ Output Range:           $E$1                   │
 │                                                  │
 │  ○ New Worksheet Ply:                            │
 │                                                  │
 │  ○ New Workbook                                  │
 └──────────────────────────────────────────────────┘
```

Complete the form as shown and click on the [OK] button.
You should get the output on the right of Table 9.7.

(c) Is there a significant difference across the three groups?
(d) Repeat the process, but change **Alpha**: to 0.05. Is there a significant difference now?
(e) Try changing some of the data or enter your own into the
worksheet.

Post hoc *analysis*

For analysis of variance, one further set of tests can be performed if a significant difference is found across the groups. The F-test will only confirm that
the three groups did not belong to a common population, but will *not* tell
whether any combination of pairs belonged or did not belong to a common
population. A *post hoc* analysis will allow the researcher to determine
whether or not pairs of groups were significantly different. There are a number of these tests, all of which are more conservative than using multiple
t-tests (in other words, it will be more difficult to find statistical significance
among pairs). These include tests in order of increasing conservatism:
Duncan, Neumann–Keuls and Tukey, and Scheffé. Each test requires the calculation of a statistic that is in turn compared with its own table of probabilities. In fact the use of multiple t-tests is highly regarded as inappropriate
and likely to enhance the commitment of a Type I error, finding a difference
that does not really exist. Although it is the most conservative, the Scheffé
test is the easiest to perform, so it will be used to illustrate the process.
Details of other tests can be found in more advanced texts such as Winer
et al. (1991), Howell (1997) and Black (1999).

TABLE 9.7 Data for ANOVA and the results of the test from Excel

	A	B	C	D	E	F	G	H	I	J	K
1	Group A	Group B	Group C		Anova: Single Factor						
2	23	32	31								
3	22	34	20		SUMMARY						
4	26	43	23		Groups	Count	Sum	Average	Variance		
5	25	36	26		Group A	10	282	28.20	17.96		
6	29	27	35		Group B	9	313	34.78	20.19		
7	33	32	37		Group C	8	233	29.13	34.13		
8	35	34	32								
9	28	38	29								
10	30	37			ANOVA						
11	31				Source of Variation	SS	df	MS	F	P-value	F crit
12					Between Groups	231.97	2	115.98	4.953	0.016	5.614
13	28.2	34.8	29.1	= mean	Within Groups	562.03	24	23.42			
14											
15	α =	0.01			Total	794.00	26				

There are two ways to view the test: to calculate a critical minimum difference, or to provide a significance test for each difference. Since they are relatively easy to do, both will be illustrated. First, the test of significance is related to the F-test, where the F'-ratio for each pair is found by

$$F'_{B-A} = \frac{(\bar{x}_B - \bar{x}_A)^2}{2 \times MS_{within}/n} \tag{9.8}$$

where

$\bar{x}_A, \bar{x}_B$ are the means of the two groups in question

MS_{within} is the mean square within from the ANOVA table

n is the sample size. If the samples are not all the same, then the harmonic mean is used, which for three samples is found from

$$\frac{3}{n} = \frac{1}{n_A} + \frac{1}{n_B} + \frac{1}{n_C}$$

which is a built-in Excel function. The critical value is for Scheffé's test found from

$$F'\text{-}crit = df_{between} \times F(\alpha, df_{between}, df_{within}) \tag{9.9}$$

where

df are the degrees of freedom from the ANOVA test (Table 9.7)

$F(\alpha, df_{between}, df_{within})$ is $F\text{-}crit$ from the ANOVA test

which is easily found in Excel, as we will see in the next activity. From $F'\text{-}crit$, it is possible to find a minimum difference in means from the next equation,

$$\Delta\bar{x}_{min} = \sqrt{\frac{2 \times F'\text{-}crit \times MS_{within}}{n}} \tag{9.10}$$

Let us return to the case illustrated in Table 9.5, Figure 9.2 and Table 9.6. Having found a significant difference across the three approaches when $\alpha = 0.05$, the question remains whether or not those experiencing Approach A are significantly different from B or C, and whether those experiencing Approach B are significantly different from C: three combinations, A − B,

TABLE 9.8 *Summary of Scheffé post hoc analysis of pairs of means for ANOVA in Table 9.6*

B - A	C - A	C - B		Harmonic mean =	14.96
0.8	1.3	0.5	= diff	Scheffé min diff =	0.87
6.03	14.88	1.96	= F'	Scheffé F'-crit =	6.44

A – C, and B – C. Looking at Figure 9.2, one might expect the difference between Approaches A and C to be significant and between Approaches B and C not to be, but be uncertain about the difference between Approaches A and B. But visual checks are not very accurate. In fact, if the Scheffé test is applied, it is found that only Approaches A and C are significantly different and the combinations of Approaches A and C and Approaches B and C are not, as shown in Table 9.8. Here we see that only the difference between C and A is greater than the minimum. Alternatively, we can see that the F'-ratio for C and A is the only one that is greater than F'-crit.

Now try an example yourself on Excel in Activity 9.7.

ACTIVITY 9.7

Make a copy of Table 9.9 on another worksheet. If you have not already done so, carry out the analysis of variance but using $\alpha = 0.05$. This should produce the table on the right. Now all that has to be done is add what is shown in rows 17–20.

Which, if any, of the pairs are significantly different?

We will consider non-parametric tests in the next chapter before looking at some more articles and reports that used statistical tests to resolve hypotheses.

TABLE 9.9 Data for ANOVA and the results of the test from Excel with Scheffé post hoc comparison of cell means

	A	B	C	D	E	F	G	H	I	J	K
1	Group A	Group B	Group C		Anova: Single Factor						
2	23	32	31								
3	22	34	20								
4	26	43	23		SUMMARY						
5	25	36	26		Groups	Count	Sum	Average	Variance		
6	29	27	35		Group A	10	282	28.2	18.0		
7	33	32	37		Group B	9	313	34.8	20.2		
8	35	34	32		Group C	8	233	29.1	34.1		
9	28	38	29								
10	30	37			ANOVA						
11	31				Source of Variation	SS	df	MS	F	P-value	F crit
12					Between Groups	231.97	2	115.98	4.95	0.02	3.40
13	28.2	34.8	29.1	= mean	Within Groups	562.03	24	23.42			
14											
15	α =	0.05			Total	794.00	26				
16											
17	Post hoc analysis of differences in means:										
18	B - A	C - A	B - C		Harmonic mean =	8.93					
19	6.6	0.9	5.7	= diff	Scheffé min diff =	5.95					
20	8.25	0.16	6.09	= F'	Scheffé F'-crit =	6.81					

=HARMEAN(F5:F7)

=SQRT(2*F20*$H13/9)

=G12*FINV(0.05, G12, G13)

=(C19^2)/(2*$H13/$F18) and Copy left

=B13-C13 and similarly for the other two

10

Non-parametric Tests

Experimental, quasi-experimental and *ex post facto* designs often generate results that are not interval data, continuous numbers, but nominal or ordinal data instead. Thus parametric tests are not the appropriate tools to resolve the hypotheses. There is a need for tests that basically do not have all the constraints of parametric tests, some for which there are no assumptions about the type of data, or normal distributions for interval/ratio data. Not surprisingly, these are referred to as non-parametric tests, and they are appropriate for analysing nominal and rank/ordinal data. They do have some requirements of their own and their disadvantage is that their use is more likely to incur a Type II error than a parallel parametric test. They are often rated against comparable parametric tests in terms of *power efficiency*, which Siegel and Castellan (1988) describe for a test that has a power efficiency of 90% as 'when all the conditions of the parametric statistical test are satisfied the appropriate parametric test would be just as effective with a sample which is 10% smaller than that used in the non-parametric analysis'.

The number and variety of tests are considerable and beyond the scope of this book (see Siegel and Castellan (1988), probably the most comprehensive book available), but one of the more common ones will be used in an example to illustrate the basic differences with parametric tests: *chi-square* or χ^2. This is primarily used with nominal data, but is sometimes used with ordinal data where frequencies of ranked categories are used, due to its simplicity, though it may increase slightly the probability of making a Type II error. We will go back over the three basic types of research design used to describe parametric tests and show the non-parametric equivalents.

Before looking at the tests themselves, it is worth considering the types of research questions they can resolve and what the differences are between these and the ones answered by parametric tests. Sometimes the questions have to be changed owing to the nature of the data that can be collected. Imagine the situation where the research question asked whether there was a difference between two groups in the conservativeness of their political views. If the study were to use, say, an instrument on strength of conservative political views and generate a score for each person, then the mean scores of the two groups could be compared to see if there were a difference using the *t*-test. On the other hand, if one were to record what party each group said they voted for in a recent election, assuming one party were identifiably conservative, then the frequency of voters for each party for each group would constitute the data. To resolve the difference in voting patterns for the two groups, the χ^2-test would be appropriate. But note that two different questions are being answered:

1 Is there a difference in voting patterns between the two groups?
2 Is there a difference in level of conservatism between the two groups?

Thus one must be aware that the type of data collected may influence what question is being answered. In both cases, one might wish to infer whether there is a difference in conservatism between the two groups, but only the first really answers that question. We will come back to a numerical example of this question, but let us first look at some examples of non-parametric tests that are parallel to the z-test and t-test.

ONE-SAMPLE TEST

As seen earlier, the question to be answered by such tests is whether or not the sample or group at hand is typical or representative of a larger group (population). Non-parametric tests are appropriate for situations where the data is not interval or ratio. Therefore, instead of measuring a characteristic of a group and filling a frequency table with frequencies for different intervals, the frequencies are for nominal or ordinal characteristics.

Take the (fictitious) case of a survey carried out in an English village pub one evening, to ascertain the political affiliation of the patrons. The question was, are they, the sample, a typical cross-section of voters in that ward, the population? The first column of numbers in Table 10.1 provides the results of the survey. Note that the patrons are grouped not according to a measurement on an interval scale (height, IQ, etc.), but according to a *nominal scale*: political affiliation. There is no mean or standard deviation – these have no meaning here. To resolve the question, there is a need to compare these results with the characteristics of the larger population. It was decided that the recent village council election would provided a valid indication of the voting tendencies of the ward (the population), and thus the results of the last election appear in the second column of numbers as percentages. Using the total number of persons in the pub survey, the third column shows the expected frequencies for a sample this size based upon the percentages in the recent council election. The fourth column of numbers is the difference between the observed and expected frequencies squared divided by the expected frequency, to give an indication of the relative size of the variation from the expected. These are all added together to form the chi-square statistic, and, again, this is checked against a probability table. The addition in the last column is usually represented by the equation for the chi-square test, which says in mathematical symbols, add up all of the values in the last column,

$$\chi^2 = \sum \frac{(O - E)^2}{E} \quad \text{(one sample)} \quad (10.1)$$

TABLE 10.1   *Chi-square test of political affiliations of patrons of the Green Toad pub on a given night, using expected affiliations based upon recent voting patterns in the ward*

Parties	Observed frequency (O)	Recent election (%)	Expected frequency (E)	$\dfrac{(O-E)^2}{E}$
Labour	24	32	27.84	0.53
Conservative	18	30	26.10	2.51
Liberal Democrat	33	32	27.84	0.96
Raving Loony	12	6	5.22	8.81
Totals	87	100	87.00	$\chi^2 = 12.81$
				$p < 0.05$

The results in Table 10.1 show that the null hypothesis, no difference between the political affiliations of those in the pub and the ward as a whole, was rejected and that the group in the Green Toad on that night would not be considered representative of the recent voting population. For those of you who are not familiar with British politics: yes, there is a Monster Raving Loony Party, though its membership is rather small.

Carrying out chi-square test for one group on a spreadsheet

Since there is no automatic way of carrying out a chi-square test in Excel, it is necessary to set the data out on a worksheet and do the calculations, which is still easier than doing it on paper with a calculator. The chi-square goodness-of-fit test to check whether a sample is typical of a larger (known) population is quite straightforward. Table 10.2 uses the data in Table 10.1 with the raw frequencies shown in the shaded cells. The rest of the cells contain formulae to calculate the required values. In several cases, as you will see, it is easiest to type in the formula in one cell and then use the **Copy** facility to copy it down a column or across a row. This requires one to be careful about the use of $ when designating cells that you do *not* want to change during copying, since without it the cell designations will change.

For example, the calculation of the **Expected frequencies** is based upon the product of the **Total** number of participants and the **Expected probability** for each group. Thus for Labour voters, it is the product of the contents of **B6** and **C2** (note the dashed arrows). We use **B$6** so that when the contents of **D2** are copied down the page, the total stays the same but the expected frequency changes in column **D** depending on the expected probability in column **C**.

The test of significance is again one that depends on a distribution of all possible samples. Here the distribution is one of possible chi-square ratio values for all samples having four categories being compared with the

TABLE 10.2 *Chi-square goodness-of-fit test from Table 7.6 displayed on a worksheet, using **Tools, Auditing, Trace Precedents** to show contributors to cell **D2**, Expected freq (E) for Labour with dashed arrows*

	A	B	C	D	E	
1	Parties	Observed freq (O)	Expected prob	Expected freq (E)	$(O-E)^2$ / E	=B$6*C2 & Copy down column
2	Labour	24	0.32 -->	27.84	0.53	
3	Cons	18	0.30	26.10	2.51	=(B2-D2)^2/D2 & Copy down column
4	Lib Dem	33	0.32	27.84	0.96	
5	Rav Loon	12	0.06	5.22	8.81	=SUM(D2:D5) & Copy across row
6	Totals:	87	1.00	87.00		
7	df =	3		χ^2-ratio=	12.81	
8	α =	0.01		p =	0.005	
9				χ^2- critical=	11.34	

=COUNTA(A2:A5)-1

=SUM(E2:E5)
=CHIDIST(E7,B7)
=CHIINV(B8,B7)

population expected frequencies (essentially two groups). Thus the degrees of freedom are found by

$$df = m - 1 \qquad (10.2)$$

where *m* is the number of categories. Thus for this situation with four categories, *df* = 3, and Figure 10.1 shows the corresponding chi-square distribution. There is a different chi-square distribution for each number of degrees of freedom, but most books just have the tables for the critical values for α = 0.10, 0.05, 0.01 and 0.001 for a list of degrees of freedom. The distributions become shorter and spread more to the left as the degrees of freedom (and number of groups) increase, and thus the critical values increase.

Rather than use a table, the worksheet in Table 10.2 generates a critical value (cell **E9**) with which you can compare the actual ratio (in cell **E7**) to see if it is significant. The *p* value in cell **E8** simply gives a rough probability for the ratio in **E7**. Carry out Activity 10.1 at this time.

ACTIVITY 10.1

(a) Open a new worksheet and set up the one shown in Table 10.2.
(b) Change the level of α to 0.005. Is the difference in voting patterns still significantly different? One cannot always go by what is in cell **E8** as it is subject to being rounded off. Compare the χ^2-ratio to the critical value.

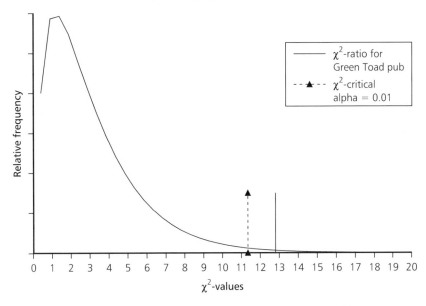

Chi-square sampling distribution for *df* = 3

FIGURE 10.1 *Sampling distribution for the problem shown in Table 10.2,*
with the chi-square ratio and critical values both shown

TWO GROUPS

As can be seen from Table 10.11 at the end of this chapter, there are several
possible non-parametric tests for two groups. The following example only
covers one, again using the chi-square test for simplicity, to illustrate the use
of such tests.

Carrying the above example a little further, in an effort to resolve whether
the patrons of the Green Toad and the nearby Red Herring pub had much
the same political preferences, since they were in the same ward, the patrons
of the Red Herring were interviewed as well. (Consider the sampling and
data collection problems: they would not be trivial!) The question here is, can
they be considered to be from the same population with respect to voting
pattern? Here, there is no comparison with the rest of the ward, but rather a
comparison with each other. They could have comparable voting preferences and still both be atypical for the ward. The results for both pubs are
listed in Table 10.3, called a contingency table.

To use the chi-square test in this situation, the expected frequencies
column is generated from the percentages derived from the combined
frequencies of both surveys. These in turn are used to determine the
expected frequencies, as listed in Table 10.4. The same calculation is carried
out, this time for eight groups, to see if the sum produces a significant chi-
square statistic, which it does not. What does this tell us? Though there is a
difference in voting patterns, it is not significant (n.s.) and it could be attributed to chance alone or natural variation between samples.

TABLE 10.3 *Contingency table (2 × 4) showing the results of the surveys on political preference at the Green Toad and Red Herring pubs*

	Green Toad	Red Herring	Totals	Percentages
Labour	24	16	40	24.5
Conservative	18	10	28	17.2
Liberal Democrat	33	36	69	42.3
Raving Loony	12	14	26	16.0
Totals	87	76	163	100.0

TABLE 10.4 *Chi-square test comparing political affiliations of patrons of the Green Toad and Red Herring pubs on a given night, using expected affiliations based upon combined patterns*

Parties	Observed frequency (O)	Expected percentage	Expected frequency (E)	$\frac{(O-E)^2}{E}$
Green Toad:				
Labour	24	24.5	21.35	0.33
Conservative	18	17.2	14.94	0.62
Liberal Democrat	33	42.3	36.83	0.40
Raving Loony	12	16.0	13.88	0.25
Red Herring:				
Labour	16	24.5	18.65	0.38
Conservative	10	17.2	13.06	0.71
Liberal Democrat	36	42.3	32.17	0.46
Raving Loony	14	16.0	12.12	0.29
Total	163		163.00	$\chi^2 = 3.44$
				n.s.

This table can be represented as an equation that adds up the final column, the variations for the two groups:

$$\chi^2 = \sum_{\text{Group 1}} \frac{(O-E)^2}{E} + \sum_{\text{Group 2}} \frac{(O-E)^2}{E} \quad \text{(two groups)} \quad (10.3)$$

The degrees of freedom are still $df = 3$, since there are two groups and four categories and since for this test,

$$df = (m-1)(k-1) \quad (10.4)$$

where m is the number of categories and k the number of groups.

This second common non-parametric test is the analogue to the *t*-test: comparing two groups to see if they belong to a common population for a trait. In this case, it is the distribution of frequencies in categories for the two

TABLE 10.5 *Worksheet for frequency data in Table 7.7, showing how to carry out the chi-square test, with **Tools**, **Auditing**, **Trace Precedents** to show contributors to cells **E3** and **F2***

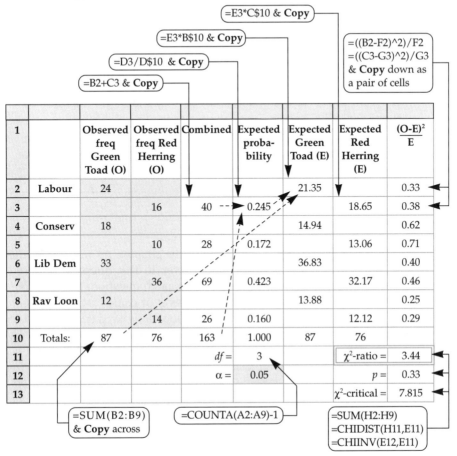

1		Observed freq Green Toad (O)	Observed freq Red Herring (O)	Combined	Expected proba-bility	Expected Green Toad (E)	Expected Red Herring (E)	(O-E)² E
2	Labour	24				21.35		0.33
3			16	40	0.245		18.65	0.38
4	Conserv	18				14.94		0.62
5			10	28	0.172		13.06	0.71
6	Lib Dem	33				36.83		0.40
7			36	69	0.423		32.17	0.46
8	Rav Loon	12				13.88		0.25
9			14	26	0.160		12.12	0.29
10	Totals:	87	76	163	1.000	87	76	
11				df =	3		χ²-ratio =	3.44
12				α =	0.05		p =	0.33
13							χ²-critical =	7.815

Formula callouts (top):
- =E3*C$10 & Copy
- =E3*B$10 & Copy
- =D3/D$10 & Copy
- =B2+C3 & Copy
- =((B2-F2)^2)/F2
- =((C3-G3)^2)/G3 & Copy down as a pair of cells

Formula callouts (bottom):
- =SUM(B2:B9) & Copy across
- =COUNTA(A2:A9)-1
- =SUM(H2:H9)
- =CHIDIST(H11,E11)
- =CHIINV(E12,E11)

groups. But as we will see below, it does not necessarily answer the same kind of question as a *t*-test.

Carrying out chi-square test for two groups on a spreadsheet

To illustrate how this is calculated, the data for comparing the patrons of the two pubs shown in Table 10.4 is displayed in the worksheet in Table 10.5. The raw frequencies for selecting political preferences are placed in the shaded cells. The other cells with numbers actually contain the formulae shown.

The data from the two are essentially combined to set up expectations as if there were a common population for the two. As this example has $df = 3$, where do the ratio and critical values appear on the distribution in

Figure 10.1? Setting up the problem on a worksheet allows you to change values, for example, in this case, see what it would take to make a significant difference in Activity 10.2.

ACTIVITY 10.2

(a) Open a new worksheet and set up the one shown in Table 10.5. The totals at the bottom of each column allow you to check yourself: those for the observed frequency should be the same as those for the expected.

(b) Change the number of Raving Loony voters in the Red Herring pub from 14 to 24. Is the difference in voting patterns now significantly different?

WHICH TO USE: *t*-TEST OR CHI-SQUARE?

This question was raised at the beginning of the chapter. As was noted, the most obvious criterion for deciding the answer to this question is based upon the type of data collected to answer a research question. For example, if the question were 'Is there a difference in level of conservatism between patrons of two pubs?' then we would have to look at what data was used to answer the question. Simply put, if the data were scores that would meet the criteria in the left column of Table 10.6, then the parametric *t*-test would be appropriate. But if patrons were classified into categories, and frequencies belonging to each category tallied, then the data would require the non-parametric chi-square test.

To be more specific, let us map out two answers to the question by elaborating on two ways the variable could be operationally defined. We could define 'level of conservatism' by designing a purpose-made test that would give a score relative to the level of conservatism and then administer it to patrons. Alternatively, we could take the view that action speaks louder than words and simply ask them which party they voted for (or would vote for) in an election. Following the two lines of logic results in two different tests as outlined in Table 10.7, and logically following, the two statistical tests.

We can even illustrate the results with hypothetical data to show what could be the kind of outcomes in each case. This is shown in Table 10.8, with sample data for each of the two approaches. This raises a question about the measurements of the variable, 'conservatism': are they really measuring the same thing with two different instruments? Or could there be other components or factors that might influence the outcomes of either instrument that may distort their responses? This is where the arguments begin.

The researcher using the questionnaire on conservatism could maintain that the instrument is independent of *who* is running for office, the argument being that personality may encourage or discourage voters regardless of

TABLE 10.6   *Criteria for choosing between parametric and non-parametric tests*

Parametric	Non-parametric
Continuous data (scores)	Nominal data (frequencies in categories)
Normal distributions for all groups	Ordinal data (ranks)
	Non-normal distributions of continuous data

TABLE 10.7   *An example of two ways to answer ostensibly the same question*

Parametric	Non-parametric
Are patrons of one pub more conservative than another?	Do the patrons of two pubs vote along the same party lines?
Questionnaire (20 questions, 5-point scale) as a measure of 'conservatism'. The higher the score, the more conservative a person is. Individual score range: 20–100.	How many voted for (or would vote for) each of the political parties represented in local elections (frequencies in for each party)?
Compare mean scores for each pub with a *t*-test	Compare voting frequencies for the two pubs using chi-square

TABLE 10.8   *Data and results for the example of two ways to answer ostensibly the same question*

	Parametric			Non-parametric	
	Green Toad	Red Herring		Green Toad	Red Herring
Mean	78	68	Labour	24	16
Std dev.	22	24	Conservative	18	10
Number	87	76	Liberal Democrat	33	36
			Raving Loony	12	14

$t = 2.76$ ($p < 0.05$)

∴ Reject H_0: there probably is a difference in level of conservatism

$\chi^2 = 3.44$ (n.s.)

∴ Accept H_0: there is probably no difference in voting patterns

their political affiliation. The researcher asking patrons to indicate which party they will vote for claims that this avoids abstractions and gets them to commit their beliefs to action, focusing on issues. What becomes apparent is that the statistical tests are definitely the most appropriate for the data collected, but there is some question as to which is most appropriate to answer the research question. In other words, the potential for disagreement lies with the choice of operational definition (i.e. instrument) and *not* the statistical test! You can address this as you consider the question in Activity 10.3.

ACTIVITY 10.3

There are other strengths and weaknesses to both arguments for the measurement approaches taken. Can you elaborate on these?

CROSSTABS, A SPECIAL CASE

Many statistical packages will carry out cross-tabulations, calculations relating to χ^2 on pairs of binary variables, like gender, responses to pairs of yes/no questions (a dubious practice since single questions have such low reliability and validity), etc., from 2×2 contingency tables. How these should be reported depends on the nature of the research question and the sample or samples. Let us take a simple example to illustrate the problem. A research study wanted to know whether there was any relationship between gender of secondary school teachers and a propensity to be a cigarette smoker. Two approaches could be taken to the problem of sampling:

(a)   A random sample of 50 male teachers and a random sample of 50 female teachers could each be surveyed to find out whether they were smokers or not.
(b)   A random sample of teachers could be taken from the rolls and a simple survey conducted to find out whether they smoked or not, and their gender.

Now the difference does not seem important, but the second might reflect differences in proportions within the profession. Also, though both are *ex post facto* designs, the questions they are answering are slightly different:

(a)   Two samples from the two populations would allow us to answer the question, is there a difference between the genders in the propensity to smoke? This would be tested using a chi-square test on a 2×2 table.
(b)   A single sample should provide us with a description of strength of association, analogous to correlations between continuous variables seen earlier, using the phi, ϕ, coefficient of association, based upon a 2×2 table.

The phi coefficient is found simply by

$$\phi = \sqrt{\frac{\chi^2}{n}} \tag{10.5}$$

Two difficulties arise: most statistical packages give both, *and* the test of significance of the ϕ coefficient is the chi-square test. Confused? Let us put some numbers to this problem to illustrate how the results could be interpreted.

Table 10.9 provides a special 2×2 contingency table for χ^2, adapted from the one in Table 10.5 (by **Deleting** the unneeded cells), and includes a

TABLE 10.9 *A 2 × 2 contingency table with both χ^2 and ϕ coefficients reported*

1		Smokers	Non-smokers	Combined	Expected prob	Expected smokers (E)	Expected non-smokers (E)	$(O-E)^2/E$
2	Men	20				26.25		1.49
3			36	56	0.583		29.75	1.31
4	Women	25				18.75		2.08
5			15	40	0.417		21.25	1.84
6	Totals:	45	51	96	1.000	45	51	
7				$df =$	1		χ^2-ratio =	6.72
8				$\alpha =$	0.05		$p =$	0.01
9	phi =	0.26					χ^2-critical =	3.841

=SQRT(H7/D6)

calculation of the ϕ coefficient. The results would be reported in one of the following ways, using the letter labels as before:

(a) There is a difference in smoking/non-smoking tendencies between men and women.
(b) There is a moderate (but significant) relationship between smoking and gender.

Carry out Activity 10.4 at this time.

ACTIVITY 10.4

Implement the worksheet in Table 10.9. Investigate the impact on ϕ and χ^2 of changing frequencies of responses.

THREE OR MORE GROUPS

There is a non-parametric χ^2 analogue to the analysis of variance for testing differences across three or more groups, but it lacks the clear-cut equivalances for testing each of the pairs. To illustrate the type of questions that could be answered, let us consider the following hypothetical study. Bernard Bean wanted to know if there was any difference in smoking habits among coffee drinkers. He negotiated with the local coffee shop that let customers drink as many cups as they like to ask questions of a random selection of each group: those who drank only a single cup, two-cup drinkers and those who drank three or more cups at a sitting. He simply asked these people about their smoking habits. His results are summarized in columns B, C and D in Table 10.10.

TABLE 10.10   *Chi-square for three groups of coffee drinkers*

Annotation boxes (top):
- =$F$7*B$11 & **Copy diagonally**
- =$F$10*B$11 & **Copy diagonally**
- =$F$4*B$11 & **Copy diagonally**
- =(B2-G2)^2/G2 Similarly each cell below so that it includes the difference for that row

	A	B	C	D	E	F	G	H	I	J
1		One cup	Two cup	Three or more	Combined	Exp prob	Exp one cup	Exp two cup	Exp three or more	(O-E)²/E
2	Smokers	12					19.90			3.135
3			24					21.60		0.266
4				20	56	28.43%			14.50	2.088
5	Ex-	25					24.87			0.001
6	smokers		30					27.01		0.332
7				15	70	35.53%			18.12	0.538
8	Non-	33					25.23			2.394
9	smokers		22					27.39		1.061
10				16	71	36.04%			18.38	0.308
11	Totals:	70	76	51	197	100.00%	70	76	51	
12							$df =$	4	χ^2-ratio =	10.123
13							$\alpha =$	0.05	$p =$	0.04
14									χ^2-critical =	9.488

Annotation boxes (bottom):
- =SUM(B2:B10) & **Copy across the row**
- =B8+C9+D10 & **Copy up to other two cells**
- =E10/E$11 & **Copy up to other two cells**
- =CHIINV(H13,H12)
- =SUM(J2:J10)

Column E combines each group and is used to generate expected percentages in column F, which are in turn used to provide expected frequencies. The variations for each group are calculated as before. The degrees of freedom for this 3×3 design are

$$df = (3 - 1)(3 - 1) = 4$$

As can be seen from the results, there is a difference in smoking patterns across the three groups of coffee drinkers, but it is difficult to tell the source (see Siegel and Castellan (1988) if you are interested in taking this further). Note that to answer the alternative question 'is there a difference in coffee drinking patterns across smoking habits?' would require that random samples be taken from smokers, a subtle difference considering the data would look much the same. Thus which question is answered depends on how the samples were drawn. Carry out Activity 10.5 at this time.

TABLE 10.11 *Some typical parametric and non-parametric tests (after Black, 1999)*

Measure (optimal)	One-sample	Two groups Independent	Two groups Related/ matched	Three or more groups Independent	Three or more groups Related/ matched
Interval/ ratio	z-test t-test ($n < 30$)	t-tests	$t_{related}$-test	One-way ANOVA Factorial ANOVA	Randomized block ANOVA ANCOVA (Analysis of covariance)
Ordinal	Kolmogorov– Smirnov test	Kolmogorov– Smirnov test Wilcoxon– Mann– Whitney test	Wilcoxon signed ranks test	Kruskal–Wallis one-way analysis of variance	Freidman two-way analysis of variance by ranks
Nominal	χ^2-test goodness-of-fit	χ^2-test, $k \times 2$ table	McNemar change test	χ^2-test for $m \times k$ tables	Cochran Q-test

---

ACTIVITY 10.5

Implement the worksheet in Table 10.10. Investigate the impact on χ^2 of changing frequencies of responses.

SUMMARY

As noted earlier, Table 10.11 lists comparable non-parametric tests to the parametric ones described before, including tests for three or more groups. The tests that use ordinal and nominal variables for correlations shown in Table 10.11 are also non-parametric tests.

Choosing an appropriate test is often a matter of matching the test to the research question and the consequential type of data and, for parametric tests, making sure that all of the assumptions have been met. There is the danger of degradation of data by using a 'lower' test by considering interval data as rank-ordered data and using a non-parametric test. This can increase the risk of making a Type II error, that is not finding significance when it really is there. It is also

continued

possible to degrade data by considering ranked data as nominal when selecting a less appropriate test. On the other hand, sometimes the reverse happens where a parametric test is used with ranked data, particularly when total scores on questionnaires are used, a choice that can be argued when the range of scores is large. Justification for deviating from what might be expected, going either way, should be presented by researchers in their reports.

Much more complex designs than those used as examples above appear in the literature, employing multidimensional schemes, examining the potential interrelationships among an even larger number of variables. The statistical tests exist, but the interpretation becomes increasingly complex. Yet this is to be expected, since rarely do we find that any one human characteristic, trait or event has a single cause. As noted before, the task that faces the social science researcher is complex simply because of the nature of his/her subjects, so it is not surprising that the tools are not simple either. Like any complex tool, measurement and statistics applied to complex designs require care and skill if they are to be employed appropriately. All too often, though, it is not the choice of statistical test that is at fault, but any one of the other criteria that are being considered in this book.

CRITERIA FOR EVALUATING INFERENTIAL STATISTICS (PARAMETRIC AND NON-PARAMETRIC)

The following are some guidelines for applying the criteria in this column of the Profiling Sheet, with an emphasis on choice of tests.

Appropriate choice of statistical test (and design) for the research question
This and the next criterion can be difficult to judge. While the statement of the question and the null hypothesis form the basis for the study, a study may not tell you enough to know whether or not the design is the best. What can be judged is the logical consistency across the questions, the variables measured and the statistical test chosen. Does the test resolve the question? Also, some studies could have considered the interaction of more variables, but have not done so through oversight, or insufficiently large sample to fill all the cells in the design. Sometimes the limitations are resources, which influence the sample size and therefore the complexity of the study.

A more powerful test could have been used   This criticism can be levelled at some correlational studies; based upon the research questions asked, an experimental or another *ex post facto* approach would have produced more profitable results. Alternatively, the test does not take advantage of the level of data; for example, a non-parametric test has been used where a parametric one was appropriate, thus increasing the risk of a Type II error (not finding a significant difference when there was one). This judgement can be based upon the type of data (nominal, ordinal, interval or ratio), which will determine the variety of appropriate tests. Tables 8.1 and 10.11 can be used as a first reference, though if there is still doubt, ask someone who has more experience with statistics.

Missing analysis where needed   The data was collected or available (e.g. *ex post facto*), but not analysed. Hypotheses could have been tested.

Inappropriately analysed, tests performed not appropriate   This ranges from using repeated tests on pairs (multiple *t*-tests), where a more complex design would have been appropriate, to using a parametric test on data (nominal or ordinal, or non-normally distributed data) when a non-parametric test would have been more appropriate. Because of the nature of the statistical tests, there is often a greater risk of a Type I error because of this (finding significant differences where they do not really exist). It can also result from choosing a statistical test that simply does not answer the research question.

No justification for analysis, post hoc *data snooping*   There are those who are like young stamp collectors – they gather data but for no planned reason. Then there is the magic trip to the computing centre where some kind soul puts the data into a statistical package and, miraculously, out comes statistical significance! Articulate researchers can cover up this approach, with clever words and conclusions. Reading reports can be a bit like looking for the small print in a legal document. One must understand the rules of the game to be able to spot the more subtle violations or not meeting the assumptions of a test.

To pull all these criteria together, now try Activity 10.6.

ACTIVITY 10.6

Obtain articles that have used non-parametric inferential statistical analysis such as χ^2 (often easily identified by the presence of probabilities, e.g. $p < 0.05$, for significance levels). Evaluate each using copies of the Profiling Sheet at the end of the chapter.

Profiling Sheet: *Understanding Social Science Research,* © Thomas R. Black, 2001

Article: _____

Type of Study: ☐ Descriptive, ☐ Survey/correlational, ☐ *Ex post facto,* ☐ Experimental/quasi-experimental.

Questions/ hypotheses	Representativeness	Ethics and Confidentiality	Data Quality I	Data Quality II	Descriptive Statistics	Inferential Statistics
Valid question or hypothesis based on accepted theory with well-justified referenced support	Whole population	Ethical standards met and data sufficiently confidential that no individuals or institutions can be identified	Educationally, sociologically, psychologically, etc., significant and manageable number of concepts	Commercially or professionally produced/tested with high validity, reliability and objectivity (V, R, O)	Appropriate display of data and results as statistics or in tables and/or graphs, clearly labelled	Appropriate choice of design and statistical tests for resolving H_0
Valid question or hypothesis based on own theory, well justified	Random selection from a well-specified population		Limited academic significance, very narrow perspective	Project or personally produced/tested with high V, R, O	Some inadequacies in presentation of tables/graphs	A more powerful test could have been used
Credible question/ hypothesis but alternative possible, or too extensive/global, or support missing	Purposive sample from a well-specified population, with justification for representativeness	Ethical issues not addressed or confidentiality not discussed when it should have been	Large number of concepts, potentially confusing	Commercially or project produced with moderate V, R, O	Other methods of display of data/results would have been more appropriate	Missing analysis where needed
Weak question/ hypothesis, poorly stated, or justified with inappropriate references	Volunteers or convenience, with no justification of representativeness	Ethical issues not addressed and/or some loss of confidentiality	Too many concepts and variables investigated to provide meaningful results	Commercially or project produced with low V, R, O, or no information provided	Serious misconceptions encouraged owing to nature of graphical display of results	Inappropriately analysed data, tests performed not appropriate
No question or hypothesis stated, or inconsistent with known facts	Unidentified group	Ethical standards violated and/or subjects endangered owing to no confidentiality	Trivial concepts, not academically significant	Inappropriate instrument for the variables/concepts described	Intentionally misleading use of descriptive statistics	No justification for statistical analysis, just *post hoc* data snooping

Comments and justification for classification:

11

Controlling Variables and Drawing Conclusions

Up to this point, a wide variety of interrelated criteria for judging the appropriateness of the design and employment of sampling techniques, measuring instruments, presentation of data, and statistical tests has been introduced. Interrelationships have been identified as often as possible, showing where decisions at one level will affect the quality of the procedure at another, which in turn will affect the *strength* of the inferences and conclusions the researcher can make. The main problem is that usually it is just the relative value of the conclusion that is affected and rarely is a piece of research totally useless. This places the onus on the reader to decide just how much value to place on the outcomes of a given piece of research when citing them as a basis or justification of his/her own study. This is not a trivial decision and is one that requires careful consideration. Just how far from the ideal can the procedure of a study deviate from accepted standards and still have the results be considered as valid? By now, the criteria in the previous ten chapters should have been applied to a variety of articles. This alone should provide you with some insight into the answer to this question, since every situation is going to be different.

It must be remembered that research is an ongoing process, social science research rarely produces earth-shaking discoveries, and every researcher builds on the works of others, no matter how imperfect they may be. As researchers, we all should be able to learn from our own and others' mistakes. Ideally, it is the researcher's task to collect (in a replicable manner) and present evidence dispassionately. It is recognized that it is impossible to separate researchers from their beliefs, particularly since these are often the motivation for carrying out the research in the first place. Yet most researchers should endeavour to carry out their research in such a way as to survive public scrutiny and not produce unwarranted conclusions. As a reader, you will have to contend with the imperfect real world, with a knowledge gained from this text of what ought to be. To this end, the final chapter will bring together the criteria presented earlier, showing how earlier procedures in a research project can affect the appropriateness and strength of conclusions in reports.

CAUSE AND EFFECT

Not surprisingly, this is very difficult, and sometimes impossible to prove, even when a study has been rigorously planned. There are a number of ways to maintain 'control' over variables, ensuring that the effect observed is due to the limited number in which the researcher is interested and not some other *extraneous* variables. For example, this is achieved through representative sampling in *ex post facto* studies where life events are equivalent to treatments. True experimental studies will require some form of random distribution of subjects across groups to receive different treatments. All studies endeavour to avoid the introduction of their own unwanted variables by careful design and administration of the measuring instruments. Yet structuring a study so that it is possible to justify any tendency for cause and effect relationships requires the researcher to plan and execute the study with extreme care, including making an appropriate choice of variables. Global variables, such as social class or amount of education, lack sufficient specificity to be the cause of events or traits.

Statements often appear in reports such as 'there was a significant difference between the scores of two groups', which subsequently are used to justify the existence of a cause and effect relationship between the two variables. Unfortunately, statistical tests can only confirm or refute that the difference is so great that it is unlikely to be due to natural variation across samples. In addition many of the more interesting events in the world, particularly human-influenced ones, have multiple causes and many that may not be at all obvious. This is partially due to the fact that the events do not occur with the definite predictability of everyday happenings. For example, when someone hits a table with a hammer, unless you are deaf, you will hear a noise. The probabilistic world is equivalent to expecting a noise, but recognizing that there is a finite probability there will not be one. In statistically based social science research, the problem is even more complicated: while statistical significance does tell us that whatever difference that exists probably did not occur by chance alone, it does *not* tell us what did cause the difference. This is somewhat like watching a magician about whom we have a considerable amount of suspicion: if he hits the watch rolled up in the cloth with a hammer, is the noise we hear that of the hammer hitting the watch? The proof may require careful investigation to confirm or refute what the appropriate inference is (what caused the sound) for our observation (seeing the cloth struck and hearing the sound). While the magician may deny us the opportunity for closer observation, the researcher when writing a report should not.

Let us consider a simple example. If you measure how tall all of the 10 year olds and 8 year olds in a school are, within each group the heights will not be the same. While 10 year olds will *tend* to be taller than the 8 year olds, not all the children in the older group will be taller than all those in the younger group. They may overlap since age is not related to a certain single height. Even if a representative group of all children having the same birth date were chosen, the heights would vary. Not surprisingly, if a graph were plotted of the heights versus number of people for a large sample, we would find that the heights would vary normally around a mean for an age group. Also, the mean height of the 10 year olds would probably exceed that of the 8 year olds, and a statistical test (e.g. a *t*-test) would show that they did indeed not belong to the same population for height. But from this data alone, we are still none the wiser as to the *cause* of the differences in height, either within the groups or between the groups.

While direct cause and effect is difficult to define in the same way as the sound produced by a hammer, with such *ex post facto* studies we can say that there is a *tendency* for older children to be taller than younger children, based on observations such as those described. Describing this relationship as height associated with age is better than saying age causes one to be taller. Age itself does not cause a child to be taller: there are underlying biological processes that are the actual cause – age is only a convenient marker. What makes it even more difficult to analyse is the fact that we all have known an 8 year old who was taller than a 10 year old.

Carrying the example one step further, let us now introduce an imaginary situation: in visits to classes of 12 year olds, a researcher unexpectedly visits a class that has a mean height of 1 metre (think about it: these kids are short!). By taking the mean and standard deviation of such a group and comparing it with population parameters using a *z*-test, it is possible to determine the probability of this group of 30 short students belonging to the overall population of 12 year olds, at least with respect to this single trait. In reality, they could be a concentrated group out in the tail of that distribution. If the probability that the sample is typical of those randomly selected from the main population is less than 5% (1 in 20), then it is significant, which is likely in this case. In other words, we would reject the null hypothesis that the group is not different from a truly representative sample from the whole population. Well, the researcher, wanting to be *really* sure, sets the significance level at 1%. In other words, if the probability that this group of apparently exceptionally short students is part of the population of 12 year olds is less than 1%, the researcher will reject the null hypothesis (that they are not different) and accept there is a difference. Theoretically, there is no such thing as a zero probability: the tails of the bell-shaped curve never reach zero, never touch the horizontal line – they just get closer and closer. But we know that in reality, there is a tallest and a shortest (see e.g. the *Guinness Book of Records*).

Assuming the researcher has found a statistically significantly different group of exceptionally short 12 year olds, the question arises, what does it mean? It is probably easier to tell what it does not mean. The statistical significance does not tell us the cause of this shortness, and any researcher trying to ascertain the cause will have to be a good detective to isolate it. And there is the real chance that there is no individual cause. Also, there is the finite probability (1 in 100) that this collection of short 12 year olds in one place is perfectly 'normal', and it is only a chance occurrence (remote as it may be) that they are all in the same class in a school. The statistical test strongly suggests that this is highly unlikely, but it is possible. Now as the researcher is only an observer of life and must employ another *ex post facto* design, it is much less likely that he/she will be able to prove that any cause(s) identified are the correct ones and not something else, since there is no direct control over competing variables.

Following the case of the short 12 year olds a bit further, the researcher proceeds to search for a cause. Through questionnaires and interviews, he discovers that all their parents work at the local bean canning factory and, therefore, have as a bonus a free supply of beans. Since salaries are low, understandably the families eat considerable quantities of beans, again (statistically) significantly more than the national average. Is this the cause of the observed short stature? Our researcher is now obligated to investigate a multitude of other possible causes, ranging from genetics to diet to water, and is unlikely to isolate a single cause in such an *ex post facto* study. Even if a diet of beans were the physiological 'cause', this might satisfy the biologist, but not others. Would a sociologist accept this or prefer to attribute the cause to the position of the parents in the class structure of society? Would an educationist prefer to attribute the cause to lack of knowledge and understanding of proper diet? Would a psychologist wish to pursue the approach that it was manipulation by the bean factory and the parents were inappropriately convinced of the value of a high bean diet, or enticed to eat beans? Each discipline brings along its own perspective of the world, which can influence conclusions.

This conveniently leads to the reason why there is such an interest in true experimental designs. If an experiment is performed where the researcher has control over the independent variables (the possible causes), then justifiably drawing conclusions is a little easier. For our example, it would be advantageous to be able to take a random sample of new-born children from all over the country and raise them on varying proportions of beans in their diet, and monitor their growth over time, but ethics prevents this. Would guinea pigs do for an experiment? Or monkeys? It is apparent that the problem is not with the statistics, it is with the multitude of possible variables and the difficulty in actually carrying out what appears to be the most satisfactory experiment. Studies in the social sciences are no easier to devise. In such situations, it may be that detective techniques based on better designed *ex post facto* studies and other investigative techniques will be needed to resolve the dilemma as to the cause of the observed effect.

The challenge for readers of research reports is to decide how well the researcher has accounted for all the possible causes and how well he/she has justified the identification of the cause of the observed effect, if this is the case. When a report omits a discussion on this, then the reader begins to wonder about the quality of the research and/or the depth of understanding about research design possessed by the researcher. Later discussion will point up some subtle and not so subtle potential sources of weak and inadequate conclusions. In addition, readers would reasonably expect a conscientious researcher to identify limitations of the present study and make recommendations for further work.

CONTROLLING VARIABLES

To be able to justify adequately any cause and effect relationship, a researcher aims to 'control' all the variables in a study. This requires the researcher to ensure that the desired independent variables do have the opportunity to demonstrate an effect on the measured outcome (dependent variable) and eliminate any possible influence by any other specific, potential, independent variables. There are two basic ways to accomplish this: (a) as seen in earlier chapters, design the study actually to use certain characteristics of the sample group as possible independent variables to see if these affect the measured dependent variables; and (b) randomly select or distribute the sample(s) essentially to spread all other possible variables evenly across all groups. Thus, the more complex the study, like multidimensional factorial analysis of variance, the more variables one is trying to control by observing their possible influence on the measured dependent variable. The simpler the study, such as a *t*-test comparing two groups, the more variables one is trying to account for through random sampling and/or random assignment.

Thus, if a study is centred on one set of potential independent variables, those others recognized by the theory being applied as affecting the dependent variables being studied are considered to be *mediating variables*. For example, a study investigating the effect of a new learning situation would want to ensure that each group was initially the same with respect to distribution of intelligence (thus one group should not have a higher mean IQ score), previous learning, interest in the subject matter, resources available outside the learning situation, etc.

To illustrate this further, consider the researcher who wishes to investigate possible variables associated with cognitive emphasis of examinations given by university teachers. In other words, having seen professors' and lecturers' examinations, how might we explain why some papers demand much more intellectually of the learners, and consequently have a larger proportion of questions requiring, say, problem solving than others? There are a number of possible independent variables: age, sex, academic background, subject taught, size of institution, years of non-academic and academic experience, etc. Even choosing the three potential independent variables, academic experience (0–2 years, 3–10 years, 11 or more years), subject taught (science, engineering, humanities) and size of institution (less than 5000 students, 5000–10,000 students, over 10,000 students) means a $3 \times 3 \times 3$ design, as shown in Figure 11.1. This would allow one to check not only the possible relationship between each of these variables individually, but also combinations of variables (the interactions represented by the 27 individual cells in the matrix), on the proportion of problem-solving questions included on examination papers. Thus, one could test not only whether or not different levels of experience were associated with higher level question asking, but also whether one combination of experience, size of institutions and subject were associated with higher level question asking. Unfortunately, there would be 351 possible pair-wise comparisons! The problem then becomes one of making sense of the results. For example, taking just one of these possible pair-wise combinations, what would one say about the result showing that science teachers with 3–10 years' experience at institutions of 5000–10,000 students ask significantly more problem-solving questions than humanities teachers with 0–2 years' experience at institutions with less than

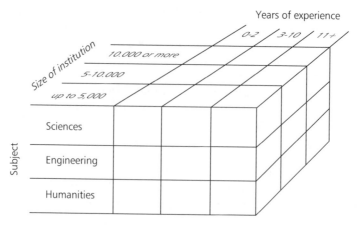

FIGURE 11.1   *A 3×3×3 design with percentage of problem-solving questions on examinations as the dependent variable*

5000 students? This forces us to return to the original plan: were the hypotheses and variables well-thought out in the first place?

Returning to the design, it still would be necessary to control the possible influence of the other potential, independent mediating variables mentioned by random sampling. This would mean each cell would have lecturers of both sexes, of a range of ages, having a variety of academic qualifications, etc. – in other words, typical of lecturers and professors in general. To have a sound sample, it would be preferable to have 30 subjects in each of the 27 cells, or 810 persons! Even if these were randomly selected from institutions, it is likely not all would respond to the request for sample examinations, so that the percentage of questions at higher levels can be determined (dependent variable).

Taking this example on one more stage: when applying for a grant to carry out this investigation, the researcher gets significantly less funding than what was asked for (not surprising). The consequence is that there are resources for a study of 100 lecturers, so it is decided to investigate only one variable, academic subject (three cells). Thus the role of sampling requires that all the other mediating variables (including type of institution and number of degrees) be accounted for by the representativeness. Consequently, in each cell, there will now also be lecturers from all three sizes of institutions having years of experience 'typical' of academics. Though this design does not allow the researcher to comment on any potential contribution of the variables size of institution and relative amount of experience, these have been controlled. Alternatively, the researcher could have fewer persons in each cell for a two-dimensional design (9 cells with 11 each), but finding significance will be more difficult in that the differences in mean number of questions will have to be greater than for larger cell sizes.

And finally, none of these *ex post facto* designs would allow the researcher to determine causal relationships. At best, the outcome would be to describe associational relationships between personal/institutional traits and tendency to ask higher level questions. While this would be a good start, further research would be required to identify 'why' for any significant differences found.

Sources of invalidity

In addition, there are other variables that can affect the outcome(s) of any study. The actual mechanism of collecting the data can interfere with the quality of the results and affect the reliability, validity and objectivity of that data, and consequently the validity of any conclusions. For example, the time at which a test is given, questionnaire completed or observations made could inadvertently introduce a variable that could affect the results. Such a variable might be introduced in such an obvious way as measuring some of the subjects before lunch and some after, or a much more subtle influence such as the presence of an observer, which can affect the performance of some tasks. These extraneous variables not included in the theory or model underlying the study could influence the outcomes. When considering the overall validity of a study, we can distinguish among four types or components:

1 *Internal* validity refers to the logical consistency across the question, hypotheses, choice of variables and choice of instruments.
2 *Construct* validity, as we have seen, is concerned with whether the instrument measures what it is purported to measure.
3 *External* validity relates to the generalizability of results to a larger population.
4 *Statistical* validity is determined by the appropriate choice of statistical test for the data collected and question asked.

Most of these sources of confounding have been mentioned in conjunction with aspects of research design described in earlier chapters, but Campbell and Stanley (1963) have provided a succinct list of 12 factors that can jeopardize validity. These were expanded to 13 by Black (1999) who has included some interactions to provide the set of 15 described below:

1 *No comparison across groups.* With single samples, one can find correlations, but often being able to compare groups provides stronger inferences about relationships between variables.
2 *Time: other events.* Something other than what was intended happens to the subjects between the first test or observation and the second that produces an effect(s) that can be confused with that produced by the independent variable(s). This could range from members of a group watching a television programme to political events.
3 *Time: maturation.* As the name indicates, the subjects mature in some way, becoming older, wiser, hungrier, or even more tired. As can be seen, the time scale will depend upon the nature of the variables involved and could be as short as minutes or as long as years.

4 *Selection: sample (and assignment).* The sample may not be representative of any population, as discussed in Chapter 3. All too often it could be described as 'convenience sampling', using a convenient group, which means that the researcher is really using a whole population, should not be using inferential statistical tests and will not be able to generalize legitimately to any larger group. It is also of prime concern for *ex post facto* studies where representative sampling from the groups that have had the designated life experiences is the basis for justifying the validity of the independent variable. Assignment is particularly important when established groups are selected to be experimental or control groups, subsequently subjected to some experience, and then measured: whether it was the experience or the original group characteristics that made the difference becomes unclear. This is one of the reasons for random assignment to groups (Chapter 3).

5 *Selection: regression.* There is a tendency for some traits to have subjects regress towards the mean with increasing time. In other words, those who did well on the first achievement test tend to come closer to the mean the second time; those who score low on an attitude survey the first time, will score close to the mean, the second.

6 *Selection: sample stability.* Even if one starts with random selection or assignment to groups, there will sometimes be attrition, loss of subjects. Those that are left may well be a different group from that originally selected and mediating variables may no longer be accounted for. Knowing why subjects dropped out can help to discount this extraneous variable, particularly if it can be shown that the reason had nothing to do with the study. Large numbers of subjects can also minimize any effects.

7 *Interaction of time with sample.* For example, selection bias may interact with maturation by selecting one group that was subject to maturation where another was not.

8 *Interaction of independent variable with sample.* Sample selection bias, for example, could influence the effect of an experimental treatment, making it impossible to tell which was the cause of the observed result.

9 *Direction/nature of causality uncertain.* Time delays and choice of variables can result in indeterminacy of direction of relations in experimental designs. *Ex post facto* designs can often tell us there is a difference in groups, but like the study about coffee drinking and smoking, it can be impossible to determine, from the quantitative data alone, whether there is a causal relationship or, if so, in which direction.

10 *Unnatural/invalid experiment/treatment.* Some studies involve multiple treatments over time and the effects of earlier treatments are not erasable. This is particularly true for single groups in learning situations: determining which treatment after the first is the determining factor will be difficult. Just knowing that they are part of an experiment can sometimes affect the performance of subjects and contaminate results, often referred to as the Hawthorn effect. The use of double-blind designs that result

in no one knowing who is in the experimental group and who is in the control group is widely used in medicine to control for psychological effects interfering with medicinal ones. This is more difficult to achieve in social science designs.

11 *Invalid measure of variables.* Instruments can inadvertently measure something other than what was intended. On the other hand, if the categories to which subjects are assigned are not clearly defined, it will not be possible to replicate the study. For example, there is considerable disagreement on how social classes are defined among sociologists, and thus one would expect an explicit operational definition in any study employing this concept. Lack of validity can also result in outcomes only being seen in research situations and not in real life. For example, career choice indicated on a questionnaire may not be matched by true commitment or ability to pursue that career in reality. This is one of the reasons for the emphasis on validity of operational definitions in Chapter 4.

12 *Instrument reliability.* The measuring instruments lack reliability, either inherently or over time. Observers may change their criteria or simply flag with time. This can be checked through the various means of determining the reliability coefficient for an instrument discussed in Chapter 4.

13 *Learning from instrument.* Sometimes the actual measuring instrument or measuring process will affect the outcome(s) on a second, later measure. For example, this could involve subjects actually learning some subject matter from a test, the instrument could constitute practice of a skill in itself, or subjects might become test-wise, just better at that type of test. There is also the possibility that the first measurement increases or decreases the subjects' sensitivity to whatever the experimental treatment is. For example, a before-experience attitude questionnaire could make subjects more sensitive to the experience than in non-experimental situations. Thus, the experiment would not be comparable with real life and the results could not be generalized to the population from which the sample was taken.

14 *Instrument reacts with independent variable.* Recall the example of the considerable discrepancy between pollsters' predictions and the actual outcome in the parliamentary election of 1992 in the United Kingdom described in Chapter 4.

15 *Other interactions.* The possibilities are numerous, but look for idiosyncratic characteristics of groups having a differential effect on outcomes owing to exceptional interactions with treatments, instruments, conditions, or even the researcher.

Obviously, there are numerous potential sources of confounding of results, so that even if one does find a statistically significant result, it will take considerable care to ensure that the identified independent variable in an experimental study is the real cause or contributor to an association between variables. Not always will the reader be able to determine the validity of claims from the information provided in the report or article, but the above does provide an indication of key points to look for when considering a document.

Put in more mathematical terms, Kerlinger and Lee (2000) make the point that the choice of research design and subsequent statistical test is based upon having as great a control over variance as possible: 'Maximize systematic variance, control extraneous variance, and minimize error variance'. These all relate to issues raised earlier:

(a) to maximize systematic variance indicates a need to make sure that as much of the variability round the mean as possible is attributable to those variables in which the researcher is interested;

(b) to control extraneous variance can be interpreted to indicate a need to reduce the amount of variability of scores round the mean that can be attributed to extraneous variables as much as possible; and

(c) to minimize error variance requires that the measuring instruments are as reliable as possible (recall how reliability coefficients are calculated).

These are of obvious importance to parametric statistical tests since they employ variance (standard deviation squared) in the calculations and decisions about significance levels, though analogous sources of variability can be found for non-parametric tests as well.

CRITERIA FOR VARIABLE CONTROL

In summary of the above, the following are the criteria for this column on the Profiling Sheet.

All mediating and extraneous variables accounted for, internal validity maintained   A reader would expect to find a detailed description of the design of the study that described the theory including all possible variables, noted those to be included in the study and how mediating variables were to be controlled, provided sufficient information to have a high mark in the Data Quality II column, and indicated how extraneous variables were controlled.

Most mediating and extraneous variables accounted for   The degree of transgression or omission that will be tolerated is up to the reader. Obviously, most studies will not be perfect, but you will have to decide whether this or the next is appropriate. Comments entered on the Profiling Sheet would clarify such a classification.

Mediating variables controlled only, confounding possible   The researcher has not controlled extraneous variables, thus leaving the source of the effect unclear. Comments as to what you think are the confounding variables would be appropriate.

Inadequate control of variables, confounding probable   Not only are extraneous variables not accounted for, but also mediating variables have not been controlled. Sometimes this results from lack of a clear model or theory, or a lack of a clear research question and hypothesis.

Control of mediating and extraneous variables not discussed, confounding possible   Sometimes this results from a lack of understanding of research processes, or there is a deficiency in writing skills to convey what has been done. Whatever the cause, it is not clear that any variables have been controlled, though something has happened to the subjects and data has been collected; just what has been done to avoid confounding is not clear.

DRAWING CONCLUSIONS

There is the statement supposedly made by a politician that there was a definite problem with the Navy, since half the sailors were below the Navy's average for intelligence. (If you did not laugh, recall what the mean tells us; see Chapter 6.) This points up two main sources of problems that researchers will encounter when drawing conclusions from a measurement-based study: (a) a basic understanding of (or lack of) what research and statistics can tell us; and (b) the problems of controlling extraneous and mediating variables. These ultimately end up being linked when one finds a study making unwarranted claims.

A key suspected source of unreasonable conclusions (here is a study in itself!) is the ubiquitous computer and the vast amount of statistical software available to help carry out calculations. As has been noted before, it is all too easy for a researcher (if he/she can be called that) to collect data unsystematically, trot over to the computer centre, and find a friendly soul who will help enter the data into an apparently appropriate program that will do all the number crunching. Out comes the statistical significance, but what does it all mean? The reason for this speculation comes from reading articles that in one sentence state 'and the difference was significant at the 5% level ($p < 0.05$)', followed by the claim 'thus we can safely say that A caused B'. There is no mention of design structure for the study, much less possible mediating or extraneous variables, and sometimes the sample description leaves much to be desired. Statistical tests only confirm that the differences observed did or did not (probably) happen by chance alone, indicating (in some cases) indirectly how likely that there was some cause. Justification of what the cause might be is a separate matter for the researcher. It also seems a shame to read a report that appears to be the product of a conscientious researcher who has carefully designed instruments and collected data, only to have left it unprotected at the computer centre, allowing someone else to 'squeeze as much as possible out of the data'. A researcher does not have to be a computer wizard to use this tool properly, just informed about what a statistical test will reveal, and to be able to defend his/her choice of test.

The last column of the Profiling Sheet could be considered as the summary of all of the others. Basically, having arrived at the end of the report or article, you are asking, are the results justified? What relative value will I place on these findings? How much will they influence my own research and thinking? There are few perfect reports and there are few totally useless ones, at least in refereed journals, so the evaluation should rarely result in a binary classification of rubbish or perfect. Evaluation implies careful analysis, identification of implied meanings, and deciding how well supported the results and conclusions are. To make matters more complex, the justification for any conclusions is not given just at the end of a report or article; the entire structure of the study and procedure followed constitute part of the justification (or limitations) of the results. The processes involved are much too complex, as this book has endeavoured to demonstrate, to allow the rationalization of results to be confined to a few sentences.

Some common pitfalls

While the following list is not exhaustive, it does include many of the common sources of misleading conclusions in reports and articles (Shipman, 1972; Blum and Foos, 1986; Cohen and Manion, 2000):

• Inadequate theoretical framework leads to poorly or weakly defined variables, for example teacher effectiveness, social class, intelligence (IQ tests are not the only measure), violence on television (are Bugs Bunny and Rambo equally violent?), levels of crime or unemployment, to mention a few.

• The conclusion refers only to data that supports the hypothesis. There is a difficulty in detecting this in a journal article, but it may be more apparent when referring to the full report, thesis or dissertation behind it. Too often, beliefs govern what is selectively reported.

• Conclusions are extended to individual behaviour when the study has focused on group tendencies. Statistical studies involve data collected on groups and the tests of significance use means and standard deviations, for example, and thus individuals within the groups will perform/behave divergently, providing variance round a mean. To use a mean as an indicator of expected individual behaviour/performance is inappropriate. For example, if the average annual income of accountants were £25,000, would you expect your neighbour Fred the accountant to make exactly £25,000?

• The conclusion appears to ignore the data and yet includes arguments for the support of the original hypothesis in the face of negative evidence. The first possible reason for this is a lack of logical consistency in the report. Blum and Foos (1986) describe this as a form of rationalism, which can degenerate into a set of excuses for not finding what was expected. On the other hand, it is possible that the researcher is being honest about procedural faults, documents them, and is actually suggesting a replication of the study to resolve this issue. Considering the complexity of social science research, one is surprised that more of this type of evaluation of procedure does not occur.

• Even with a non-representative sample, conclusions are extended to a larger population (see Chapter 3). This happens all too often when a convenient group or volunteers are used as subjects for a study. Even when a research project starts with a random selection of subjects, often there is some attrition. As long as there is a follow-up of those who did not continue and the reason they did not participate had nothing to do with what was happening to them as part of the study, then there is still justification for extending the results to the original population. For example, questionnaires can be lost in the post, subjects become ill or move, jobs or roles change which can make participation inappropriate or impossible. If the reason for not continuing is not identified, then there is always the suspicion that something going on in the study has caused the subjects to drop out, like the wording of a questionnaire, reluctance to be observed in the manner planned, or their role in an experiment. In such cases, the research approach itself could have provided a confounding variable.

- The conclusions are based upon the researchers applying their own operational definition to a set of existing statistics. In other words, the data was collected by another group, for example government statistical offices collecting census data, and the researchers assign their own meaning, like using income as the sole indicator of social class. The study then reports various correlations with other data (again defined by the researchers as indicators of their own variables) and conclusions are reported. While this may seem harmless, the reader must be assured that such definitions are valid. Wide-searching surveys are often conducted as a general data trawl, though sometimes there are hypotheses to be tested. Government agencies are looking for trends in society to predict housing, school and medical needs for coming years. Reports using such data for some other purpose should stimulate the reader to ask searching questions about the validity of the operational definitions.

- Conclusions sometimes include an attempt to relate the study's findings to other studies. Unless there has been a definite effort to replicate a study, the reader ought to ensure that the data (operational definitions) is comparable. There are frequent problems when trying to make cross-cultural or cross-national comparisons, for example when difficult-to-define variables such as social class are employed. Does 'lower middle class' mean the same thing in Spain as in Canada, for example? Such problems can occur with longitudinal studies where definitions can change over time. Are teachers, civil servants or doctors as 'well-off' today as they were 100 years ago? Has the purchasing power of the middle class improved or declined since the Second World War? How purchasing power is defined by those who collected the two sets of data will determine the relative validity of any conclusions.

- There are still the occasional papers in which the conclusions confuse statistical significance with sociological, psychological or educational significance. If a study were to show that the reading age of 12-year-old girls was 2% higher than that for 12-year-old boys (assume that the difference was statistically different), would this be educationally significant? Should a national programme be started to rescue boys from a fate worse than death? This is not to say there is not a difference, but is it large enough to generate any concern?

- Conclusions have been known to provide claims that go beyond the evidence provided, taking one more 'logical' step. For example, if a study were to show that there was a high positive correlation between the number of books in homes and the ultimate achievement of educational qualifications, would it be reasonable to recommend that sets of books should be given to families that lack sufficient reading material?
- It is still possible to find conclusions that automatically attribute cause and effect relations for simple correlations, just because the correlations are significant. As seen in Chapter 8, correlations are an indication of strength of association, but by no means proof of cause and effect.
- Parallel to the previous item, there are conclusions that maintain a cause and effect relationship for experimental or quasi-experimental studies based on finding statistical significance alone. Again, as noted in Chapters 9 and 10 and earlier in this chapter, the burden of proof rests with the researcher, who must prove that all other possible causes have been controlled, *and* even then should really only state the relationship in probabilistic terms.

With time and experience, you surely will be able to add to this list.

CRITERIA FOR EVALUATING CONCLUSIONS

The following are summary criteria for the last column on the Profiling Sheet.

Appropriately drawn based on data shown   A well-designed and executed study, not necessarily using inferential statistics, but clear in its presentation, defending and justifying any conclusions; basically a sound study worth referring to in your own research.

Some lack justification or are poorly defended   Not all the conclusions are fully justified or some are poorly defended. This could be due to a weak design (see other columns) or poor writing ability of the researcher.

No justification of conclusions   The results and conclusions are presented, but no justification for these. This requires the reader to 'read between the lines' to try to infer why, and to consider the design, sampling and data collection procedures carefully to determine whether the conclusions are justified. This can be due to something being hidden, but more than likely, it is poor writing ability.

No conclusions drawn, only description of data and process   Some reports of studies (but very few articles) lack any real conclusions. These tend to present the data but draw no substantive conclusions nor make any recommendations. This can indicate a poor design, lack of initial research question or hypothesis, and/or poor data collection procedures.

Inappropriate conclusions for data   Occasionally, a research paper draws conclusions that are not substantiated by the results presented. The researcher goes well beyond what is justifiable from the study at hand.

SUMMARY

How you, the reader, intend to use the result may well influence how you ultimately rate overall a given report or journal article. If you are carrying out a literature search, looking for justification for your own research, then you may tend to be more lenient in your classification, or at least in how much credence you attribute to a weak study. On the other hand, if you are an administrator or teacher looking for justification of a change, for example in policy, administrative structure or teaching style, then the strength of the supporting evidence for conclusions must be very strong. Belief may be a strong motivator, but evidence to the contrary should not be ignored.

The aim of this book has been to provide comprehensive coverage and, consequently, some readers will require a greater depth of understanding for some topics to be found in more advanced texts. Quantitative studies in the social sciences are complex, partially because using numbers requires some understanding of the mathematics behind their use, and partially because such studies contend with very difficult subjects: human beings. Hopefully this book will help you the reader overcome any reluctance to read quantitative studies, and for some of you, help you on the road to competently designing and carrying out your own studies. You should now be well equipped to carry out Activity 11.1.

ACTIVITY 11.1

(a) As a concluding exercise, you will find a fictitious article in Appendix A to be critically analysed as a practice assessment. Use the entire Profiling Sheet and give reasons for your classifications. I have provided the outline of a 'model' answer with my classifications for each column with justifications after the article that you can compare with only *after* you have carried out your own analysis.

(b) Select an entirely new article/report and carry out a complete evaluation using the entire Profiling Sheet.

Finally, by keeping your expectations of quality of research high and communicating this to such bodies as the editorial boards of journals, you will be contributing to the improvement of quantitative research – which is an interesting hypothesis for someone's research!

Profiling Sheet: _Understanding Social Science Research_, © Thomas R. Black, 2001

Article: _____

Type of Study: ☐ Descriptive, ☐ Survey/correlational, ☐ _Ex post facto_, ☐ Experimental/quasi-experimental.

Questions/ hypotheses	Representativeness	Ethics and Confidentiality	Data Quality I	Data Quality II	Descriptive Statistics	Inferential Statistics	Variable Control	Analysis and Conclusions
Valid question or hypothesis based on accepted theory with well-justified referenced support	Whole population	Ethical standards met and data sufficiently confidential that no individuals or institutions can be identified	Educationally, sociologically, psychologically, etc., significant and manageable number of concepts	Commercially or professionally produced/tested with high validity, reliability and objectivity (V, R, O)	Appropriate display of data and results in tables and/or graphs, clearly labelled	Appropriate choice of design and statistical tests for resolving H_0	All mediating and extraneous variables accounted for, internal validity maintained	Appropriate design for the question(s) posed and conclusions justifiably drawn from data shown
Valid question or hypothesis based on own theory, well justified	Random selection from a well-specified population		Limited academic significance, very narrow perspective	Project or personally produced/tested with high V, R, O	Some inadequacies in presentation of tables/graphs	A more powerful test could have been used	Most extraneous variables controlled or accounted for	Some lack of justification or conclusions poorly defended
Credible question/ hypothesis but alternative possible, or too extensive/global, or support missing	Purposive sample from a well-specified population, with justification for representativeness	Ethical issues not addressed or confidentiality not discussed when it should have been	Large number of concepts, potentially confusing	Commercially or project produced with moderate V, R, O	Other methods of display of data/ results would have been more appropriate	Missing analysis where needed	Mediating variables only are controlled, some extraneous variables could cause confounding of results	No justification of conclusions provided or conclusions not supported by this study
Weak question/ hypothesis, or poorly stated, or justified with inappropriate references	Volunteers or convenience, with no justification of representativeness	Ethical issues not addressed and/or some loss of confidentiality	Too many concepts and variables investigated to provide meaningful results	Commercially or project produced with low V, R, O, or no information provided	Serious misconceptions encouraged owing to nature of graphical display of results	Inappropriately analysed data, tests performed not appropriate	Inadequate control of variables, confounding probable	No conclusions drawn, only description of data and processes provided
No question or hypothesis stated, or inconsistent with known facts	Unidentified group	Ethical standards violated and/or subjects endangered owing to no confidentiality	Trivial concepts, not academically significant	Inappropriate instrument for the variables/concepts described	Intentionally misleading use of descriptive statistics	No justification for statistical analysis, just _post hoc_ data snooping	Extraneous variables not considered, confounding likely	Inappropriate conclusions for data provided

Comments and justification for classification:

12

Planning Your Own Research

Up to this point, the primary emphasis of this book has been on evaluating other people's research, trying to determine the credibility of claims and research outcomes. We all do this as part of our own research in order to base our own efforts on a good foundation of sound earlier studies. No one starts from nothing; we all build on the work of others. And even if we have no intention of using a quantitative approach ourselves, we may wish to base our research on quantitative studies in our own area, since such studies can be a valuable source of information on *what* is happening. Of course, the same should be said of researchers who plan to carry out a quantitative study: they need to know how to evaluate qualitative research in order to be able to determine which studies are best to support arguments for their research proposal.

Let us briefly consider how one could use what has been learned by examining other people's research as a guide in the design of our own project. The criteria espoused in the previous eleven chapters need some reorganization if they are to help in the planning of a study so that not only do you have the greatest potential to answer your question, but you do it using your resources efficiently and in such a way that the results could be replicated. This last statement points out a major concern of research: it should be carried out with sufficient rigour and care that if someone else were to carry out the same with another representative sample, the results would be much the same. Like most endeavours in life, careful planning is the key.

A SYSTEMATIC APPROACH TO PLANNING YOUR RESEARCH

In Chapter 1, a summary of the processes involved in designing and carrying out a study were presented in Figure 1.3. Such a skeleton plan highlights where key decisions have to be made, without being simplistically prescriptive. In reality, what researchers often find is that later decisions can compel one to change earlier choices. For example, having decided on the research question, later it is found that the question in its entirety cannot be answered and only part of it may be resolved. The process could look like this, responding to the numbered steps in Figure 1.3 up to the point where the researcher changes his/her mind:

1 *Overall research question:* How can we improve middle-level management?
2 *Specific question:* Which of two management schemes will be most effective in an organization?
3 *Hypothesis:* One of the two possible management schemes will be more effective in the management of a given level.
4 *Population:* This should apply to all middle management.
5 *Sample:* Two separate, purposively selected, 'typical' departments will be used (quasi-experimental design) to implement the contrasting schemes.
6 *Instrument:* How do we measure 'effectiveness'? If we use the views of employees who have to function under each of the schemes, are we really evaluating effectiveness, *or* are we comparing their perception of effectiveness? While employee satisfaction is one part of effective management, it is important and the one we really want to know about at this stage, so we will have to go back and adjust the question.
2 *Specific question* (again): Which of two management schemes will be best suited to the employees and be seen as most effective by them and likely to enhance their performance?

The principle to keep in mind is to maintain logical continuity across the parts of the research. Thus it does not matter if you change your mind during the planning stages, as long as you recognize the need and do it conciously. What you want to avoid is finding (or not finding) after you have collected your data that you cannot answer your original question, or for that matter any question. In such a complex process, it is not difficult to lose continuity of thought and process. It would not surprise me if you have found during the process of evaluating articles some which seem to ask one question at the beginning and answer a different one at the end. My students have in my classes.

To avoid this outcome, it is recommended that you carry the planning through right to the end, including selecting the statistical process you will use to resolve any hypotheses, *before* collecting any data. This does not mean you will know what the answer will be, but you should be able to determine whether or not the process will provide an answer at all. An inappropriate choice of instrument, unrepresentative sample group(s) or the wrong statistical test can leave you with no answer. While a sound study may provide you with surprises and answers you did not expect, at least you will get answers. Too many studies have been conducted without sufficient planning and rigour to provide outcomes that are justifiable.

You should keep a record of the planning process and decisions that are made, along with justifications and rationale. This is not just for purposes of writing up a thesis or dissertation for a degree, but as part of a learning experience. Doing research is like playing tennis: you should get better with experience, but unless you note what you have done and evaluate the processes, it is unlikely you will know where improvements are needed.

To start the process, carry out Activity 12.1.

ACTIVITY 12.1

Outline your plans for organizing your research process (you can use Figure 1.3, but keep in mind that you may want to modify it with experience). Decide how you are going to keep a log of decisions and activities for analysis later.

PLANS TO PROCEDURES

Planning is not just making a map and following it. There will also be points in the process where it is necessary to try out the developed instruments and planned procedures for data collection to ensure they will function as expected on the important day. Each of the notional stages of the process involves numerous decisions to ensure the quality of the process and continuity throughout. In the following sections, each stage will be summarized and important decisions to be made noted.

Research question

For many research students, this can be the most difficult decision, since there is almost totally free choice as to what to do. On the other hand, even experienced contract researchers often have to translate somewhat vague questions of the commissioning organization into more precise research questions and hypotheses. These then have to be taken back to the organization to ensure they are consistent with what is wanted, which can present problems of communication among interested parties. For example, a funding body provides support to answer a general question in a school district, local education authority or even another country, with the proviso that the host institution participates in the process. Consequently, you as the contractor must also be a good negotiator.

Individually originated research for a higher degree often has its sources of questions from personal experience and interest. The difficulty with these is that they can initially sound like find the cure for all evils in your area of interest. While this is not unreasonable, you may have to cut out a bit for the research for the degree, and leave the remainder for the rest of your research life. This is where your supervisor will be of greatest assistance, helping you to take on enough, but not too much.

Preparation for asking a sound question should include surveying the literature to see what has gone on before. Drafts of research questions should be discussed with colleagues and your supervisor or contractor, with the rationale and justification based upon other research. I would recommend this be initially kept to a couple of paragraphs each, with the expectation that the questions will change and evolve into a sound starting point. It is worthwhile ensuring that the questions clearly identify the variables involved and suggest relationships to be explored.

A hypothesis is an expression of the nature of relationships between variables. This could be an expectation of correlational or associational relations from a survey, or differences in traits or outcomes from an *ex post facto* or experimental design. At this stage you want a fairly explicit translation from a research question to a description of anticipated relationships.

Document this stage in Activity 12.2.

ACTIVITY 12.2

Describe your overall question, research question and any hypotheses.

Research design

If this is your first research endeavour, keep it simple. In particular, for

- *descriptive* – recognize the limitations of inferences that can be made.
- *survey* – keep it small, but large enough to find significant correlations if they exist (e.g. over 50 but below 200 if you are on a limited budget).
- *ex post facto* – the samples hold the key to the valid definition of the groups who are who they are because of their life experiences. Make sure that they are defined so that they are mutually exclusive: an individual should not fit in more than one group. Limit groups to two or three.
- *experimental or quasi-experimental* – ensure the 'treatments' are different and relatively easy to administer. Limit groups to two or three for your first endeavour.

Identifying potential extraneous variables that need to be controlled can be quite a challenge. You will then have to decide how they will be 'controlled'. For example, for the ones you have identified, the following questions are examples of the type to guide you:

- Can they be controlled simply by random sampling and/or random assignment, making sure that all groups have an equal distribution of the traits or variables in question?
- Is it a matter of ensuring that the measuring or data collection process does not inadvertently introduce unwanted influences, particularly differentially for just one of the groups?
- Does it require that you trial your measuring instruments to make sure they measure what they are supposed to measure, and do it reliably?
- Is it necessary that the groups are kept separate so that the data satisfies the requirement that the groups are independent?

Different designs in specific situations will present a variety of opportunities for extraneous variables to influence the outcomes.

The choice of statistical test should be considered at this point and possibly the first attempt at expressing outcomes as null hypotheses, since they will express outcomes in terms of the statistical differences. Remember, you want to ensure that whatever you choose for a design, it will eventually answer the research questions.

Carry out this next stage in Activity 12.3.

ACTIVITY 12.3

Outline a preliminary design structure. Describe how you plan to control any possible extraneous variables that might influence the outcomes.

Populations and samples for inferential statistics

Just defining a population is not a trivial task. We use the term population in a general sense, to mean any defined group that has a set of common traits of interests. The difficulty comes in the definition such that the subjects will fit in one and only one group. Therefore, we could be interested in chemistry, physics and biology teachers, but where does the person who teaches both physics and chemistry fit? Such groups are not mutually exclusive, a large number of people could belong to more than one population.

Remember that inferential statistics are based upon the premise that you will be making inferences about a larger population on the basis of a representative sample. While traditionally direct random selection has been the assumed best way, other techniques were introduced that include aspects of randomness which can achieve the same end.

Randomness is always desirable, not only for purposes of representativeness, but also to control for unanticipated extraneous variables. Random selection allows samples that include the entire range of characteristics in proportions typical of the population in question. Random assignment allows the distribution of characteristics or traits that have the potential to be extraneous variables evenly across all the groups. Thus no one group is differentially affected by having a disproportionate number of, say, highly intelligent children, more experienced managers, less qualified nurses, or whatever.

If a purposive sample is the only way to secure an equitable distribution of traits, it should include as many characteristics as possible. This can be an essential part of the sampling strategy, for example purposively selecting a few typical organizations and then randomly selecting individuals within each.

Also, now is a good time to obtain a list of ethical standards for your discipline or organization. This will help you avoid any unfortunate oversights in procedure or process.

Document this next stage in Activity 12.4.

ACTIVITY 12.4

(a) Describe the characteristics of the population to which you wish to extend any inferences, and how you intend to draw your sample.
(b) Justify your choice of sampling strategies.
(c) What ethical issues need to be addressed?

Measuring instruments

Obviously the underlying variable needs to be clearly defined and preferably based upon concepts the research community understands and shares. Validity can be ensured by having instruments considered by another expert to see if they have the potential to measure what was intended.

Instruments must be unambiguous and clearly understood by subjects. Reliability can be enhanced by having a small sample (that covers a cross-section of subjects, but not including subjects you will subsequently use) complete the instrument and then you carry out the item analysis process described in Chapter 4. The item total correlation will flag up suspect items that can be improved, once you have decided why they are producing responses inconsistent with the rest of the instrument. This may require you to interview some respondents to determine how they interpreted the suspect items. Remember, it is not difficult to word items in such a way that respondents interpret them differently than you would. You are the expert and wording may include vocabulary they are not used to using. Trialling instruments can include data collecting processes like structured interviews, *before* real data collection in the field, to ensure that the process of data collection does not inadvertently introduce unwanted extraneous variables.

Now carry out Activity 12.5.

ACTIVITY 12.5

Outline what your instrument will be and how you plan to trial it (step 6 in Figure 1.3).

Checking your design, choosing statistical tests

Now that you have planned your sample and decided on your instruments, you should review your choice of designs. What statistical test will you use? Ensure that the outcomes of any statistical test will resolve your hypotheses and ultimately answer your research questions.

At this point, it is useful to decide what you will use as your value α. In doing so, consider the consequences of making a Type I error, finding a difference when it does not really exist. This should be determined by what sort of decisions will be made based on the outcomes of the study. If the only consequence of making a Type I error is to spend more time doing research, then the adverse consequences are minimal. On the other hand, someone is going to decide whether or not to spend a considerable sum of money, so then you may want to be a bit more cautious.

It is not possible to calculate a value for β, the probability of making a Type II error, from what has been given here. You should remember that the probability of not finding a difference when it is there is dependent on

- your choice of α (as this gets smaller, β increases);
- the reliability of your measuring instruments;
- the representativeness of your sample;
- sample size;
- choice of statistical test.

Weakness in the last four will increase the probability of making a Type II error and reduce the probability of finding a significant difference when it really exists (power). So we see that the decision about α is primarily one based upon the consequences of decisions to be made resulting from the research, where *how* rigorously the study is conducted will determine β.

Finally, ensure that there is still logical continuity across the questions, the design, the data and the statistical tests, and that the last will actually answer your question. You should also check again for possible extraneous variables that might have crept into the design. This should all be done before real data is collected in the field.

Document this stage of your research by completing Activity 12.6.

ACTIVITY 12.6

(a) Describe your research design and justify why you think it is survey, *ex post facto*, experimental or quasi-experimental (step 7).
(b) Describe which statistical test you plan to use to resolve your hypotheses.
(c) What have you chosen for your α (probability of making a Type I error), and why?
(d) What do you plan to do to keep β (probability of making a Type II error) to a minimum?

Collecting data in the field

Now you are ready to carry out the design. For each of the general types of research, there are pitfalls to look for, such as

- *descriptive* – Trying to describe the situation descriptively with too much enthusiasm and detail can lead to instruments that are too long. As a consequence, subjects simply do not complete them fully or do not return them.

- *survey* – If the sample does not respond, how will you determine whether the instrument itself was a deterrent, or other unrelated events intervened?
- *ex post facto* – Locating lists for specific populations for life events can be challenging, if not impossible. Creative ways of identifying subjects representative of the populations of interest will be needed. In some cases, it may be possible to identify them through institutions (e.g. teachers, nurses) rather than directly.
- *experimental or quasi-experimental* – Obtaining representative samples in order to assign them randomly to treatments can be difficult. Once the groups are established, how do you keep them from interacting and consequently introducing extraneous variables?

In all cases, how do you avoid becoming a variable yourself? In other words, your presence as an observer or someone who administers a questionnaire or achievement test can influence the outcomes. Now is when you focus on *how* you will do it as well as what you will do. It is also appropriate to check for ethical considerations, such as establishing procedures for ensuring confidentiality.

Describe your plans for this stage in Activity 12.7.

ACTIVITY 12.7

Outline field data collection and how ethical standards will be maintained (step 8).

ANALYSING YOUR RESULTS

Planning ahead, it is good practice to think about how your results will resolve the stated hypotheses. How will you explain the results, no matter what they are? You will need to avoid speculation on why, or at least make sure it is obviously speculation and hypotheses for future research. The key issue to consider is whether or not you will have enough evidence to answer your research questions, or will you only be able to answer part of them?

When you have completed your research, it is always sound practice to evaluate your processes, use this as a learning experience, determine what was good and what you would do differently next time. This may even be a section in your dissertation or thesis if that is the final report of your study.

Finally, it is worthwhile suggesting future research that could follow yours. There will surely be unresolved issues or new ones that arise. This gives your work not only a past derived from earlier research, but a future in subsequent studies. Remember, research is an ongoing process and never really ever finished.

Looking at the whole plan, consider Activity 12.8.

ACTIVITY 12.8

Justify why you think this process will resolve your original research questions.

SUMMARY

If you have responded to each of the above eight activities in this chapter, you should now have an outline for your research proposal. The last page of this chapter shows a criteria sheet that I use in guiding my evaluation of research projects that my students submit. Obviously, it is based upon the criteria described earlier. Learning to evaluate your own work will save you considerable time and effort in the end. Best wishes in your efforts!

Research Design Evaluation Criteria

Type of Study (may be more than one): ❑ Accounts, ❑ Interviews, ❑ Document Analysis, ❑ Development/Evaluation, ❑ Descriptive Qualitative, ❑ Descriptive Quantitative, ❑ Correlational, ❑ Normative, ❑ *Ex post facto*, ❑ Experimental/quasi-experimental.

A. Initial Planning

Aims/Questions/Hypotheses

Valid aims, question or hypothesis based on accepted theory with well-justified referenced support	Valid aims, question or hypothesis based on own theory, well justified	Credible aims/ question/ hypothesis but alternative possible, or too extensive/global, or support missing	Weak aims/ question/ hypothesis, or poorly stated, or justified with inappropriate references	No aims/question or hypothesis stated, or inconsistent with known facts

Representativeness

Whole population or case study	Random selection from a well-specified population	Purposive sample from a well-specified population, with justification for representativeness	Volunteers or convenience, with no justification of representativeness	Unidentified group

Documentation of Development Processes (for Development/Evaluation Study)

Well documented	Random selection from a well-specified population	Purposive sample from a well-specified population, with justification for representativeness	Volunteers or convenience, with no justification of representativeness	Unidentified group

Ethics and Confidentiality

Ethical standards met and data sufficiently confidential that no individuals/ institutions can be identified	Some ethical issues addressed, but some omitted	Ethical issues not addressed or confidentiality not discussed when it should have been	Ethical issues not addressed and/or some loss of confidentiality	Ethical standards violated and/or subjects endangered owing to no confidentiality

B. Data or Evidence Collection

Data Quality I

Educationally, sociologically, psychologically, etc., significant and manageable number of concepts	Limited academic significance, very narrow perspective	Large number of concepts, potentially confusing	Too many concepts and variables investigated to provide meaningful results	Trivial concepts, not academically significant

Data Quality II

Commercially/ professionally produced/tested instrument or procedures with high validity, reliability and objectivity (V, R, O)	Project or personally produced/tested instrument or procedures with high V, R, O	Commercially or project-produced instruments or procedures with moderate V, R, O	Commercially or project-produced instruments or procedures with low V, R, O, or no information provided	Inappropriate instrument or procedures for the variables/ concepts described

C. Data Handling and Analysis

Descriptive Statistics

Appropriate display of data and results in tables and/or graphs, clearly labelled	Some inadequacies in presentation of tables/graphs	Other methods of display of data/results would have been more appropriate	Serious misconceptions encouraged owing to nature of graphical display of results	Intentionally misleading use of descriptive statistics

Inferential Statistics

Appropriate choice of design and statistical tests for resolving H_0	A more powerful test could have been used	Missing analysis where needed	Inappropriately analysed data, tests performed not appropriate	No justification for statistical analysis, just *post hoc* data snooping

Qualitative Evidence

Appropriate choice of approach and evidence to resolve questions	A more powerful approach could have been used	Missing analysis where needed	Inappropriately analysed data, evidence not appropriate	No justification or planning of approach or analysis, just *post hoc* evidence snooping

Variable Control

All mediating and extraneous variables accounted for, internal validity maintained	Most extraneous variables controlled or accounted for	Mediating variables only are controlled, some extraneous variables could cause confounding of results	Inadequate control of variables, confounding probable	Extraneous variables not considered, confounding likely

Analysis and Conclusions

Appropriate design for the question(s) posed and conclusions justifiably drawn from data or evidence provided	Some lack of justification or conclusions poorly defended, lack of evidence or data	No justification of conclusions provided or conclusions not supported by this study	No conclusions drawn, only description of data and processes provided	Inappropriate conclusions for data or evidence provided, considerable speculation

D. General Dissertation/Thesis Processes

Use of Literature

Appropriate use of literature to support theory, aims, questions, processes and decisions about procedures	Some use of literature to support theory, aims, questions, processes and decisions about procedures	Little use of literature to support theory, aims, questions, processes and decisions about procedures	No use of literature in supporting theory or decisions, just an annotated bibliography	Little or no survey of literature

Integration of Course Content

Appropriate use of concepts and skills acquired in taught modules/courses	Reasonable employment of content and skills from taught part where needed	Considerable lack of use of content, thesis dissertation has little consistency with taught modules/courses	Total lack of use of content, thesis dissertation has no consistency with taught portion	Unacceptable, needs complete revision to be considered a thesis dissertation for this course

Presentation of Dissertation/Thesis

Appropriate layout, organization, good grammar and spell-checked	Some lack of quality in presentation	Considerable lack of quality, poor grammar, no spell-check	Poor quality, need much revision and improvement, but can be rescued	Unacceptable, needs complete revision in layout and presentation

Appendix A: Sample Article

The following article is fictitious to save embarrassment. It was designed specifically to incorporate a variety of good practices and faults. You can use it as an example for practising evaluating a complete article, not only to identify the individual strengths and weaknesses, but also to describe how they are interrelated.

It is suggested that you use a copy of the final Profiling Sheet and write up your justifications for the classifications in each of the columns. This could then be a source of class discussion, or, if working individually, you can find a model answer on the resource web site.

When I teach this course, the final assignment (and a major part of the grade) is for each student to select an article of interest to him/her that uses quantitative approaches, carry out a critical analysis using the Profiling Sheet, and submit the ratings with justifications. I then do my own analysis and compare it with the student's, a time-consuming task but one that provides comprehensive feedback to each person.

Appendix A: Sample Article

International Journal of *********** in Education
(1999) Vol 1, 2, 345–347

Teacher-pupil Interaction in the Computer-based Classroom

G. Farnsworth Bloggs, Department of Education, Estuary University

Abstract

A number of studies have shown that in mixed-sex classes, boys dominate the computer facilities and receive more help from the teachers, though the amount of attention received varies across studies. This study systematically observed 30 Primary 5 classrooms during periods of computer-based learning activities. It found that overall boys received more attention than girls, with some notable exceptions. Interviews indicate which children had computers at home and subsequently it was found that these tended to be the more dominate users of computers in class.

Introduction

Studies of classroom interaction in general and of gender have frequently shown that in mixed classrooms boys often receive more teacher attention than girls and dominate discussions. This has been recorded in the United States (Brophy and Good, 1970; Good, Sykes and Brophy, 1973) and Britain (Spender, 1981; Stanworth, 1981; Clarricotes, 1980; French and French, 1984; Galton, Simon and Croll, 1980).

While this has been documented in general classroom interaction, the results have not all been consistent. Also, less has been done to see what the nature of interaction centred round computer media is. The assumption of many studies has been that attention seeking varies (Spender, 1981) and the consequences depend on teacher responses. Even when boys are in the minority, they tend to attempt to dominate discussion and gain attention (Stanworth, 1981). The underlying reason for either the attention seeking or granting attention has not been widely investigated.

Methodology

This paper presents the results of the systematic observation of 30 Primary 5 classrooms in 20 schools in three local education authorities. The average class size was 32 pupils of widely mixed ability as reported by the teachers.

Previous studies have shown (e.g., Croll and Moses, 1985) that children seen to have learning problems receive much more individual attention than do other children in a class. Boys tend to be in the majority for having special educational needs. Thus, observations were carried out on 40 above average and 40 below average children, as classified by their teachers, to see if ability was a factor. There were equal numbers of boys and girls in each group. During periods of computer use, these children were observed using a schedule that required recording the type of activity and interaction every ten seconds.

Four observers observed 30 sessions, one per class, over a period of four weeks. In addition at the beginning, they jointly watched a lesson each and compared notes on observation recording. Interactions were coded differently depending on whether they were teacher or child initiated. The number of time periods for each type of interaction was found and percentages for each type were recorded. For this paper, the percentage of the session each pupil was engaged in interactions with the teacher was used as the independent variable.

Results

During these computer-based learning sessions, the teachers spent most of their time circulating round the room working with the children. The boys in all cases engaged in interactions with the teachers on average 4.5% of their time while girls were engaged with the teachers 3.4% of their time. These results are consistent with other studies on classes using computers. The data was further broken down to see whether ability had an effect on demand for attention. Table 1 provides a summary of the observations.

Table 1. Gender and ability differences in individual teacher attention (20 in each group).

	Average interaction time	
	Above average	Below average
Boys	3.5%	4.6%
	sd = 0.52%	sd = 0.58%
Girls	3.4%	4.2%
	sd = 0.48%	sd = 0.55%

From this it would appear that there is no real difference between boys and girls in their demands for attention, but there might be between ability groups. The results of a two-way analysis of variance on the data are provided in Table 2. This confirms there was a difference between ability groups ($p < .05$), but no significant interaction between ability and gender.

In addition, the frequency which children or teachers initiated the interaction was recorded. The summary of this data is

Table 2. Analysis of variance summary table for data in Table 1.

	SS	df	MS	F	P-value	F-crit
Ability	7.5	1	7.5	6.47	0.0130	3.97
Gender	1.2	1	1.2	1.03	0.31	3.97
Interact	0.1	1	0.1	0.04	0.84	3.97
Within	88.13	76	1.2			
Total	96.88	79				

shown in Table 3. The difference between the pattern of interaction for boys and girls was significantly different ($\chi^2 = 4.85$, $p < .05$). This would seem to indicate that boys were more demanding of teachers' attention than girls.

Table 3. Frequencies of teacher and pupil initiated interaction by boys and girls.

	Boys	Girls
Teacher Initiated	122	138
Pupil Initiated	146	112

Finally, the researchers interviewed the 30 teachers, asking each of them to describe why they felt that boys were more demanding than girls. There were five commonly reported reasons by teachers, based upon their experiences. These were

- Deprived of attention at home
- Need to prove they are better than girls
- Like to have the teacher praise them
- Boys are naturally more assertive
- Girls are shy
- Others

Their responses are summarised in Figure 1, showing how many teachers gave each response.

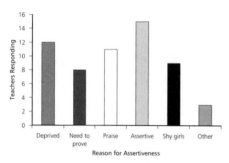

Figure 1. Teachers' reasons for boys being more assertive than girls.

Teachers also noted that sometimes their time would be dominated by one or two individuals who had problems out of school, or were being bullied in school.

Interviews with children who were particularly assertive in their use of computers in the classroom revealed that they had computers in their homes. They were more confident in the use of these tools and tended to get on with the work with no inhibitions. It was found that as many girls as boys had access to computers in their homes.

Conclusion

These results are consistent with other findings that indicated boys tend to dominate computers and computer-based lessons. The more frequent asking for attention confirmed that boys were more demanding than girls. Teachers provided a consistent set of reasons for such behaviour, some that were intrinsic to typical behaviour of boys, others that were typical of differences between boys and girls. These indicate a need for teachers to be aware of external pressures on boys, and differentiate these from common differences in behaviour due to gender.

Allowing boys to dominate lessons and in particular computer-based learning exercises, will only continue the trend for girls to avoid using computers. This in turn will prevent their participating in new technology in the future. Teachers need to find ways of preventing boys from dominating resources, including their own time, if there is to be equitable development of skills in information technology.

Future research should investigate ways of ensuring equal access to computer resources in the classroom by girls.

References

Brophy, J. E., and Good, T. L. (1970) Teachers' communications of differential expectations for children's classroom performance: some behavioural data. *J. of Educ. Psychol.*, **61**, 5.

Clarricotes, K. (1980) The importance of being Ernest... Emma... Tom... Jane. The perception of gender conformity and gender deviation in primary Schools. In Deem, R. (Ed.) *Schooling for Women's Work*. London, Routledge & Kegan Paul.

Croll, P., and Moses, D. (1985) *One in Five*. London, Routledge & Kegan Paul.

Dillon, J. T. (1982) Male-female similarities in class participation. *J. of Educ. Res.*, **75**, 6.

French, J., and French, P. (1984) Gender imbalances in the primary classroom: An interactional account. *Educ. Res.*, **26**, 2.

Galton, M., Simon, B., and Croll, P. (1980) *Inside the Primary Classroom*. London, Routledge & Kegan Paul.

Good, T. L., Sykes, J., and Brophy, J. E. (1973) Effects of teacher sex and student sex on classroom interaction. *J. of Educ. Psychol.*, **72**.

Spender, D. (1981) Women and educational research. *Research Intelligence*, April.

Stanworth, M. (1981) *Gender and Schooling: A Study of Sexual Divisions in the Classroom*. London, Women's Research and Resources Centre.

Outline of a Model Answer for Evaluating Quantitative Research Exercise

Article by G. Farnsworth Bloggs (1999)

Classification

I would suggest this is an *ex post facto* study, since both independent variables are life determined (gender and ability).

Question/Hypothesis

There is a reasonably argued rationale with literature support for the aim of the study. In fact there are two separate questions: (a) is there a difference in attention applied to boys and girls; and (b) is the reason for any difference due to ability? Unfortunately, I do not think that either was stated clearly at the beginning and consequently had to be inferred from reading the introductory summary and later reading. Therefore, I would classify this as 'poorly stated' even though it is 'well justified'.

Representativeness

In this case, it is not clearly stated *how* the 30 classrooms were selected, nor how the 20 schools were chosen, nor how the three LEAs were picked. Children in each class above and below average ability were *chosen* by the host teachers. I see no evidence from the paper that suggests this is a representative sample, based either upon a random selection or upon a purposive sample that would represent population traits, nor any justification that the schools were in any way typical of a larger population. Thus from the paper (which may reflect poor communication skills) I would classify this as an unidentified group.

Ethics and confidentiality

Permission was acquired for the project from the LEA, acting one assumes as *in loco parentis*, and consequently we assume it has vetted the procedures. Teachers were briefed on the study. It would not appear from the report that specific schools could be identified. Therefore, at least indirectly, the issues of ethics and confidentiality have been addressed.

Data quality

While there were only a few variables being considered, based on concepts of interest, there is no information provided on the instrument development process. We are not told what interactions were considered of interest to record as an indication of receiving attention, the source of any such list, nor any information on trials. Interview schedules were developed to determine the reasons for domination differences in boys and girls, but no details or rationale were provided. In fact, these assumed that boys would dominate. Thus there is no justification of the validity of the instruments. A major source of lack of reliability, not commented on by the authors, was that of possible lack of consistency between the four observers. One might question the objectivity of the instrument, since there is simply no evidence provided that efforts have been made to ensure objectivity of observations through (say) parallel observations of groups. Again, the reader is confronted with a dilemma as to whether there is a lack of good practice or just poor communication skills. Another major data issue that should have been addressed is one of classification of children as being above or below average ability by the teachers: how valid and reliable was this? Was there any check on the criteria (if any) applied by the (possibly as many as) 30 teachers? As a result, I would classify this as 'Educationally significant and manageable number of concepts' but 'Project-produced instrument with no information provided on V, R, O'.

Descriptive statistics

Three tables are presented in the paper, which relate to the statistical tests and a bar chart summarizing the interview data. They are understandable, Table 2 being a typical table for two-way ANOVA, but it could be confusing without reading the text carefully. Overall, I would classify this as 'Appropriate display of data...'.

Inferential statistics

The two-way ANOVA test shown in Table 2, based on the summary data in Table 1, would seem appropriate for the type of data collected (keeping in mind the measurement issues raised earlier). The chi-square test is used in Table 3, which would seem to be a valid test considering it is frequency data for groups and gender. One should at least ask, from where did the author obtain the divisions? Did the test contribute to the answer of either of the research questions? What evidence is there that the differences between groups are attributable to something other than chance due to sampling? Since there is little justification for the choice of test or how the variables for the test were determined, I would classify this as both an 'Appropriate choice of test', but at the same time 'No justification for analysis, *post hoc* data snooping'.

Variable control

Some possible uncontrolled extraneous variables that may have influenced the results are the lack of a representative sample (selected groups may not behave consistently with the whole population), teacher differences that might stimulate differential behaviours (again were the teachers typical?), any impact of the external observer in the classroom, possible gender-associated traits (such as those learned traits brought to class rather than genetically determined ones), and the bias of the interviews to try to determine why the boys dominated (a potentially unwarranted assumption). Therefore, I would classify this as 'Inadequate control of variables, confounding probable'.

Data analysis and conclusions

Were the conclusions supported by sound evidence or are they speculation? The first that 'boys tend to dominate computers' was almost a self-fulfilling prophecy, considering how the interviews were conducted. Statistical tests are very good for determining the existence of differences in groups, but unless carefully constructed instruments are used, it is often difficult to tell why these differences exist. Many of the reasons are based upon other studies. Are there any other possible conclusions that could have been reached based upon the evidence provided? I think so. While it might be suggested that the study be replicated, I suspect the whole process needs restructuring to resolve the second question about dominance, and a study that includes the design of some improved complementary qualitative approaches. Consequently, conclusions would merit a 'Some lack of justification or are poorly defended'.

Appendix B: An Introduction to Spreadsheets

WHY USE A SPREADSHEET?

With all the various statistical packages available for micro- and mainframe computers, one might ask, why bother to use a spreadsheet utility package? The simple answer is mainly because with such software it is relatively easy to enter and see one's raw data in a worksheet, and recent versions now allow you to carry out many common statistical operations. Some advanced statistical packages also allow you to import your raw data from a spreadsheet-generated worksheet rather than typing it in using their own (sometimes rather unfriendly) systems. For example, SPSS/PC+ has a **TRANSLATE** command that allows you to import data listed on a worksheet and vice versa. Thus if you wish to use such a package later, it will not be necessary to retype your data.

A second advantage in using a spreadsheet is that you have control over which equations are used in carrying out calculations, since you can enter some yourself. This means that you are not limited by the functionality of the statistical package itself. It does have the same requirement that you have to set up your data carefully and in addition enter some of the equations yourself, but, as will be shown, it is possible to build in checks to ensure that errors are identified if they occur. This will also allow you to explore mathematical relationships that would be difficult to consider on statistical packages.

Third, any basic operations can be carried out easily to generate visually pleasing graphs, a function that can be missing in some more specialized statistical packages. This makes it easier to transfer results to a written report, particularly if it is word processed, or to print out the graphs directly for inclusion in a report.

Fourth, there are a number of basic statistical functions built into Excel that are easy to use. These allow one to process small data sets simply.

Finally, almost everyone has a spreadsheet on their computer. It is easier to learn about statistics this way and then decide later which statistical package is best for you. One of the greatest sins that can be committed in the world of statistics is to use a statistical package without understanding what it is doing. They often generate every possible statistic and carry out all operations for a set of numbers, leaving it to the user to decide which is most appropriate or even legitimate. This has led the uninitiated to use inappropriate statistical tests just because the package generated them. Computer software is incredibly powerful and immensely time saving, but *you* must be in control.

Spreadsheets: Some basics

Most spreadsheet packages come with either paper-based or computer-based learning materials to acquaint you with their functionality. This book uses Excel, though there are many similarities with other packages. If you are new to the world of spreadsheets, just think of a *worksheet* as a huge sheet of paper with a grid of boxes called *cells* (see Figure B.1). In these cells, we can put words, numbers or even formulae that will automatically calculate numbers. When you first call up a spreadsheet, you are presented with a blank worksheet of cells, each of which has an address based upon a combination of its column (**A, B, C, ...**) and its rows (**1, 2, 3, ...**), with one cell highlighted, the *active cell*, equivalent to the cursor in a word processor (cell **J2** in Figure B.1). Usually, a new worksheet will begin with the cell pointer in cell **A1** in the upper left-hand corner. You could enter something in that cell by typing the words or numbers and pressing the return or enter key, sometimes marked with a ⏎, and then move to another cell using the arrow keys on your keyboard or your mouse.

A spreadsheet such as Excel will appear with a menu across the top as illustrated in Figure B.1. One selects an operation either by using the mouse and clicking on an operation, or by calling up the menu choice by typing the underlined letter.

In Microsoft-Windows-based systems, choosing a menu option will bring down a further menu, such as shown in Figure B.1 for Excel where the choices for **Edit** are shown. This tree-like structure can cause a bit of confusion, but there is usually a built-in help facility and there are usually books on how to use the package in addition to the issued reference.

Spreadsheets are very versatile and flexible utility packages, and for purposes of exercises here, you will only use a very limited range of commands and facilities. This book will refer to Excel, which will load a Lotus or Works worksheet and convert it to an Excel worksheet, if necessary.

Summary of cell formats and symbols

Listed in Table B.1 are common symbols that appear in cells when entering calculations. Every cell that has an equation, calculation or refers to another cell for its data begins with an equal sign. Therefore, if you want cell **B2** to contain the same number as **A1**, you would type in cell **B2** the following, =**A1**, and press the return key.

	A	B	C
1	45		
2		45	
3			

=A1

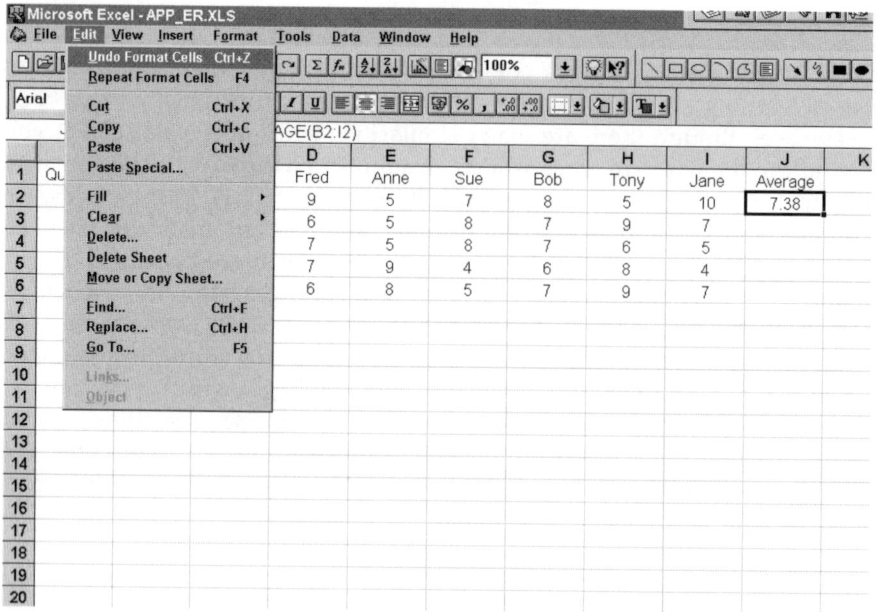

FIGURE B.1   *An Excel worksheet with main menu and **Edit***
submenu shown

There are a few simple rules one must follow when entering an equation in a cell, which if not followed may result in a message that there is an error in the cell, or you may just get a wrong answer. These are as follows:

- There must be an equal number of left and right brackets, ( ), in a cell.
- To indicate some operations, they need to be enclosed in brackets. For example, to multiply the sum of the contents of **B2** and **C5** by 6, use =6*(B2+C5). When in doubt, use brackets.
- When you **Copy** a cell designation to another cell, it will change by the difference in the number of rows and columns unless it is *absolute*, that is it has **$**. For example, if the contents of **B2** (=A1) were **Copy**ed to **C3**, the new contents would become whatever is in =B2 (add one row and one column), and if **Copy**ed to **C2**, they would become the contents of =B1 (add one column). If the contents of **B2** had been =$A$1, then **Copy**ing them to **C3** would mean that **C3** or **C2** or any cell would also contain the contents of =$A$1. *If you do not want cell designations to change when* **Copy***ing, use absolute designation.*

Wizards

Excel has several facilities that make specific tasks much easier, which are referred to as 'Wizards'. The ones shown here are from Microsoft Excel 97; though screens from earlier and later versions may differ slightly, they will

TABLE B.1 *Symbols used in cell equations*

Symbol	Meaning
=	Equals, precedes every equation, function or cell reference
:	Colon, used between cell designations to indicate a range, e.g. **B6:B9**
( )	Brackets, to isolate parts of an equation
+	Plus, indicates addition
–	Minus, indicates subtraction or a negative number
*	Asterisk, indicates multiplication, e.g. =**3*B6**, 3 times the contents of **B6**
/	Slash, indicates division, e.g. =**A5/12**, the contents of **A5** divided by 12
^	Hat, indicates power, e.g. =**C5^2**, the contents of **C5** squared
$	Dollar, to make a cell designation *absolute* regardless of where it is copied

	A	B	C	D	E	F	G	H	I	J
1	Quest	John	Mary	Fred	Anne	Sue	Bob	Tony	Jane	Average
2	1	8	7	9	5	7	8	5	10	7.38
3	2	6	8	6	5	8	7	9	7	
4	3	3	5	7	5	8	7	6	5	
5	4	5	5	7	9	4	6	8	4	
6	5	7	9	6	8	5	7	9	7	
7	Totals:									

FIGURE B.2 *Data set for eight subjects answering five questions*

be very similar. The two that will be commonly used here, with their icons as they appear on the menu bar at the top of a worksheet, are:

fx Function Wizard, which takes you through the necessary steps to insert a function in a cell.

📊 Chart Wizard, which takes you through five steps to generate a chart from a frequency table.

The steps within representative windows will be shown below for you to refer to when setting up charts or worksheets in the activities in the text.

FUNCTION WIZARD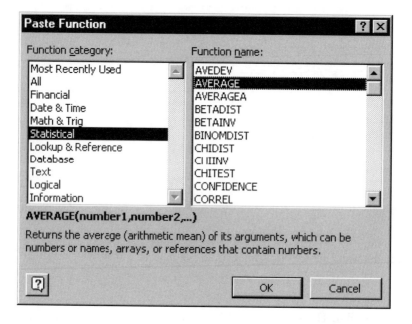

There is a very large number of built-in functions in Excel, which can carry out simple and complex actions on data. These are what make a spreadsheet powerful, providing functionality that saves an immense amount of time and makes it possible to model and illustrate graphically many statistical concepts. We will use a relatively small proportion of these, but the Function Wizard makes it unnecessary to type in everything, minimizing errors due to wayward fingers. It presents a series of windows that prompt you to fill in boxes, and then deposits the resulting function in the chosen cell, complete with all the parameters.

Call up a new worksheet with which to experiment. Type in the contents of cells from Figure B.2, to serve as data, but leave cell **J2** blank for now.

To use the Function Wizard, first of all place the cursor in the cell where you want the outcome of a function to appear, in our case cell **J2**, and then click on the Function Wizard icon. This brings up the following window:

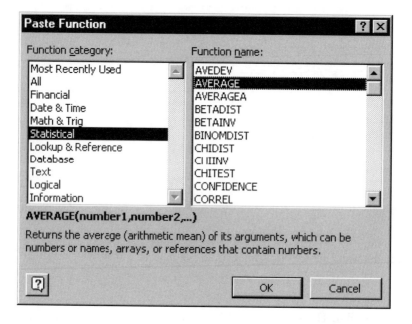

First you choose a category on the left (I have chosen **Statistical**), and then the function on the right. There is a description of the function that is highlighted and if you click on the button, more information will be revealed. Each function has a unique window, so it is not possible to show them all, but let us consider two to see how it works. The first is a simple function for finding the mean of a set of numbers, **AVERAGE**, second from the top of the statistical function list. Having placed the cursor in cell **J2**, we select **AVERAGE** and click on **OK**, which results in the following window:

AVERAGE

Number1 B2:I2   = {8,7,9,5,7,8,5,10}

Number2   = number

= 7.375

Returns the average (arithmetic mean) of its arguments, which can be numbers or names, arrays, or references that contain numbers.

Number1: number1,number2,... are 1 to 30 numeric arguments for which you want the average.

?   Formula result = 7.38   OK   Cancel

For this example, I clicked on cell **B2**, held the left mouse button down and swept over to include all cells up to **I2** in the row. The result appears in the lower part of the box, which will appear in cell **J2** when **OK** is clicked on. Note that in Figure B.1 the answer has been rounded to one decimal place fewer, **7.38**, since I formatted the cell to have only two places. Carry out Activity B.1 at this time.

ACTIVITY B.1

(a) Now you try to find the standard deviation of row 2 scores for question 1.

(b) What is the total score for Mary? (*Hint*: Look for the word **SUM**.)

Answers: (a) 1.65 if you used **STDEVP** or 1.76 if you used **STDEV**; (b) 34.

Copying by click and drag

To copy the contents of a cell to another cell, you can

- highlight the cell
- click on **Edit**
- select **Copy**
- highlight the new cell
- return to **Edit**
- choose **Paste**.

If the cells are adjacent, there is an easier way you can copy using just the mouse. First, click on the cell you want to copy, for example **J2** in the worksheet above. It will look like the following:

7.38

If you then place the mouse over the lower right-hand corner, it will look like this:

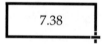

Press the left mouse button and drag over adjacent cells to copy the contents. For example, if dragged down over the next three cells, it would look like this:

When the mouse button is released, the cells will fill with the adjusted formula from the initial cell, here **J2**. Remember the rules above about the use of **$** to specify absolute (unchanging) cell designations in formulae.

CHART WIZARD

This section provides details on the process of using the Chart Wizard. You should load Excel and start a new worksheet to try out the following activity. The sequence uses the frequency table below, the results of a survey of patrons of the Green Toad pub one Saturday night. This should be typed into a worksheet and the data in these cells will be used in the example below. The five windows that appear in the Chart Wizard are presented so that you can refer back to them as needed.

	A	B	C
1	Party	Male	Female
2	Labour	6	2
3	Conserv	3	3
4	Lib Dem	3	9
5	Rav Loony	3	1
6	Total	15	15

It is easier if you block out the data with the mouse, and then click on the Chart Wizard icon. If you click on the icon first, you will be asked to identify the data range, which can be done with the mouse. You will be able to **Copy** the resulting chart to another document, like a Microsoft Word file, for a report later. The first window to appear will be

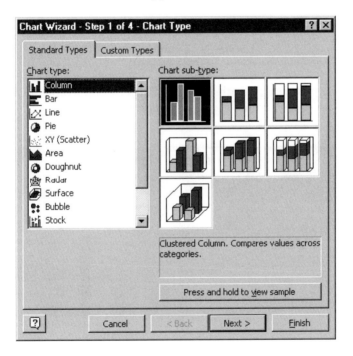

The Chart Wizard will automatically select what it thinks is the most appropriate chart for the data, but it may not always be the best. To change it, simply place the mouse pointer in the cell for the chart type you want and click on the left mouse button. The **Column** chart has been chosen for this example. When you are satisfied with the choice (which you can change later), click on the Next > button to go to Step 2, shown below:

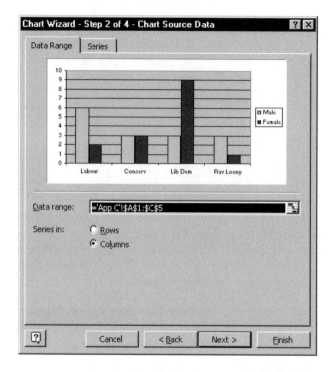

Assuming this is the appropriate type of chart (an opportunity to make alterations follows), click on the [Next >] button to go to Step 3:

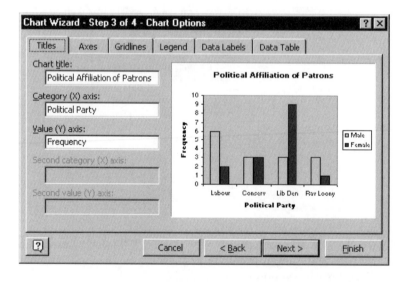

This window allows you to add a title and labels for the axes. Click on the **Gridlines** tab to remove or add gridlines (I removed them), the **Legend** on the right, alter the axes, etc. The final image is shown on the right as a miniature. When complete, click on the [Next >] button for the final window:

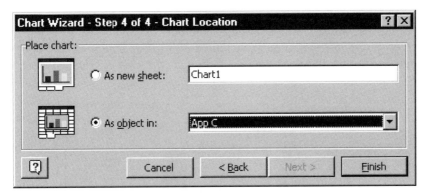

Here you can choose to have the chart on a separate sheet or next to your data. I prefer to have it next to the data to view better the consequences of changes.

This is the limit to what you can do in the Chart Wizard. You can go back to previous steps by clicking on the [< Back] button or place the chart on the page by clicking on the [Finish] button. If along the way you decide you do not want to continue, then click on the [Cancel] button and start over later.

Editing a chart after the Chart Wizard from the menu bar

The chart can be further edited by double clicking on the chart to activate it and the menu on the right. Several of the items have pull-down menus like the one shown, which allow you to make changes. If this does not appear, you may have to add it under **View**, **Toolbars** and click on **Chart**.

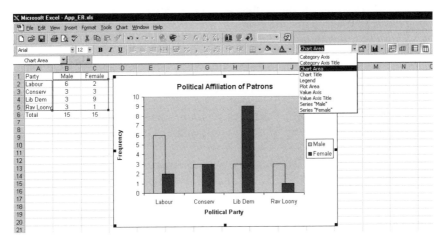

Editing charts directly using the mouse

The most fundamental change that can be made in a chart is its size, which can be adjusted by clicking on the chart and dragging one of the selection handles.

In addition to the menus above, you change specific aspects of the chart by using the mouse pointer. To select the part of the chart you want, click once on the item (like an axis), at which point little squares will appear at either end or on the components shown in the case of the *x*-axis in the chart below:

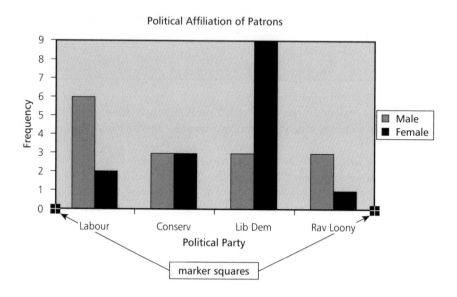

Then double click on a specific part of the chart to produce a window with menus and option 'tabs' for you to choose. Positioning the mouse pointer can be a bit tricky, since the mouse is very sensitive as to where it is when you click. If you are just a little bit off from where you should be, you may get a window other than the one you want. The ease of use may depend on the resolution of your monitor and the type of mouse, but, with practice, you can select parts of the chart, raising the following windows, with the number of 'tabs' to choose from in each case:

- **Format Chart Area** (3) **Patterns** (colour/shading around chart), **Font** (only if you want one font/size for whole chart), **Properties** (object positioning).
- **Format Plot Area** (1) border (if any) and colour/shading inside.
- **Format Axis** (5) either *x*- or *y*-axis: **Patterns** (of axis line), **Scale** (max/min, categories, where axes cross), **Font** (of numbers), **Number** (decimal places/style), **Alignment** (of numbers/categories).
- **Format Data Series** (6) **Patterns** (to change line and bar shapes/colours), **Axis** (range etc.), **Y Error Bars**, **Data Labels**, **Series Order**, **Options** (overlap of bars, gap between bars, etc.).
- **Format Data Point** (3) only if you want to highlight a single data point, pie section or column: **Pattern**, **Data Labels**, **Options**.

- **Format Legend** (3) **Patterns, Font, Placement.**
- **Format Axis Title** (3) **Patterns, Font, Alignment** (vertical/horizontal).
- **Format Chart Title** (3) the same as **Format Axis Title**.

With the numerous combinations of tabs, it is not possible to show them all, but they are fairly self-evident in what function they perform. You can also change the contents of the legend and titles by clicking on them and activating an outline box, after which you can place the cursor inside and type.

Finally, sometimes it is desirable to place a label somewhere specific on a chart that is not accessible by the above. On the main menu is the icon for the text box ▤ which allows you to mark out a rectangular area anywhere and type in it.

All of these choices and options can be a bit bewildering when you start, but with use, and using the help facilities, it will become easier. It is worth making notes of commonly used procedures to save time later.

References

Adams, D. (1979) *The Hitch Hiker's Guide to the Galaxy*. London: Pan Books.

Anastasi, A. (1990) *Psychological Testing* (6th edn). London: Collier-Macmillan.

Atkinson, R.L., Atkinson, R.C., Smith, E.E., Bem, D.J. and Hilgard, E.R. (1990) *Introduction to Psychology* (10th edn). San Diego, CA: Harcourt Brace Jovanovich.

Beauchamp, M. (1988) 'Hard facts to sleep on', *Guardian*, 25 May: 21.

Black, T.R. (1999) *Doing Quantitative Research in the Social Sciences: An Integrated Approach to Research Design, Measurement and Statistics*. London: Sage.

Black, T.R. (2000) 'Parental education and fertility in Africa: testing the link', Unpublished manuscript, University of Surrey.

Blalock, H.M. (1979) *Social Statistics* (rev. 2nd edn). Tokyo: McGraw-Hill Kogakusha.

Blum, M.L. and Foos, P.W. (1986) *Data Gathering: Experimental Methods* Plus. New York: Harper & Row.

Bourner, T. and Hamad, M. (1987) *Entry Qualifications and Degree Performance*. London: CNAA.

Campbell, D.T. and Stanley, J.C. (1963) *Experimental and Quasi-experimental Designs for Research*. Chicago: Rand McNally.

Chase, C.I. (1985) *Elementary Statistical Procedures* (3rd edn). New York: McGraw-Hill.

Cohen, L. and Manion, L. (2000) *Research Methods in Education* (5th edn). London: Routledge.

Cronbach, L.J. (1990) *Essentials of Psychological Testing*. (5th edn). New York: Harper & Row.

Dorfman, D.D. (1978) 'The Cyril Burt question: new findings', *Science*, 201 (4362): 1177–1186.

Ferguson, G.A. (1976) *Statistical Analysis in Psychology and Education* (4th edn). New York: McGraw-Hill.

Gephart, W.J. and Bartos, B.B. (1969) 'Occasional Paper 7: Profiling Instructional Package', Phi Delta Kappa.

Glass, G.V. and Hopkins, K.D. (1996) *Statistical Methods in Education and Psychology* (3rd edn), Allyn & Bacon.

Greer, S. (1978) 'On the selection of problems. Reading 6', in J. Bynner and K.M. Stribley (eds), *Social Research: Principles and Procedures*. Harbour: Longman, pp. 48–52.

Grimm, L.G. (1993) *Statistical Applications for the Behavioral Sciences*. Wiley.

Grosh, M.E. and Glewwe, P. (1995) 'A guide to living standards: measurement study surveys and their data sets', LSMS Working Paper No. 120. Washington, DC: World Bank.

Guba, E.G. (1978) *Towards a Naturalistic Inquiry in Educational Evaluation*, Monograph 8. Center for Study of Evaluation, UCLA.

Guilford, J.P. and Fruchter, B. (1973) *Fundamental Statistics in Psychology and Education* (5th edn). New York: McGraw-Hill.

Howell, D.C. (1997) *Statistical Methods for Psychology* (4th edn). Belmont, CA: Duxbury Press.

Huff, D. (1954) *How to Lie with Statistics*. Harmondsworth: Penguin. (Recently reprinted.)

Katz, J., Aspden, P. and Reich, W.A. (1997) Public attitudes towards voice-based messaging technologies in the United States: A national survey of opinions about voice response units and telephone answering machines. *Behaviour & Information Technology*, 16(3): 125–144.

Kerlinger, F.N. (1986) *Foundations of Behavioral Research* (3rd edn). New York: Harcourt Brace.

Kerlinger, F.N. and Lee, H.B. (2000) *Foundations of Behavioral Research* (4th edn). New York: Harcourt.

Kline, P. (1991) *Intelligence: The Psychometric View*. London: Routledge.

Lehmann, I.J. and Mehrens, W.A. (1979) *Educational Research: Readings in Focus* (2nd edn). New York: Holt, Rinehart and Winston.

Lockard, J.D. (1980) *UNESCO Handbook for Science Teachers*. London: Heinemann.

Mehrens, W.A. and Lehmann, I.J. (1984) *Measurement and Evaluation in Education and Psychology* (3rd edn). New York: Holt-Saunders.

Minium, E.W., King, B.M. and Bear, G. (1993) *Statistical Reasoning in Psychology and Education* (3rd edn). New York: Wiley.

Moore, D.S. (1991) *Statistics: Concepts and Controversies* (3rd edn). New York: W.H. Freeman.

Muijs, R.D. (1997) Predictors of academic achievement and academic self-concept: A longitudinal perspective. *British Journal of Educational Psychology*, 67: 263–277.

Murphy, K.R. and Davidshofer, C.O. (1991) *Psychological Testing: Principles and Applications*. (2nd edn). Englewood Cliffs, NJ: Prentice-Hall.

Nisbett, J. and Watt, J. (1978) *Case Study* (Rediguide 26). Nottingham University.

Open University (1973) *Methods of Educational Enquiry, E341. Block 2: Research Design*. Milton Keynes: Open University Press, pp. 19–21.

Oppenheim, A.N. (1992) *Questionnaire Design, Interviewing and Attitude Measurement* (2nd edn). London: Pinter.

Popper, K.R. (1978) 'The unity of method. Reading 3', in J. Bynner and K.M. Stribley (eds), *Social Research: Principles and Procedures*. Harbour: Longman, pp. 17–24.

Reynolds, P.D. (1979) *Ethical Dilemmas and Social Science Research*. San Francisco: Jossey-Bass.

Rowntree, D. (1981) *Statistics without Tears: An Introduction for Non-mathematicians*. London: Penguin.

Sear, K. (1983) 'The correlation between A Level grades and degree results in England and Wales', *Higher Education*, 12: 609–619.

Shipman, M.D. (1972) *The Limitations of Social Research*. London: Longman.

Siegel, S. and Castellan, N.J., Jr (1988) *Non-parametric Statistics* (2nd edn). New York: McGraw-Hill.

Slevin, C. and Stuart, A. (1978) 'Data-dredging procedures in survey analysis. Reading 21', in J. Bynner and K.M. Stribley (eds), *Social Research: Principles and Procedures*. Harbour: Longman, pp. 278–284.

Thorndike, R.L. and Hagen, E.P. (1977) *Measurement and Evaluation in Psychology and Education* (4th edn). New York: Wiley.

Winer, B.J., Brown, D.R. and Michels, K.M. (1991) *Statistical Principles in Experimental Design* (3rd edn). New York: McGraw-Hill.

Wright, D.B. (1997) *Understanding Statistics: An Introduction for the Social Sciences*. London: Sage.

Index